Future Morality

Future Morality

Edited by
DAVID EDMONDS

OXFORD
UNIVERSITY PRESS

OXFORD
UNIVERSITY PRESS

Great Clarendon Street, Oxford, OX2 6DP,
United Kingdom

Oxford University Press is a department of the University of Oxford.
It furthers the University's objective of excellence in research, scholarship,
and education by publishing worldwide. Oxford is a registered trade mark of
Oxford University Press in the UK and in certain other countries

First Edition published in 2021

Impression: 1

Published in the United States of America by Oxford University Press
198 Madison Avenue, New York, NY 10016, United States of America

British Library Cataloguing in Publication Data

Data available

Library of Congress Control Number: 2021942732

ISBN 978–0–19–886208–6

Printed and bound in Great Britain by
Clays Ltd, Elcograf S.p.A.

Editor's Preface

There are scientific, medical, and technological breakthroughs that are likely to happen, but that have not yet happened. As a result, there are ethical issues that we can predict are likely to occur, but that we do not at the moment face.

I have always been fascinated by such topics. And I have long been sceptical that our instinctive intuitions about new moral dilemmas should be relied upon. To take just one example: Louise Joy Brown was born on 25 July 1978—the first human conceived by *in vitro* fertilization. At the time, the pioneering scientists behind IVF were heavily criticized by the medical establishment and by the church. The Brown family received a deluge of hate mail. Since then, millions of children have been born through IVF, and, within most circles, IVF has long ceased to be controversial. It now seems odd that it was ever contentious.

Thinking philosophically about fresh ethical dilemmas can help us distinguish between developments that we should welcome, and those that we need be concerned about. And in some areas, there are steps we could be taking now to prevent problems occurring in the future.

This book is an attempt to get to grips with some of the ethical issues confronting our rapidly changing world. I have divided it into several, somewhat arbitrary, categories: Future People, Future Lives, Future Machines, Future Communication, Future Bodies, and Future Death. It is by no means a comprehensive list of future moral dilemmas, but I hope it offers a useful snapshot.

The book includes questions such as whether we should seek an alternative to meat, whether social relationships of the future—especially friendship—will be very different from those of today, whether in the future artificial intelligence will help us to identify criminals, and whether AI will eventually make human doctors redundant.

One chapter examines whether it might be possible to shape persuasive technologies—those that are designed to change our attitudes and actions—so that they work for and not against us. Another asks what can be done about the rise of fake news and conspiracy theories, now spreading and proliferating in our digital world.

In the future we may have the power to read minds, to create artificial wombs, to 'improve' humans and livestock genetically so that both humans and livestock are less susceptible to disease. Technological advance seems to promise progress and improvement to our lives. Is there a downside?

Then there's a section on death. Machines can now keep us functioning at some level for longer than before. In fact, new technology is already forcing us to reconsider what counts as death and what's valuable about life. How far should we go to avoid death? A chapter on cryonics asks whether there's any point in freezing our bodies in the hope that one day we might be resuscitated. And we end with a chapter that questions whether what we should really be concerned about is not human future, but the future of posthumans.

William Shakespeare has the Roman nobleman Cassius tell Brutus in *Julius Caesar* that destiny "is not in the stars, But in ourselves". A similar thought is the motivating impulse behind this book. The history of human existence has been a history of scientific and technological development. We should assume that discoveries and innovations will continue to be made—almost certainly at a faster pace than ever before. But we have the power to sculpt the future; and the earlier and more clear-sighted we are about our options, the more malleable that future will be.

*

The Uehiro Centre for Practical Ethics, where I am a Distinguished Research Fellow, specializes in the philosophy of Future Morality. Most of the contributors in this book have a connection with the Centre. I would like to thank each and every one of the contributors, Hazem, Bridget, Ruth, Anne, Brian, Rebecca, Erica, Seumas, Angeliki, Xaroula, John, Jess, Carissa, James, Steve, Stephen, Julian, Gabriel, Tom, Dominic, Lydia, Alberto, Tess, Katrien, Jonny, Mackenzie, Francesca, and Anders. They put up with my chivvying and nagging, and my unreasonable demand that when it came to deadlines, they should adopt an approach more befitting the world of journalism than philosophy. Collectively they've produced a great book.

At the Uehiro Centre I would particularly like to thank the director Julian Savulescu for his enthusiasm for this project, as well as all the hard-working people who keep the Centre running, Rachel Gaminiratne, Liz Sanders, Deborah Sheehan, Rocci Wilkinson, and Miriam Wood.

Thanks too, to the OUP team: Jenny King, OUP copy editor Martin Noble, and OUP philosophy supremo, Peter Momtchiloff, for whom I've now edited many books, and who never deviates from his calm good nature.

Thanks, as always, to my tireless, unpaid proofreader and text improver, Hannah Edmonds. Thanks, as always, to three other fab Edmonds—Liz, Saul, and Isaac—with whom I shared a locked-down existence during the book's 2020 gestation.

Contents

Future Communication

Future Bodies

Future Death

Future People

1

Future versus Present Morality

Hazem Zohny

Is this book moral?

This is not a confused query about the book's personality or behaviour; it's about the time and attention that went into it—time and attention that could have been differently used. The future, after all, is uncertain; the present dire. Shouldn't ethicists focus primarily on the latter?

Let's express this sentiment along these lines:

> Ethicists are a scarce resource. The present is ethically fraught. The richest 1% own over half the world's wealth; hundreds of thousands of children die each year from malnutrition; millions live in slavery or as forced labourers. The future, on the other hand, is unknowable, and the impacts of emerging technologies—like AI, cryonics, gene editing, and mind-reading devices—largely unforecastable. Surely ethicists should focus their attention on the present, rather than on future hypotheticals.

We can call proponents of this view *Presentists*. In response, those we'll call *Anticipators* might say:

> In fact, ethicists aren't a scare resource—nearly anyone can do ethics (as opposed to, say, brain surgery). Moreover, present problems like inequality are political, not moral. Ultimately, a failure to anticipate moral problems would render the future far worse than the present.

Who is right: Presentists or Anticipators? The unexciting conclusion that both reflect some truth seems inescapable. But I'd like to suggest there is a lot to be said for Presentists, and for the claim that this book—and the way ethicists have been allured by future visions—is a little bit morally bad. This is because questions of distributive justice—of justly allocating resources—are relevant to what ethicists focus on. And ethicists—especially the applied variety who appeal to the implications of moral theories or principles for specific situations—have been overly preoccupied by the promises and perils of emerging and future technologies.

Specifically, while applied ethicists readily delve into the science behind AI, gene editing, brain–machine interfaces, nanotech, etc., they have not bothered learning much about economic theories and the conflicting values and difficult trade-offs directly raised by economic policy. Why this contrast with economics? Economics is about what is produced, distributed, and consumed. It fundamentally affects the ethical implications of all goods, including technological ones. It is ironic, therefore, how little attention applied ethicists afford it.

This claim about how applied ethicists generally focus their energies is an empirical one, and no study yet exists to vindicate it. But at the time of writing it is easy to see how applied ethicists author the most relevant of the 3.8 million results Google Scholar provides for "human enhancement," but virtually none of the 3.1 million results for "moral economics." Output on human enhancement outstrips "poverty ethics" (1.7 million), "preventable disease ethics" (100,000), "discrimination" (2.3 million), and even "abortion" (1.4 million). Even a subtopic like "moral enhancement" (460,000) dwarfs output on preventable disease ethics.

This Google Scholar survey is not, of course, meant to stand in for scholarship. And we should be extra cautious about reading too much into these figures since there is no clear dividing line between applied ethicists and other experts. Nonetheless, the numbers are indicative of a disproportionate focus on the future in what occupies those working on the ethics of concrete issues.

This book is yet further evidence of this tendency.

There may be many reasons for this trend, some of them obvious: technologies that might enhance, say, our moral dispositions are simply more interesting to think about than preventable diseases in the world. But another reason—especially when it comes to economic matters—is that applied ethicists largely relegate the ethics of economics to economists or political philosophers, where libertarians, socialists, and those in between fight it out by appealing to large, abstract principles or assumptions about things like the proper role of the state. But this is akin to relegating the ethics of emerging technologies to scientists or historians and philosophers of science. There is an asymmetry here and it's a neglected one.

The Scarcity of Ethicists

But we are getting ahead of ourselves. Let's begin with the Anticipators' retort that ethicists are not a scarce resource. Most mentally intact adults can indeed appeal to reason to answer ethical questions, and typically do so repeatedly throughout their lives. If anything, a scroll through social media suggests an overabundance of people espousing reasons for ethical stances. In contrast, few have any clue about, say, brain tumour removal. We would rightly tell our non-brain surgeon friend to be quiet if they had strong opinions about the specifics of a relative's impending brain surgery, but we might in contrast hear them out if over dinner they explain why they are vegetarian (unless they are being infuriating about it).

On the other hand, a trained ethicist is presumably better than average at justifying an ethical stance or presenting an ethical argument. They are more likely to take the time to learn the relevant empirical backdrop to ethical problems, to uncover hidden premises, and perhaps to adopt a healthy scepticism towards certain intuitions. More crucially, an ethicist is trained to make their arguments on the basis of claims that most reasonable people can appreciate, as opposed to idiosyncratic, religious, or other evidence-free claims.

Ultimately, it comes down to this: relatively few people are paid to be ethicists. The position "ethicist" is clearly a scarce one—just ask anyone trying to get a job at a philosophy department! If only a tiny minority can be paid to think about and offer resolutions to ethical problems, some justification seems required for what they will focus on. And so we should ask whether focusing on the future to the current extent is a good use of that position.

Presentists are therefore right about their first claim: ethicists are a scarce resource. Let's award them a point: Presentists 1–Anticipators 0.

Present Problems

What about the second claim that the present is fraught with pressing problems? Are the failures of our political and economic systems moral problems—that is, ones arising from disagreement over how to ethically resolve them? Or do these failures merely reflect an insufficient number of political decision makers supporting the obvious ethical path forward? In other words, are these ethics problems or "political will" problems?

It might be tempting to side with Anticipators that the most pressing problems at present are political rather than ethical. Most ethicists might agree that, of course, current concentrations of wealth are ethically unjustifiable; of course it is immoral so many are malnourished while over a billion tonnes of food are wasted each year; and of course slavery and forced labour are abhorrent and should be stopped. There are no moral dilemmas here, no conflicting values. These are problems for politicians and global institutions, not ethicists. And the same holds for other big crises of our times like climate change, authoritarianism, poverty, and preventable disease: these reflect failures of political will, not moral disagreement.

This, however, is a cop-out. Merely agreeing that much of the status quo is not morally justifiable is as vague and inane as noting that, "if emerging technologies have a really bad impact, that would be morally bad." Clearly, there's a lot more to be said. Applied ethicists (generally) take the time to understand the science and limitations behind these emerging technologies before analysing in detail the values at play, the conflicts between them, and the trade-offs entailed by the manner of embracing or rejecting them.

For instance, the possibility of genetically enhancing children has led applied ethicists to draw battle lines between reproductive freedom and prospective children's autonomy, with small libraries being written on what autonomy even means in such contexts, what the risks of banning these technologies are (e.g. might black markets for them emerge?), and what the merits of genetic enhancement might be.

In contrast, far fewer applied ethicists take the time to understand economic theories or policies and their political backdrops in order to formulate new or more cogent arguments in response to the most pressing present problems. In fact, mitigating inequality, malnutrition, slavery, preventable disease, or poverty *does* entail promoting or protecting some values at the expense of others—especially when asking *how* exactly to ethically tackle these problems. Just how much state or interstate coercion should be used to redistribute wealth, and what exactly are the trade-offs between what we value, or ought to value, in terms of equality and liberty? And what do we do when the empirical data about inequality or the effects of mitigating it are unclear?

Similarly for malnutrition and modern slavery: how do we weigh the trade-offs entailed by reordering state spending to have the resources necessary to track and tackle these, and whose burden ought that be? These are normative questions that are as applied as things can get, but they continue to be largely left to political philosophers—who tend to focus on how things ideally should be—or policymakers, who aren't trained to think systematically about the ethical implications of their policies.

Which is all to say, applied ethicists have a lot to offer in moving economic ethics forward, but—with some exceptions[1]—they remain largely either uninterested or unable to get the funding to expand onto that turf. But seeing as it's our economic and political systems that will set the path for how future technologies unfold, it seems applied ethicists should be giving economics far greater attention. To that end, I think Presentists deserve a further point: Presentists 2–Anticipators 0.

Forecasting Futures

What about the third claim Presentists make: that future technologies are largely unforecastable, so best focus on the present? Anticipators face a problem here as well, sometimes called the Collingridge dilemma: while controlling the impact of technologies is easier at their early stages, it is precisely at those early stages when we lack the necessary knowledge to beneficially influence the course they take.[2] We simply cannot tell what final shape the technology will take, how it will be deployed, or how people will react to it.

One way to resolve this is to enhance our forecasting abilities; to basically beat the Collingridge dilemma. There is much to be said for such an endeavour, but first I want to suggest that, even if we are mostly hopeless at predicting specific technological trends, Anticipators' interest in the future can be important to the present in at least three ways.

The first is this: scientific research is itself a scarce resource. To minimize the chances of squandering it, we need some anticipation of its ethical implications. If the implications are clearly unethical, we should prioritize researching something else. Of course, how far into the future we need to venture to anticipate the effects of current scientific research is a key question, but it's worth conceding that at least some assessment of future impact is required.

The second relates to a side-effect of anticipatory ethics: evaluating the ethics of a future prospect often brings us back to the present. Take the idea of powerful cognitive enhancement drugs in the classroom— should they be allowed? Aside from side-effect concerns, answering this question requires thinking about the purpose of education, of medicine, and of what, if anything, is inherently different about a drug compared to an external device like a calculator or word processor. So we might ask whether education is unavoidably competitive, helping ensure the best students get the best jobs. If so, these drugs might lead to a cognitive arms race. What would that entail? And if education is competitive, *should* it be? And should physicians prescribe these drugs, or would that violate the proper scope of medicine since they would not be used for treating or preventing disease? What exactly is the purpose of physicians? By triggering these questions, the mere prospect of these drugs leads us to re-evaluate the purpose of present institutions and norms in a new light—a valuable exercise even if these drugs never materialize.

Similarly, consider publicly funding a research project on the ethics of generation spaceships. These spaceships set out to colonize other planets, but the vast travel distances involve supporting not only those who first embark on them, but their descendants too. Is it permissible to have children in such a constrained domain, where life projects are limited and one is effectively imprisoned to a ship, and where passengers are coerced to procreate and work in areas deemed necessary for the success of the journey?[3] Generation spaceships are no impending possibility, so why bother asking let alone funding those asking these questions instead of tackling presently pressing issues? But carefully considering these questions has huge implications for the generational spaceship we all currently inhabit: Earth—a rock also hurtling through space on which we are all stuck. Our intuitions about procreating on Earth, about what we owe others, and how much sacrifice an individual should make for others, are often shackled by our overfamiliarity with Earth. Contemplating possible, far distant futures can help us to evaluate those intuitions anew.[4]

There is another way anticipating the future links back to the present: it may alter what we ought to presently value and invest in. This links to the first point raised about the scarcity of scientific research, but it goes much further.

Take a school of thought called "Longtermism."[5] Its premises go something like this: given the average life of a species (1–10 million years), with the right technology and forethought it is reasonable to expect a huge number of future human generations, with a much larger number of people in each future generation. If we are impartial about our concern, the interests of future generations matter just as much as our own. We therefore have a strong duty to care very much about the future.

Even if we reject that the interests of very distant future generations count as much as our own, it seems implausible that they do not matter at all. If it is reasonable to expect there to be many more people in the future than are currently alive, this has potentially radical implications for the present, including a far more heightened concern over existential threats like nuclear war or engineered pandemics. It shifts the question of how we ought to improve the present for us, or those soon to exist, to how we ought to improve the present to the benefit of those in the very long-term future. This still entails a focus on the present, albeit about what the present can do to promote or respect the (likely far more numerous) interests of future people.

Which is all to say, even if we are fairly inept at forecasting technological trends, there is a lot to be said for thinking about the future anyway: it might be the only way we can get the present right. That's a big win for Anticipators, so I think they deserve two points, bringing the score to 2–2.

(Im)plausible Visions

This, however, is not the final tally. I suggested scientific research itself is a scarce resource, and that by not anticipating its ethical implications, we risk squandering it. But how far into the future do we need to anticipate the effects of a scientific investigation? Often this will be deeply uncertain. For instance, there were over forty organisations in the world researching artificial *general* intelligence in 2017;[6] this is AI that can reason across a wide range of domains, with the potential to master any intellectual task that a human can. It might be invented tomorrow, a hundred years from now, or never. It likely has huge, world-rattling ethical implications, and so getting it right seems crucial.

The question remains how to ascertain the plausibility of something like artificial general intelligence (or cryonics or artificial wombs), and how much of our time its implications should occupy relative to other issues. If ethicists focus on a technology that is unlikely to be realized any time soon at the expense of present problems, or if they focus on an implausible vision of how that technology will likely be used, they risk squandering their efforts.

So it seems that, while Anticipators are justified in worrying about the future, something needs to be said about their *methods* of foresight. And yet ethicists have so far neglected formulating or adopting any framework for what constitutes a plausible vision of a future technology. Instead, the typical methodology suffers from what's sometimes called an "if and then" syndrome:[7] *if* technology x becomes available, *then* its consequences will demand immediate attention. This conditional statement can be enough to instigate an entire subfield of ethical inquiry about a hypothetical future technology.

The problem, as scholars of science and technology studies keep reminding us, is that taking certain technological developments for granted fails to credit the interplay between science and society. Ethicists all too often think about an emerging technology in isolation, worrying about the implications of, say, radical life extension, while assuming that if/when it is possible, that future will largely have the same economy, same population problems, and same values. But acknowledging this co-evolution of science and society requires taking into account myriad interacting socio-cultural, economic, political, and historical factors—an analysis which calls into question the relative value of much of the work Anticipators do.

Scholars in science and technology studies and the philosophy of technology have in fact developed numerous approaches to evaluating the plausibility of future technologies that recognize these indeterminate, interacting factors. These published frameworks are variously called ethical technology assessment, anticipatory technology ethics, constructive technology assessment, and socio-technical scenarios, to name a few.[8] All these methods are rooted in the idea that the assessment of a technological vision should explicitly acknowledge the complex and contingent nature of technological developments and their effects.

And yet it remains rare to see ethicists worried about emerging technologies making use of these, let alone building on them or refining them. I think this warrants a further point for Presentists.

That leaves us with a concluding score of Presentists 3–Anticipators 2. It is an admittedly highly arbitrary score, but it reflects what I think should concern ethicists thinking about the future: there is indeed a distributive justice question about how ethicists focus their attention; ethicists (especially the applied variety) have been neglecting the hugely pressing economic problems of our time, expending a lot of energy learning science but not so much learning economics; and even though anticipating the future is crucial not just for future people but for the present, ethicists largely remain unconcerned with any systematic method for thinking about what makes those future visions plausible.

It isn't the most sexy of topics, but there's a lot to be said for the ethics of doing ethics. I suggest ethicists have been, not horrendous at this, but moderately bad. The point, therefore, of this chapter, is to raise a question mark about the value of many of the subsequent chapters. Sorry!

Further Reading

Tetlock, P. and Gardner, D., *Superforecasting: The Art and Science of Prediction* (Crown Publishing Group, 2015).

Notes

1. The most glaring of which is Peter Singer, who hugely influenced applied ethics and massively contributed to changing how many see our duties to the distant poor and to animals in factory farms.
2. D. Collingridge, *The Social Control of Technology* (Frances Pinter, 1980).

3. For a brief but insightful discussion of this topic, see Neil Levy, 'Would it be immoral to send out a generation starship?' In *Aeon Ideas* (2016). Available from: https://aeon.co/ideas/would-it-be-immoral-to-send-out-a-generation-starship.

4. That is indeed what many of the chapters in this book end up doing. For instance, Stephen Rainey (**Chapter 15**) considers a future of pervasive mind reading, but in doing so tackles questions about our present relationship to technology and what the purpose of technology ought to be.

5. H. Greaves and W. MacAskill, *The case for strong longtermism* (Global Priorities Institute Working Paper No. 7–2019). Available from: https://globalprioritiesinstitute.org/hilary-greaves-william-macaskill-the-case-for-strong-longtermism/

6. S. Baum, *A survey of artificial general intelligence projects for ethics, risk, and policy* (Global Catastrophic Risk Institute Working Paper, 2017), 17–11.

7. See A. Nordmann, If and then: A critique of speculative nanoethics, *NanoEthics*, 1 (2007), 31–46.

8. See for example: E. Palm and S. O. Hansson, The case for ethical technology assessment (ETA), *Technological Forecasting and Social Change*, 73/5 (2006), 543–58; P. Brey, Anticipatory ethics for emerging technologies, *NanoEthics*, 6/1 (2012), 1–13; A. Rip and H. te Kulve, Constructive technology assessment and socio-technical scenarios. In E. Fisher, C. Selin, and J. Wetmore (eds.), *Presenting Futures, The Yearbook of Nanotechnology in Society* (Springer Netherlands, 2008), 49–70.

2

How Should We Value the Health of Future People?

Bridget Williams

Introduction

Alex is the medical director of a major hospital. She has just received a report that outlines the carbon emissions of the hospital's services, and steps that could be taken to reduce them and move towards more environmentally sustainable health care services. It's possible for the hospital to implement these changes, but only by shifting focus and financial investment over the coming years away from other priorities. For example, plans for the expansion of certain patient services would be shelved and some existing services would have to be scaled back. Consequently, the quality of care offered by the hospital for the next few years would be worse than it could have been.

The main reason to implement the report would be to reduce the risk of more severe climate change. Although there's evidence that climate change is already impacting health,[1] the real benefits of dealing with climate change will come in the future. So Alex's dilemma is whether to reduce the care the hospital provides to the current population it serves, for the sake of the health of the population in the future.

How much weight should Alex give to the health of future people?

The Health of Future People vs the Health of People Now

To determine whether and to what extent Alex should care about the health of future people we must consider a prior question: why does health matter at all?

The World Health Organisation defines health as 'a state of complete physical, mental and social well-being and not merely the absence of disease or infirmity'.[2] This definition positions health as 'well-being'. The nature and value of health, and of well-being, is controversial. Philosophers have proposed several theories of both concepts,[3] but for this chapter it will suffice to say that health is both intrinsically valuable (that is, valuable for its own sake), and instrumentally valuable (that is, valuable for what it allows us to do, or the good things it brings us).

It seems difficult to see how the intrinsic value of health would change across time. A person is a person no matter when they exist. A thought experiment from the philosopher Derek Parfit[4] makes the point clear by asking us to imagine that a person, rather irresponsibly, leaves a shard of glass in a remote part of a forest. The shard lies on the forest floor for a hundred years. And then on a fine summer day in the year 2121 a child comes along and steps on the shard, cutting her foot. The pain the child feels is the same as a child in 2021 would have felt. The intrinsic value of not experiencing this pain would not change simply due to position in time.

It is similarly hard to see how the value to a person of being able to do what they want to do, without being limited by health problems, would become less over time. The satisfaction of completing a project, or the meaning that comes from developing interpersonal relationships will surely matter just as much to people in the future. However, it may be the case that ill-health will pose less of a barrier to achieving a fulfilling life in the future, because of technological advances and better design.[5] For example, the increasing availability of elevators and ramps makes having an arthritic knee less of a hindrance than it once was.

The Instrumental Value of Population Health

So far we have considered the value of health to an individual. But what if we consider the impact of the health of one person on the well-being of others? Here, it could be argued that for humanity as a whole there would be greater instrumental value in improving population health earlier rather than later. Each person's health is influenced, to an extent, by the health of people before them. Most directly, the health of parents (particularly mothers) impacts the health of their offspring, and this may affect *their* offspring and so on. More broadly, good health probably contributes to the development of better public institutions, advancement in science and knowledge, and even our understanding of morality. So the health of people earlier in history will have the potential to influence more people, as more people will come after them.

However, this doesn't necessarily mean that population health will always be instrumentally more valuable the earlier it is. There might be some point in the future that is more important than the present for guiding the direction of humanity. Having a healthy population at this other point in time might carry greater instrumental value than health earlier. As a comparison, one might generally think that it is better to have money earlier, so that it can be invested wisely. However, this might not always be the case. For example, considering their life overall, it might be better for a person to receive a large sum of money when they are aged 30 rather than when they're 15. A 15-year-old may be less likely to know how to invest well, and more likely to spend the money frivolously. Something analogous may be true for the resource of population health. As a species our knowledge has increased substantially over time, and we can expect this to increase further in the future. Future populations may be better at knowing how to 'invest' the resource of health.

Navigating Uncertainty

The future is uncertain, and, generally, we will have greater confidence that action intending to improve health in the nearer term will bring about the desired outcome. All else being equal, the further into the future the intended outcomes of our actions extend, the less certain it is that what we hope to cause will in fact be caused. Many things could happen between now and then to thwart our efforts. There may be something very specific to the project which means it doesn't occur the way we had planned. At the other extreme, .

a catastrophe could cause the extinction of humanity, so the intended beneficiaries of any project would not be around to reap the benefits. Thus, even if we value health equally across time, if we were to choose between an option that aimed to cause a health gain now and one that aimed to cause the same gain in the future, all else being equal, we should choose the nearer-term option.

Equality and Prioritizing the Worse Off

As well as maximizing health benefits, many people believe that an important function of actions to improve health is to progress towards a more equal distribution of health, and that particular effort should be made to prioritize those who are worse off. Does this give us a reason to prioritize nearer-term health outcomes?

Human health has undoubtedly improved over time. With advances in wealth, living conditions, the development of modern medicine and evidence-based interventions, we've seen vast improvements in almost all markers of human health, most obviously in the reduction of child mortality rates and improvements in life expectancies.[6] Given this trajectory, it might be reasonable to assume that populations in the future are likely to experience better health than people today. However, this is far from guaranteed. It is possible to think of scenarios where health fails to improve in the future. For the time being at least, humanity is confined to a finite world with finite resources, and climate change is posing a serious threat to future health. We are also at risk of catastrophes—such as a nuclear winter—that could derail humanity's progress in a dramatic way. If we think it is particularly important to prioritize the very worst off, this might even suggest we should prioritize preventing global catastrophes. Overall, given that it's unclear whether we should expect future people to be better or worse off than we are currently, it is unclear how concern for equality affects how we should weight future health.

Duties to Individuals

It might be argued that whether or not decision-makers like Alex should consider people in the future depends on whether they have a duty to do so. However, another thought experiment from Parfit shows the difficulties that arise when considering duties to future populations. Parfit asks us to imagine that our generation has the choice of either (i) using up all the world's resources so that there is little left for future people, or (ii) limiting our consumption so that more resources will be available for future people. Our choice will change the world substantially. This change will be dramatic enough that it will alter the course of people's lives, so much so that different sets of partners will meet and conceive different children than they would have had we chosen the other option. This means that if we choose option (i), the people that are alive after we have used up the world's resources would not have existed had we chosen option (ii). So it is difficult to say that we had a duty to provide a better environment for the people in the world where we choose option (i), because they would not have existed had we done so.

One possible interpretation of this is that we can consume the world's resources to our heart's content, as the particular people who come later will not be able to condemn us for it, as they wouldn't otherwise have existed. However, Parfit rightly rejects this interpretation. Rather than giving us licence to ignore the interests of future populations, this conundrum (termed the 'non-identity' problem[7]) suggests that relying on notions of duty to specific individuals is the wrong way to consider this decision.

Partiality

Thus far I have assumed that Alex should be impartial regarding the distribution of health outcomes. Some people believe that morality doesn't require us to be completely impartial, and that it is morally acceptable (or even required) to favour those closest to us over strangers. Such partiality seems less relevant when we are considering public decision-making rather than private action, but even so, some may argue that as a population we may be justified in favouring those closest to us in time. If this is the case, however, there must still be limits to the extent of our partiality. Most people believe that we shouldn't even favour our closest family members absolutely. If I had the option of either preventing my child from stubbing their toe, or preventing another child from losing their leg, it is clear that I should prevent the much greater injury. So, even if we think that,

as a population, we may be justified in showing partiality to populations closer to us in time, we will still have to give some weight to
the interests of more future people.

Are We Neglecting the Health of Future People?

So far, I have argued that we may have reasons to give additional
weight to nearer-term health outcomes, but that the health of people
in the future matters and that this should be factored into our health
policies. These considerations don't just apply to Alex and the decision
about whether to make environmental sustainability a priority in
health care services. They apply more broadly.

But do we give the health of future people sufficient consideration?

Globally, we invest a lot in protecting and promoting health.
Appropriately, there is growing interest in the processes, techniques,
and institutions used to direct these resources and determine health
priorities. Priority-setting processes are obviously complex,[8] but two
factors frequently come up: (i) the scale of a health problem, and
(ii) how efficiently we can make progress to tackle the problem. In the
1993 World Development Report, *Investing in Health*, it was suggested
that '[p]riority should go to those health problems that cause a large
disease burden *and* for which cost-effective interventions are available'.[9] The way we currently consider these two factors may neglect
future health benefits.

Uncounted Burden

The *burden of disease* refers to the aggregate morbidity and mortality
that can be attributed to a disease or issue in a population. This is
commonly measured in *disability-adjusted life years* (DALYs), which
combines the number of expected life years lost due to premature
death, with an estimate of the ill-health experienced due to disease.
Some diseases primarily have an impact by causing premature death
(e.g. cancer); others may not lead to early death but instead cause pain
and suffering to the living (e.g. chronic back pain). The DALY
provides a way of bringing both of these types of health impact
together, to enable comparison across different disease types in a

way that isn't possible with other health metrics such as incidence, prevalence, or mortality rate.

Estimates of burden of disease have thus far focused on the health profile of the current population, describing the relative magnitude of the health problems harming people now. But unless we expect the profile of the global burden of disease to remain exactly the same in the future, using current burden of disease estimates as our profile of humanity's ill-health will leave the health of future people improperly counted. The COVID-19 pandemic made clear the pitfalls of this approach. Burden of disease estimates have thus far not accounted for the possible emergence of a novel pandemic pathogen. Prior to late 2019, no person had ever suffered from COVID-19, so the vast harms caused by this new disease were not visible in burden of disease estimates.

With advances in computing and modelling it may be possible to develop estimates of the expected distribution of disease burden into the future, using the best available evidence to simulate how population health might change over time. An approach like this could also take into account uncertain or irregular events, such as the emergence of a novel pandemic pathogen.

The obvious limitation of trying to work out the causes of ill-health in the future is our inability to accurately predict the future, particularly to anticipate new diseases or discoveries, to predict the course of our response to climate change, or other events such as a pandemic or nuclear war. However, while there is much that is unknown, we do have some useful knowledge. To continue with the example of COVID-19, it may have been difficult to predict that a novel coronavirus would emerge in Wuhan, China in late 2019 and drastically alter global society in 2020. However, it was not difficult to predict that a novel zoonotic pathogen would cause a pandemic at some point. Health experts have been warning of this risk for many years, describing it as a question of 'when' not 'if'.[10] If we had been considering humanity's burden of disease as something that takes into account health over decades or centuries, then a new pandemic would have been much more visible in calculations of the burden of disease, and we may have been better prepared.

Uncounted Benefits

As well as leaving future health burdens uncounted, we may also be leaving future health benefits uncounted. Cost-effectiveness analyses provide an estimate of the health benefits gained per dollar spent to improve health, and are frequently a major consideration in priority-setting processes. But most health economic analyses are evaluated with respect to their impact on current people, rather than incorporating impacts on populations in the future. Time impacts cost-effectiveness estimates in at least two ways: the choice of time horizons for analysis, and the use of discounting.

Most cost-effectiveness analyses only extend into the near-term future, usually capturing the lifespan of those directly targeted by the intervention. In cost-effectiveness studies of vaccines, analyses can extend up to 100 years into the future, but this is intended to capture the age cohort vaccinated rather than the effects on subsequent generations. But the effects of vaccination campaigns will often flow on to subsequent generations through reduced disease prevalence causing reduced transmission, even in the absence of further rounds of population vaccination. For example, the campaign to eradicate smallpox involved widespread vaccination. The beneficiaries of that campaign included those who were themselves vaccinated, but also all of us in subsequent generations, who no longer live in a smallpox-endemic world.

Another relevant feature of economic evaluations is the use of 'discounting'. This is the practice of reducing the value of costs and effects, for the purposes of current decision-making, of things that occur in the future. There's considerable controversy about whether and why health effects should be discounted.[11] As mentioned, there are reasons for prioritizing actions that aim to increase health in the shorter term, over actions that aim to increase health in the longer term, and discounting can be one way to account for that. National guidelines suggest a discount rate of between 1.5% and 5% per year for future health effects.[12] However, when thinking in terms of decades and centuries, future health effects become insignificant with such rates. For example, a constant discount rate of 1.5% would see us value a single life lost during the Crusades in the thirteenth century as equivalent to the loss of almost 150,000 lives today.

Conclusion

Let us return to Alex; it seems clear that when deciding whether the hospital should take steps to reduce climate change, the benefits to future people should be taken into account. Less clear is how exactly this should be done. I have outlined some relevant factors to consider, but there are many open questions. These include: Will health become less important for a fulfilling life? How likely is it that population health will continue to improve? How should we navigate uncertainty in outcomes? Are we justified in showing partiality to people who are closer to us in time?

What is evident though is that, while we should not neglect the urgent health problems facing humanity right now, we should also not neglect the problems that, through our action or inaction, we might be failing to prevent for people to come. Currently, consideration of health priorities seems to be leaving health in the future uncounted. Working out how the health of future people fits into our health priorities should itself become a priority.

Further Reading

Broome, J., *Climate Matters: Ethics in a Warming World* (W. W. Norton & Company Inc., 2012).
Norheim, O. F., Emanuel, E. J., and Millum, J. (eds.), *Global Health Priority-Setting: Beyond Cost-Effectiveness* (Oxford University Press, 2020).

Notes

1. N. Watts, M. Amann, N. Arnell, S. Ayeb-Karlsson, K. Belesova, M. Boykoff, et al., The 2019 report of The Lancet Countdown on health and climate change: Ensuring that the health of a child born today is not defined by a changing climate, *The Lancet*, 394 (2019), 1836–78.
2. As set out in the constitution of the World Health Organisation, available from https://www.who.int/about/who-we-are/constitution.
3. For a discussion of competing theories of the value of health see D. Hausman, Health, well-being, and measuring the burden of disease, *Population Health Metrics*, 10/13 (2012), and for a discussion of theories of well-being see R. Crisp, Well-being. In E. N. Zalta (ed.), *The Stanford Encyclopedia of Philosophy* (Fall 2017 Edition), https://plato.stanford.edu/archives/fall2017/entries/well-being/.
4. D. Parfit, *Reasons and Persons* (Oxford University Press, 1984).

5. I am grateful to Tyler John for suggesting this point here, which is also made by Owen Cotton-Barratt in O. Cotton-Barratt, Discounting for uncertainty in health. In N. Eyal, S. A. Hurst, C. J. L. Murray, S. A. Schroeder, and D. Wikler (eds.), *Measuring the Global Burden of Disease: Philosophical Dimensions* (Oxford University Press, 2020), 243–56.

6. M. Roser, H. Ritchie, and B. Dadonaite (2013), Child and infant mortality. Published online at *OurWorldInData.org*. https://ourworldindata.org/child-mortality; and M. Roser, E. Ortiz-Ospina, and H. Ritchie (2013), Life expectancy. Published online at *OurWorldInData.org*. https://ourworldindata.org/life-expectancy.

7. For further discussion of the non-identity problem and how it impacts how we should consider the interests of future people see J. Broome, *Climate Matters: Ethics in a Warming World* (W. W. Norton & Company Inc., 2012).

8. For more on this topic see O. F. Norheim, E. J. Emanuel, and J. Millum (eds.), *Global Health Priority-Setting: Beyond Cost-Effectiveness* (Oxford University Press, 2020).

9. World Bank, *World Development Report 1993: Investing in Health* (Oxford University Press, 1993), p. 63.

10. When delivering the Shattuck Lecture on April 27, 2018, Bill Gates said, "We can't predict when. But given the continual emergence of new pathogens, the increasing risk of a bioterror attack, and how connected our world is through air travel, there is a significant probability of a large and lethal, modern-day pandemic occurring in our lifetimes." Available from: https://www.gatesfoundation.org/Media-Center/Speeches/2018/04/Shattuck-Lecture-Innovation-for-Pandemics

11. For a detailed discussion see H. Greaves, Discounting future health. In O. F. Norheim, E. J. Emanuel, and J. Millum (eds.), *Global Health Priority-Setting: Beyond Cost-Effectiveness* (Oxford University Press, 2020), and M. Fleurbaey and S. Zuber, To discount or not to discount, and O. Cotton-Barratt, Discounting for uncertainty in health, both in N. Eyal, S. A. Hurst, C. J. L. Murray, S. A. Schroeder, and D. Wikler (eds.), *Measuring the Global Burden of Disease: Philosophical Dimensions* (Oxford University Press, 2020).

12. A. E. Attema, W. B. F. Brouwer, and K. Claxton, Discounting in economic evaluations, *PharmacoEconomics*, 36 (2018), 745–58.

* I am grateful for very helpful comments from David Edmonds, Tyler John, Julian Savulescu, and Nir Eyal.

3

Can Alt-Meat Alter the World?

Anne Barnhill and Ruth R. Faden

Introduction

There is much that is wrong with the global food system. One major concern is the system's negative impact on climate change and the environment. Here, meat production is the primary culprit. Many experts agree that significant reductions in meat production are needed and that will require significant reductions in meat consumption. The pressing challenge—moral, political, technological, and cultural—is how to achieve dramatic, rapid reductions in the amount of meat most people, especially people in high-income countries, eat.

The food system accounts for a significant proportion of total greenhouse gas emissions (in the order of 25%). Beyond greenhouse gases, food production is the largest cause of global environmental change, involving 40% of global land and 70% of total freshwater use.

The global population is increasing—it may reach 10 billion by 2050—and this means that global food production will need to increase significantly, and environmental impacts of global food production will also increase significantly. This will result in global environmental impacts that exceed levels many scientists consider safe or acceptable. For example, agriculture-related greenhouse gas emissions will make it unlikely or impossible to meet our overall targets for reducing greenhouse gas emissions.

To address the environmental impacts of the food system, experts have converged on the necessity of three broad changes: shifts towards more plant-based diets; reductions in food waste (of around 50%); and wider adoption of agricultural practices with a smaller environmental footprint. Of these three, shifts towards plant-based diets are the most important.

Why Plant-Based Diets Are Better for the Environment

Animal source foods have the biggest impact on greenhouse gas emissions within the food system and have other negative environmental impacts such as air pollution, high water use, and surface and groundwater contamination. These effects come directly from the animals, such as from animal waste, as well as indirectly from growing animal feed and the associated fertilizer, pesticides, and land use change.

Beef, in particular, is an environmentally intensive animal source food: it "requires 20 times the amount of land, and emits 20 times the GHGs, per gram of protein compared with pulses such as beans or lentils."[1] Ruminants (i.e. cattle, goats, sheep) account for 40% of agricultural emissions. Simply reducing beef production would have significant environmental benefits, but reductions in other animal source food, along with beef, would yield even more environmental benefits. According to one estimate, adoption of a diet that excludes animal products would reduce food's GHG emissions by 49%.[2]

Other Reasons Why Plant-Based Diets Are Better

Along with its huge environmental burden, there are two other good reasons to eat less meat. The first turns on how we should treat non-human animals. Each year, 50 billion chickens, 1½ billion pigs, 300 million cattle, and 500 million sheep are killed for food across the world. Many of these animals spend most of their lives raised in large indoor facilities, where hundreds or thousands of animals are densely packed together. These animals have high rates of injury and disease, and are not able to engage in a range of normal animal behaviours. Some chickens and pigs spend most of their lives confined in cages or pens, where they don't even have room to turn around.

The second additional reason to eat less meat is because meat production and consumption have negative public health effects. For example, eating red meat (and especially processed red meat) is associated with increased risk of cardiovascular disease, diabetes, and some cancers. Meat production—not just meat consumption—also poses risks to public health, especially when animals are kept in confinement. Because these animal operations keep large numbers of animals in small spaces and often have inadequate waste management practices, they create air and water pollution. Animal agriculture also spreads some animal diseases (e.g. bird flu, swine flu) to humans: these diseases can be transmitted to humans through direct contact with agricultural animals, through air and water pollution from farms, and through food itself. The contamination of meat products with food-borne pathogens (e.g. *E. coli*, which comes from animals' digestive tracts) is another public health problem; removing animal carcasses from the supply chain would help with this. Lastly, in some countries, the animals raised in animal agriculture are routinely given antibiotics—not just when they are sick—which spurs the creation of antibiotic-resistant bacteria. This represents a major public health threat globally.

Should We Eliminate or Just Reduce Animal Agriculture?

For all its negative effects, it's important to note that animal agriculture serves important functions. Raising livestock is a significant source of food and income for 1 billion people worldwide. Livestock can also have environmental benefits. For example, grazing livestock can help to maintain grasslands when there are no longer native herbivores. Thus, from an economic, food security, and environmental perspective we would, ideally, reduce, but not eliminate animal agriculture. It is also important to note, however, that if you think that it is deeply wrong to raise and kill animals for food where humans have viable nutritious alternatives, then it is not likely that you will find the "reduce but don't eliminate" argument persuasive. But you may still get behind reducing meat consumption, perhaps because you value any incremental reduction in animal suffering and killing.

How Can We Reduce Consumption of Meat?

How can we reduce consumption of meat and drive a significant, rapid shift towards plant-based diets? One way is to make it more expensive—for example, by imposing taxes on meat, or greenhouse gas emissions-based taxes on foods. Other policies for reducing meat consumption include changing agricultural regulations to make meat more expensive, and continuing to educate consumers about the health and also the environmental harms of meat eating. There are good reasons to be sceptical that these approaches will be implemented widely or will result in significant changes in current rates of meat consumption. In response to increasing awareness of the health hazards of beef, beef consumption went down in the United States starting in the 1970s, as some consumers switched to options like chicken, but that trend appears to have plateaued.

Meat Alternatives

Another approach to meat reduction is just to accept that consumers are attached to meat and to work around the preference. This is the spirit behind *meat alternatives*, which include plant-based analogues of meat and cultured meat (aka lab-grown meat), which uses techniques in bioscience and bioengineering to create meat from animal cells in a manufacturing context.

Veggie burgers have been around for a long time. But the last few years have seen the introduction of plant-based meat alternatives that much more closely mimic meat and bioengineering to grow meat (i.e. animal tissue) from animal cells. For example, the Beyond Burger by Beyond Meat, the Impossible Burger by Impossible Foods, and the Moving Mountains Burger by Moving Mountains Foods have all been designed to mimic the taste, mouth feel, and appearance of beef burgers. These companies are also marketing other meat alternatives in addition to burgers and have products available in grocery stores, supermarket chains, table-service and fast-food restaurants across North America, the United Kingdom, and increasingly in Europe, Australia, and parts of Asia.

Along with these plant-based substitutes for beef, companies are marketing plant-based substitutes for other meats (e.g. chicken, pork) as well as substitutes for eggs, butter, and milk. Impossible Foods, for example, has said that its goal is "to produce a full range of meats and dairy products for every cultural region in the world."[3]

A different kind of alt-meat, cultured meat (aka lab-grown meat) comes from what's called cellular agriculture. Rather than creating a plant-based analogue for meat, cellular agriculture attempts to create meat (i.e. animal tissues) by growing it from animal cells. Essentially, cellular agriculture produces meat by growing it in a vat (a "bioreactor"), rather than harvesting it from a dead animal. The first "proof of concept" of cellular agriculture, a hamburger patty produced by Mosa Meats, emerged in 2013, and many companies say they will introduce products in the next few years. Companies are working on a range of foods and cuts of meat: burgers, but also meatballs, steaks, chicken and shrimp, and "cow free whey."

The long-term aspiration of alt-meat is that it will offer consumers versions of, or close analogues of, the meats they already like and consume, that these products eventually will be offered for the same price as conventional meat, and that production will be scaled up enough to meet mass consumer demand—so that eventually alt-meat will replace most conventional meat consumption. Given the burdens of meat production and consumption, could this alt-meat future be a "win–win–win" for the environment, for animal welfare, and for public health?

This future is a realistic possibility. In the United States, sales of plant-based meat substitutes are growing much faster than sales of meat. And these sales aren't just to vegetarians: Impossible Meat says that 70% of people who buy Impossible Burgers are regular meat eaters.[4] And according to one estimate, by 2040, 60% of the global meat market will be comprised of plant-based meat substitutes and cultured meat.[5]

Don't Let the Perfect Be the Enemy of the Good

Is this a future we should embrace? Were alt-meat to replace 60% of conventional meat would it really be a *win–win–win* along animal welfare, environment and human health dimensions? We judge that it is not a clear win–win–win, but closer to a *win* on animal welfare, a *mixed bag* when it comes to the environment, and it *remains to be seen* what would be the effects on human health. A 60% reduction in global conventional meat production would be a huge win for animal welfare, saving tens of billions of animals from lives in confinement conditions. However, the environmental effects of alt-meat could be a mixed bag. For example, a significant shift from beef to plant-based beef alternatives (a mix of Beyond Burger and Impossible Burger) would offer significant reductions in greenhouse gas emissions but may not have environmental benefits along other dimensions (water use, nitrogen and phosphorus use).[6]

Reducing the amount of conventional meat that's produced would have some clear public health benefits; fewer novel and antimicrobial-resistant pathogens would be created and fewer pollutants would be released. However, the impact of alt-meat on dietary health risks is currently unknown. Alt-meat products already on the market do not appear to offer obvious health benefits to consumers. Their fat content is, for example, comparable to that of their meat analogues and, though the type of fat differs, there is no consensus about whether one is clearly preferable to the other. Companies claim that future reformulations of their products will make them healthier, but the nutritional benefits of consuming alt-meat over conventional meat remain unproven.

It's worth noting that whatever the health and environmental benefits of a shift from conventional meat to alt-meat, a shift from conventional meat to other plant-based foods would have more significant benefits. Research suggests that a shift from beef to a mix of healthy plant foods may have a better environmental profile than a shift from beef to plant-based beef alternatives.[7] Also, replacing meat with fruits, vegetables, and legumes will improve people's health more than replacing meat with plant-based beef alternatives, at least for populations in high-income countries that presently consume more than enough protein and fats.

So should we be aiming for the unambiguous win–win–win of more optimal plant-based diets—a shift from beef to beans, from chicken to broccoli—rather than advocating alt-meat? No. Past experience shouldn't leave us optimistic that many consumers will significantly change their diets out of a sense of ethical duty or for health reasons. But unlike shifting to more beans or broccoli, alt-meats don't require much adaptation. If alt-meat can eventually be offered at the same price as conventional meat, consumers won't have to make much of a sacrifice: they will simply reach for one package rather than another in the grocery store. If alt-meat can eventually come in all the cuts currently envisioned, like steak and roasts, then cherished family and cultural traditions could continue relatively unscathed. The revolution will be seamless, a painless way to do the ethically better, if not best, thing.

We should ride this wave of interest in, and adoption of, alt-meat. It would be no small feat to persuade large numbers of people to consume alternatives to conventional meat. We should not reject alt-meat, or throw cold water on its rise in popularity, because we would prefer consumers to make a more optimal dietary shift (i.e. to beans, lentils, or vegetables).

The Path of Least Resistance or the Path of Moral Transformation?

But is that too quick? Is moving to alt-meat really the right thing to do? Or are we giving up too quickly on the possibility and importance of a more significant transformation of our diets and our food systems, and of an accompanying moral transformation?

Alt-meat is greeted with scepticism by some activists and researchers and, of course, by the conventional meat industry.[8] There are numerous arguments against it—for example, that some plant-based alternatives use genetically modified ingredients (which some oppose), that lab-grown meat is fake and unnatural whereas animal agriculture is simple and natural, and that alt-meat threatens the future of ranching and rejects traditional practices and values.[9] But perhaps the most compelling argument against broad adoption of alt-meat is this: at best, this move does nothing to address the root causes of what makes the food system unethical; at worst, it relies on, shores up, and helps perpetuate this unethical system.

Take Impossible Burgers, for example. They are made with soy grown on large, industrialized farms in the US Midwest. This soy is then highly processed, combined with other mysterious processed ingredients, and then sold alongside an array of unhealthy foods at fast-food restaurants like Burger King. Although the start-up companies that created alt-meat began as scrappy little guys fighting the power of Big Food, they are now getting funding from huge meat companies. In the mind of some critics, alt-meat is on track to be another highly industrialized production system that relies upon unsustainable agricultural practices (e.g. soy produced in the US Midwest using conventional agricultural practices), funded and thus to a large extent controlled by Big Food.

Many critics of alt-meat agree that conventional meat production is a broken system that must be changed. But the best way forward, they would argue, is to replace this broken meat production system with a better meat production system, one that is more just and more sustainable through and through: small farms, raising animals outdoors and providing them with good lives; using agricultural practices that conserve resources, reduce greenhouse gas emissions, and rebuild the soil; providing good livelihoods for farmers and workers; and woven into local communities.

Rather than the alt-meat future, food activists may have other visions of the future, ones in which the food system is more thoroughly transformed. Advocates of *food justice* seek better working conditions and higher wages for farmworkers and fast-food restaurant workers, and for everyone to have access to healthy, affordable food. Advocates of *local food systems* and small farms argue that we should get our food from smaller farms that are accountable to local communities, rather than relying on a global system dominated by huge companies, with food grown on the other side of the world. Advocates of *food sovereignty* work to secure the rights of small-scale and landless farmers, peasants, and indigenous people, and argue for greater local or regional control over food and agriculture. Instead of globalized food systems controlled by multinational companies and by agreements made between national governments, the food sovereignty movement proposes smaller-scale food systems that are democratically controlled at the local and regional level. Some argue for communal control of land, water, and seeds, and respect for the farming practices of peasants and indigenous peoples.

For these advocates, replacing one big, consolidated, globalized, industrialized production system (conventional animal agriculture) with another (alt-meat) does not achieve the future they envision. Fair enough. Growing our meat in bioreactors rather than raising animals for meat won't bring down globalized capitalism, and if a small number of companies dominate alt-meat, this will replicate the consolidation of power and profits in a small number of agri-food companies which rightfully troubles advocates.

On the other hand, it may be precisely because alt-meat harnesses the machinery of Big Food that it might be broadly and swiftly adopted. And widespread consumption of alt-meat would transform the food system along *some* important dimensions, with less land used for livestock and so available for other uses, fewer greenhouse gas emissions from protein production, and vastly fewer animals raised in morally troubling conditions.

Conclusion

So where does this leave us? We conclude that, despite all these concerns, we should still welcome a future in which alt-meat is widely adopted. An attainable "win–mixed-bag–remains to be seen" is better than the "win–win–win" of consumers moving to a heavily plant-based diet for the simple reason that this outcome is unrealistic and unattainable. And a "win–mixed-bag–remains to be seen" is certainly preferable to the "lose–lose–lose" of the current state of eating-affairs. But we should approach this future with three significant caveats and additional goals in mind. First, we must recognize that alt-meat addresses only some of the injustices and morally urgent problems in the global food system and that embracing alt-meat does not absolve us from working towards solutions to these problems. Second, we should embrace alternative proteins without buying into the hype. We should bring to alternative protein the same critical eye and demand for ethical improvement that we bring to the food system more generally. Thus third, we should engage in real ethical interrogation of this burgeoning industry, and articulate concrete ways in which the industry may be ethically improved.

Acknowledgements

This work is a product of the Beef, Food Choices and Values project, which was funded by the Stavros Niarchos Foundation. It is an outgrowth of our joint research on alternative proteins with Jan Dutkiewicz, Justin Bernstein, Jess Fanzo, Daniel Mason-D'Croz, Rebecca McLaren, and Travis Rieder. We would like to thank them for their substantial contributions to this work.

Further Reading

Rowe, M., *Beyond the Impossible: The Futures of Plant-Based and Cellular Meat and Dairy* (Brighter Green, 2019). https://brightergreen.org/wp-content/uploads/2019/11/Beyond-the-Impossible.pdf

Notes

1. T. Searchinger, R. Waite, C. Hanson, et al., *Creating a Sustainable Food Future* (World Resources Institute, 2018).
2. J. Poore and T. Nemecek, Reducing food's environmental impacts through producers and consumers, *Science*, 360/6392 (2018), 987–92.
3. E. Watson, Impossible Foods: 'our goal is to produce a full range of meats and dairy products for every cultural region in the world' (2018), Foodnavigator-usa.com Accessed 10 June 2020. https://www.foodnavigator-usa.com/Article/2018/04/13/Impossible-Foods-Our-goal-is-to-produce-a-full-range-of-meats-and-dairy-products-for-every-cultural-region-in-the-world.
4. Watson (2018).
5. A. T. Kearney, How will cultured meat and meat alternatives disrupt the agricultural and food industry? https://www.kearney.com/documents/20152/2795757/How+Will+Cultured+Meat+and+Meat+Alternatives+Disrupt+the+Agricultural+and+Food+Industry.pdf/06ec385b-63a1-71d2-c081-51c07ab88ad1
6. See D. Mason-D'Croz, et al., Pathways to sustainable beef production and demand in the United States (unpublished work-in-progress), p. 73.
7. See Mason-D'Croz et al. (work-in-progress).
8. See E. Jönsson, Benevolent technotopias and hitherto unimaginable meats: Tracing the promises of in vitro meat, *Social Studies of Science*, 46/5 (2016), 725–48; A. E. Sexton, T. Garnett, and J. Lorimer, Framing the future of food: The contested promises of alternative proteins, *Environment and Planning E: Nature and Space*, 2/1 (2019), 47–72; World Economic Forum, *Meat: The Future Series: Alternative Proteins* (2019) https://www.weforum.org/whitepapers/meat-the-future-series-alternative-proteins#:~:text=New%20research%20prepared%20by%20the,significant%20health%20and%20environmental%20benefits; Rowe (2019).
9. Sexton et al. (2019).

Future Lives

4

Abolishing Gender

Brian D. Earp

Some people think we should abolish gender—just get rid of it. They don't typically mean that we should do away with sex: roughly, the physical or biological distinction between females and males.[1] Rather, they think it would better if sex was not linked to socially enforced gender *roles* that prescribe how people should be and behave on the basis of their sex. And their proposal for how to bring about this better future is to banish gender roles—and associated cultural norms—altogether.[2]

To see how this might happen, consider an example. In contemporary Western culture, it is seen as normal and acceptable for females, but not males, to wear dresses. Males who wear dresses 'stand out' as being in violation of the norm. But if a coordinated campaign got a large enough percentage of males to habitually wear dresses, the norm would eventually weaken. As more traits and behaviours underwent such a process, the distinction between male and female gender roles would get less and less clear. At the limit, there would be no distinction. This limit represents the abolition of gender (i.e. prescriptive social distinctions based on sex). Let's call people who want this to happen 'gender abolitionists.'

Not everyone is a gender abolitionist. On the contrary. Many people think that gender roles are appropriate or worthwhile, perhaps even 'natural' and inevitable. On one end of this spectrum are socially conservative religious people. They might think that God fashioned humans into males and females, like other sexually reproducing animals, but also assigned certain functions or responsibilities according to sex. So, in order to be a proper man in God's eyes, a male should be, say, strong and protective (among other stereotypically 'masculine' traits), while a female should be caring and nurturing (among other stereotypically 'feminine' traits).

But it is not only religious conservatives who think we should hold on to gender in some form. At the other end of the spectrum are (some) progressive people who believe that gender can help members of certain disadvantaged groups make sense of their own minds and bodies in our social world. According to one recent articulation of this view, people with a transgender identity could find themselves effectively 'erased' from a society without gender.[3]

There are different ways of understanding this concern, as we'll see. But to get a hint of the idea, consider someone with a male-typical body who feels alienated from their sexual anatomy. Suppose this alienation is at least partly due to stable, internal factors: it is not entirely due to unjust social pressures. And now suppose that this person finds that they are least distressed and best able to flourish in a distinctly feminine gender role.[4] If such a role went out of existence, the thinking goes, it might leave this person (and others like them) worse off while threatening the integrity of their self-conception or identity. Perhaps, then, it is too risky to abolish gender? Let's look at the arguments in turn.

In Favour of Abolition (or Reform)

Start with the pro-abolition position. Why would anyone want to abolish gender? To appreciate this perspective, we should look at the status quo. There is a powerful set of assumptions in Western culture that influences how many of us think about sex and gender, even if we aren't always fully aware of it. We'll call this set of assumptions the "Dominant Gender Ideology" (DGI).[5] It goes something like this:

DGI #1.   There are two sexes, male and female, and virtually all human beings fit exclusively into one sex category or the other;

DGI #2.   There is one appropriate or 'natural' gender role each for males and females;

DGI #3. Males should 'act like' boys or men, fulfilling a *masculine* gender role, while females should 'act like' girls or women, fulfilling a *feminine* gender role; and

DGI #4. People who deviate too far from the culturally approved 'script' for their socially assigned gender role are 'acting out'—historically[6] this might be seen as a sign of mental illness or a defective moral character—and they may need to be brought back into line for their own good or for the good of society (for example, to restore social harmony, preserve the 'natural' order of things, follow God's plan, or whatever).

Something like this set of ideas probably seems like common sense to most people around the world. But critics see major problems. For one thing, the DGI ignores or downplays the existence of people with intersex traits or variations of sex development whose bodies don't neatly fit the first assumption. It also makes life difficult for transgender people and people with certain minority sexual orientations,[7] insofar as they run afoul of the third assumption. And the second and fourth assumptions build a more or less constrictive fence around pretty much everyone.

It gets worse. In many societies, the normative gender role for males (boy/man) is scripted as domineering, aggressive, authoritative, and hungry for power, while the normative gender role for females (girl/woman) is scripted as submissive, passive, and deferential to the power and authority of men. If everybody plays their assigned role, and sticks to the script, what happens? Well, it is obvious how such a drama will unfold: men will be disproportionately in charge of society and women will be kept underfoot.[8]

It's no wonder, then, that advocates for women's equality object to this situation. To stick with our thespian metaphor, if most of the 'directors' or 'playwrights' in society—those with greater ability to mould cultural norms, institutions, and public narratives as they see fit—are males, they will tend to hire male actors for leading parts, and write such parts for men. What's more, they will tend to appoint each other as fellow directors and playwrights and produce plays and stories upholding the idea that the status quo is only right and proper ("Males are *naturally* better writers and performers," they might say, "which explains why females are underrepresented in the theatre").

Such a situation seems decidedly unfair. So how should we address it? One approach would be to try to 'rewrite the script' for male and female gender roles, so they wouldn't produce such an imbalance. That way, even if people did accept their assigned roles, there would be less inequality between the sexes in terms of their power and status in society. According to this reformist approach, society might try to recharacterize traditionally masculine traits like dominance, aggressiveness, and ambition and make them more gender-neutral: equally likely to be associated with the female as the male gender role (and likewise for 'feminine' traits like being empathic or emotionally expressive).

Although promising, this approach may face certain roadblocks. One potential roadblock is practical; the other is more conceptual.

The Practical Problem

Take the trait of aggressiveness as an example. Suppose our aim is to get people to stop thinking of aggressiveness as a masculine trait, associated primarily with the male gender role, and to start thinking of it as something that is feminine, associated with the female gender role (or perhaps equally associated with both). For people who regard males and females as 'blank slates,' with no inherent psychological differences—even at the group level—apart from the ones that arise through cultural conditioning, this shouldn't be too tall an order. On this view, it is essentially arbitrary that aggressiveness should have become culturally linked to masculinity rather than femininity, and we would do well to start unlearning the association.

On the other hand, there are those who think the association is not arbitrary, but rather reflects an underlying biological difference between males and females that exists, on average, at the group level, independent of any cultural influence.[9] According to this view, such a basic difference is bound to be picked up by our brains' statistical learning mechanisms—basically, pattern detectors—and go on to structure the relevant stereotypes that end up circulating in the wider culture. If that is right, then aggressiveness (and perhaps other 'masculine' traits) might be linked to the concept of maleness in many cultures because males are, in fact, more aggressive (etc.) on average, and not only because of their gendered socialization.

But we have to be careful here. Even if there is some biological basis to the mental association people have between certain traits and masculinity or femininity, it wouldn't entitle us to jump from a descriptive 'is' to a prescriptive 'ought' (that is, to a socially enforced set of rules for how males or females *should* act, think, feel, or relate to others). To stick with our example of greater male aggressiveness, this difference could—hypothetically—be entirely biological, and we might still want to rewrite the cultural scripts for male and female gender roles to make that trait (and all the other allegedly masculine or feminine traits) equally socially prescribed for all sexes.

But now imagine that we actually succeeded in doing so. Might this create a conceptual problem?

The Conceptual Problem

Suppose you are a gender reformer, rather than a gender abolitionist. You don't want to get rid of male and female gender roles wholesale, but you do want to make them less rigid, less restrictive, more expansive, and more equal in terms of power and status.[10] So you take all the 'masculine' traits that reinforce male dominance, and all the 'feminine' traits that reinforce female subordination, and you work to change society so that over time these traits become associated with both sexes equally.

Well, you may have become a gender abolitionist despite yourself: if most 'masculine' traits are now equally 'feminine' and vice versa, the very distinction between masculine and feminine starts to break down. Accordingly, people of whatever sex could be free to be and behave however they pleased, as there would be no strict sex-specific script from which they could be said to deviate (and so be accused of 'acting out' as in DGI #4). Again, at the limit, there would simply be no gender roles or norms.

And this is exactly the future that many people want. As one gender abolitionist put it, the very existence of gender roles, no matter what they prescribe, is "inherently oppressive."[11] According to this view, there is no way to culturally endorse a trait, even a positive one, for one sex but not the other without leaving a lot of people out—thereby exposing them to social sanction and other kinds of harm. As an example, suppose that the trait of dominance comes to be seen as 'feminine' one day. That'll be great for females who possess that trait, whether by nature or nurture or some combination. But non-dominant females will be seen as deficient in some way; and dominant males will be seen as stepping out of line.

On the other hand, if dominance comes to be seen as equally feminine and masculine, it will be a gender-neutral trait available to everyone. The same goes for all the other traits that are currently considered masculine or feminine—including culturally variable ones like the propensity to wear suits or ties or dresses or make-up, or to shave certain body parts, enjoy particular color schemes, or keep one's hair short or grow it out.

This is one vision of gender justice: a world where anyone, of any sex, feels comfortable exhibiting any trait without worrying about the repercussions. Where knowing what someone's genitals look like has little or no predictive value for guessing their style of dress, their grooming habits, their physical mannerisms, sexual preferences, career ambitions, psychological profile, or ways of interacting with others. "What exactly is so scary," asks our gender abolitionist, "about individuals creating their own unique identity, regardless of their physical sex?"[12]

Against Abolition

This is where things get tricky. In a recent paper, the philosopher Matthew J. Cull argued that "we should be wary of the abolitionist position, as it imperils trans lives."[13] But how could that be so? Didn't we say that transgender people are among those who *suffer* under the dominant gender ideology (DGI)? We did, emphasizing the third assumption of that ideology: the idea that males should fulfill a masculine gender role while females should fulfill a feminine gender role. And yet, at least according to the DGI, many transgender people turn this assumption on its head. In particular, those with male-typical bodies often feel much more comfortable—or, as one might say, more 'themselves'—occupying a feminine gender role, while those with female-typical bodies often feel more themselves in a masculine gender role.[14] As a consequence, if either wishes to live according to the role—or on some views, actually be the gender—that is most authentic for them, they must 'violate' one of the core assumptions of the

DGI. This, in turn, makes them (unjustly) vulnerable to violence and other forms of abuse for supposedly 'acting out' (as in DGI #4).

So, says the gender abolitionist, why not simply abolish gender as a way of undermining the DGI? If there were no particular ways that males or females were culturally expected to act, think, feel, or relate to others, then—again—there would be no gendered 'script' from which anyone could be said to deviate, and so no basis for the perception that any particular person might be playing the 'wrong' part (for example, by being in the 'wrong' gender role for their sex). In short, there would be no gender, only sex and idiosyncratic self-expression.

But that is exactly the problem, says Cull. If there were no gender, there would also be no transgender people (as such). In other words, their existence as transgender people, or as 'gendered' people of any kind, would be conceptually impossible. And yet, being gendered in certain ways—for example, adopting a masculine or feminine appearance and/or being socially recognized as a member of a given gender category irrespective of sexual anatomy—is often central to the self-concept and well-being of at least some transgender people.[15] Accordingly, Cull writes, "one of our moral-political purposes ought to be to *maintain* the existence of gender, in order to do justice to trans people's gender identifications."[16]

Examining the Argument

Let us look at Cull's argument in more detail. Suppose that we managed to completely eliminate all gender roles, norms, and stereotypes. Gender categories like 'woman' or 'man' would then no longer refer to anything in the actual world. Instead, one could only meaningfully speak of 'females' and 'males'—and perhaps 'intersex people'—picking out humans by sex alone.[17]

Now consider the view that a trans person is anyone who does not regard themselves[18] as a member of the gender category that corresponds to their sex (as in DGI #3). For example, a trans woman on this view is someone whose sex is something other than female but who self-identifies as a woman. Where would such a person fit into our imagined scenario? Well, Cull argues, "in a society where no one identifies as women, there are no trans women." The same holds for trans men in such a society and indeed for all trans people. So, Cull concludes, "it looks like trans people need to be eliminated from society in order for the abolitionist position to be saved."[19]

That may seem a highly disturbing prospect. But there are more or less extreme ways of interpreting Cull's conclusion. On the extreme end, it could be taken to suggest that gender abolition is tantamount to genocide: if you eliminate gender (that is, work to abolish all gender roles, norms, and stereotypes), you actually exterminate transgender people. In fact, Cull does seem open to something like this interpretation: "there are potentially violent implications here, methods of elimination which are enacted upon trans people around the world on an everyday basis."[20]

Now, Cull doesn't suppose that actual gender abolitionists endorse this option. Nevertheless, Cull asks: "What might a nonviolent elimination of gender and trans identities look like? How on earth could one reach a society where trans people no longer identify as [members of their preferred] genders, and do so happily? If such a society is even possible, it seems like getting there is going to be extremely difficult."[21]

Perhaps. But then, it is not just trans women and men who would be 'eliminated' from society in the proposed sense. Rather, all women and men, including non-transgender ('cisgender') women and men— in fact, anyone with a gender identity that was not simply reducible to their sex—would be 'eliminated' from society on Cull's account. (Cull might respond that cisgender people whose gender identities matter to them under current social conditions, and who would want to retain such identities in the future, are not marginalized in the way that transgender people are, and so we should be more concerned about the potential erasure of the latter than the former. Or, Cull might see this as a further strength of the account: abolition, which Cull opposes, would threaten the identity not only of many trans people, but indeed all people with a gender identity, providing an additional reason to maintain gender in some form.)

In any case, a less extreme interpretation of Cull's conclusion can be seen by drawing a distinction. Consider Steph, someone whose sex is female but who identifies as a man (and is thus a trans man on the above conception). Now suppose that Steph identifies as a man *given* the existence of gender, but if gender did not exist, Steph would not identify as a man. And now suppose that gender is abolished so that the concept of 'man'—and hence 'trans man'—no longer refers to anyone under that description. There are at least two ways of characterizing this situation.

One way is to say that by virtue of the abolition, all trans men including Steph have been eliminated from society. That might seem to resonate with the 'violent' interpretation raised by Cull. But another characterization is this: Steph, a person who identified as a trans man when certain gender concepts had wide social purchase, still very much exists, but now has a different self-conception.

Although this latter characterization may sound less alarming, it is not actually clear how good or bad this situation is for Steph. A rough analogy should make this clearer.

An Analogy

Consider someone named Kido, a late-19th-century samurai (a special kind of Japanese warrior). Kido identifies as a samurai right up until the 1870s when the social category 'samurai' is formally abolished during the reign of Emperor Meiji. In truth, the traditional role of the samurai in society had been on the decline for a while, as Japan was becoming more industrialized, its military more modern, and its class distinctions somewhat less rigid. But there is still something psychologically jarring, and seemingly definitive, about the sudden loss of official recognition. In this real-life-inspired example, Kido himself is not eliminated from society, in the sense of being killed or exiled, but becomes a statesman in the new Meiji government. And like other former samurai, he is now considered a 'shizoku'—a novel social category with different rights and privileges, but highly overlapping membership criteria.

What about Kido's self-identity? Is he happy being a bureaucrat or shizoku? Is he able to live authentically in these new roles? We can be sure that being a samurai, prior to the 1870s, was absolutely central to Kido's understanding of himself. It framed his daily interactions with others, shaped his values and way of life, influenced how he dressed and behaved, and furnished his very existence in the world. It seems, then, that the abolition of the social category 'samurai'—both the gradual, social erosion, and the final, formal decree—might be highly distressing to Kido and disruptive to his sense of self.

But this depends on a number of factors. Did Kido have adequate support in transitioning into his new social roles? Was Kido interested in these new roles or was he forced into them through a lack of better options? Did Kido have other identities besides 'samurai' with which to structure his self-concept as the category 'samurai' began to lose social recognition? Did Kido have particular psychological or behavioral traits that made him especially well-suited to the role of a samurai? Are there other roles that might match those traits just as well? It should be obvious that Kido's ability to thrive as an ex-samurai will depend on the answers to these and other questions.

Historically, samurai were divided. Many were strongly opposed to the changes they saw happening around them, and wanted traditional social roles and norms to be preserved. When the samurai class was officially disbanded, some felt lost, confused about their place in society, and unsure of who they 'were.' Presumably, some became depressed or suicidal. Some may have continued to self-identify as samurai in private, feeling frustrated or resentful that the concept was no longer used by others to refer to any existing person. Some actually took up arms and rebelled against the changes, only to be forcibly suppressed by agents of the state.

Others, however, welcomed the changes. Some even helped to set up the incoming Meiji regime. They found new roles as government officials, teachers, artists, and farmers, among other occupations. Many felt comfortable in their new roles and identities, believing that prior social distinctions—even ones from which they may have benefitted—were an impediment to a just society.[22]

Samurai in the 1800s, like transgender people today, were not a homogenous group.[23]

Completing the Analogy

Let's return to Steph. What can we learn from the preceding analogy? Before the abolition of gender, we can suppose that, like the category 'samurai' to Kido, the category 'man' is absolutely central to Steph's self-understanding. It allows him to make personally coherent and socially intelligible his embodied experiences and interpersonal relationships in the culture of which he is a part. If the gender abolitionists get their way, therefore, what will this mean for Steph and others like him?

As with Kido, it depends. Will people like Steph—that is, people who currently identify as trans men or women—be able to adapt to the loss of gendered distinctions in the wider culture? Will this loss be gradual and informal, driven by changes at the grassroots level, or will top-down laws and policies (also) explicitly do away with gender—for example by categorizing people in terms of their genitals or chromosomes for official purposes?[24] Will new concepts be developed that are capable of doing justice to the personal qualities of people like Steph, allowing them to reconcile their minds and bodies to the social context?[25] Might some (currently) trans people thrive in a post-gender world, while others would only suffer?

It may be impossible to know the answers in advance. In the historical analogy, many samurai were in fact harmed by the abolition of the social category 'samurai,' and in some cases there were in fact violent repercussions. Now consider an important disanalogy (among others that could be raised). Prior to the 1870s, samurai were among the most privileged members of their society, whereas today, transgender people are among the least. Since abolishing gender has the potential to be very harmful to at least some significant proportion of this group, Cull suggests we should adopt a precautionary attitude and oppose the abolition of gender.

Summary and Conclusion

We seem to be at an impasse. Gender abolitionists are concerned that the current DGI is harmful and systematically oppresses women. Simply reforming gender roles, they argue, is not enough to solve these problems, so they need to be done away with completely. On the other hand, progressive opponents of abolition, although they also object to various aspects of the DGI, are concerned that abolishing gender altogether risks harming trans people. Is there a way to move forward in this thicket?

One step we can take is to be realistic. As the feminist philosopher Sally Haslanger has recently argued, whether we like it or not, there are at least some culturally salient differences between males and females at the species level independent of socialization. As such, she predicts that "[g]ender systems and gender narratives will occur in any context where humans reproduce biologically."[26] If that is right, then the total abolition of gender may not be possible—and this may be enough to assuage the worries of critics such as Cull. In other words, as long as there is some intelligible way of signaling one's (desired) membership in a socially recognized gender category, trans people—as currently conceived—need not be 'eliminated' (in any of the above senses) from society. At the same time, we must do our best to revise existing gender scripts to obliterate those aspects that tend to uphold male domination and female subordination. And above all we must do away with DGI #4: in no case should society punish those who are neither behaving unjustly nor causing harm, simply because they 'go off script.'[27]

Further Reading

Bettcher, T. M., Feminist perspectives on trans issues. In *Stanford Encyclopedia of Philosophy*, 8 January 2014, https://plato.stanford.edu/entries/feminism-trans/.

Dembroff, R., *Categories We (Aim to) Live By* (PhD thesis, Princeton University, 2017).

Serano, J., *Whipping Girl* (Seal Press, 2016).

Notes

1. For a brief account of sex as a biological classification, see N. Hodson et al., Defining and regulating the boundaries of sex and sexuality, *Medical Law Review*, 27/4 (2019), 541–52. On the relationship between sex (in this sense) and gender, see B. D. Earp, What is gender for?, *The Philosopher*, 108/2 (2020), 94–9.

2. For classic discussions of gender abolition, see R. Wilchins, *Read My Lips: Sexual Subversion and the End of Gender* (Firebrand, 1997); K. Bornstein, *Gender Outlaw: On Men, Women, and the Rest of Us* (Viking, 1995). See also D. Boyarin, Paul and the genealogy of gender, *Representations*, 41 (1993), 1–33, discussing the Pauline metaphysical tradition according to which there is neither male nor female, for all are "one" in Christ (from Paul's letter to the Galatians, 3:28).

3. Note: some people use 'gender' to refer, not to sex-based social roles or categories, but to an internal, psychological sense of oneself as being—or not being—a member of such a category (sometimes called one's 'gender identity'). But this arguably presupposes the existence of the social categories, whose respective membership criteria must substantively differ in some way for the internal sense of gender to have any (non-private) meaning. If that is correct, then abolishing gender in the social sense would also undermine gender identity. For further discussion, see K. Jenkins, Toward an account of gender identity, *Ergo*, 5/27 (2018), 713–44.

4. There are many routes to a transgender identity, and not all of them have to do with such 'internal' discomfort with one's reproductive features or sexed embodiment. For a discussion of 'external' forces (like bullying and stigma) that can contribute to such discomfort, see, e.g., R. Dembroff, Moving beyond mismatch, *American Journal of Bioethics*, 19/2 (2019), 60–3. For a positive account of feminine identity as an aesthetic and/or political aspiration, see, e.g., A. L. Chu, On liking women, *N Plus One*, 30 (2018), 47–62.

5. It's important to emphasize that both gender abolitionists and their (progressive) opponents are unhappy with the status quo. They just see different paths forward and weigh the associated trade-offs differently. Note: for a much more sophisticated and philosophically robust account of the DGI, see R. Dembroff, Beyond binary: Genderqueer as critical gender kind, *Philosophers' Imprint*, 20/9 (2020), 1–23.

6. And, unfortunately, in some places still today.

7. Socially enforced gender roles include expectations about sexual orientation. In other words, part of the dominant 'script' for males and females is that they should only (want to) have sex with members of the 'opposite' sex-and-gender category.

8. For important theoretical discussions, see, e.g., K. Manne, *Down Girl* (Oxford University Press, 2017); C. Chambers, Masculine domination, radical feminism and change, *Feminist Theory*, 6/3 (2005), 325–46.

9. For insight into some of the opposing views in this area, see the following paper and linked commentaries: J. Archer, Does sexual selection explain human sex differences in aggression?, *Behavioral and Brain Sciences*, 32/3–4 (2009), 249–66.

10. As an expression of this view, consider what one philosopher has related about her students: "As they see it, 'the feminist revolution' need not do away with gender, and being a woman or man is not primarily the problem—the real problem is how people are viewed and treated." M. Mikkola, *The Wrong of Injustice: Dehumanization and Its Role in Feminist Philosophy* (Oxford University Press, 2016), pp. 125–6.

11. G. Gillett, We shouldn't fight for 'gender equality'. We should fight to abolish gender, *New Statesman*, 2 October 2014, https://www.newstatesman.com/society/2014/10/we-shouldn-t-fight-gender-equality-we-should-fight-abolish-gender.

12. Gillett (2014).

13. M. J. Cull, Against abolition, *Feminist Philosophy Quarterly*, 5/3 (2019), 1–16, p. 1.

14. On some accounts, at least one of the reasons a transgender person might feel more themselves in a female or male gender role is because they *are* a female or male, respectively. For a thorough discussion of the various ways this claim can be understood, see T. M. Bettcher, Feminist perspectives on trans issues. In *Stanford Encyclopedia of Philosophy*, 8 January 2014, https://plato.stanford.edu/entries/feminism-trans/.

15. This is especially true of transgender people, and indeed all people, who identify within the sex or gender binary as it currently exists, and who would (want to) continue to identify within such a binary even as, for example, certain social distinctions between males and females broke down. Non-binary or genderqueer (trans) people, by contrast, might relate quite differently to the abolition of binary gender.

16. Cull (2019), p. 8, emphasis added.

17. As Lori Watson (personal communication) notes: "If we lived in this world, 'reading' someone's sex would be different than it is now. We might use secondary sex characteristics, but for many those are unclear or ambiguous. So, in this imagined world, sorting people into binary sex categories wouldn't be easy or obvious." See also L. Watson, The woman question, *Transgender Studies Quarterly*, 3/1–2 (2016), 246–53. Please note that in the above paragraph I am using a linguistic convention that presumes a gender/sex distinction: between 'man/male' and 'woman/female.' This distinction is controversial but is needed to make sense of the argument.

18. Elizabeth Barnes has made the point that infants and persons with certain cognitive limitations may not self-reflectively 'regard themselves as' a member of any sex or gender category, but this doesn't necessarily make them a trans person or someone without a sex or gender. She notes that this puts pressure on accounts of sex or gender that rely entirely upon self-identification for category membership. E. Barnes, Gender and gender terms, *Nous*, 54/3 (2020), 704–30.

19. Cull (2019), p. 12.

20. Cull (2019), p. 12.

21. Cull (2019), p. 12.

22. M. Wills, Whatever happened to the samurai?, *JSTOR Daily*, 29 December 2017, https://daily.jstor.org/whatever-happened-to-the-samurai/.

23. Indeed, on the issue of gender abolition, there are self-identified trans folks on all sides. Alison Escalante, for example, favours what she calls "gender nihilism"—a kind of abolitionist proposal—while Julia Serano has written eloquently in defence of femininity (although she would like to see the female gender role expanded, more seriously valued and respected, and less heavily policed). See, for example, A. Escalante, Gender nihilism: an anti-manifesto, *LibCom*, 26 June 2016, https://libcom.org/library/gender-nihilism-anti-manifesto; J. Serano, *Whipping Girl* (Seal Press, 2016).

24. This is not far-fetched or purely hypothetical. See for example E. L. Green, "Transgender" could be defined out of existence under Trump administration, *New York Times*, 21 October 2018, https://www.nytimes.com/2018/10/21/us/politics/transgender-trump-administration-sex-definition.html.

25. We might also want to ask about people in future generations who, had they existed prior to the abolition of gender, *would have* identified as trans

men or women, but who will not have those concepts available to them as socially recognized options for making sense of their embodied experiences. Might there be some people for whom there would then be no equivalently suitable social categories for structuring their core self-concepts? (On a related note: are there people today who, given the opportunity, *would have* identified as samurai prior to the 1870s for whom there are currently no equivalently fitting identities?)

26. S. Haslanger, Why I don't believe in patriarchy: comments on Kate Manne's "Down Girl," *Philosophy and Phenomenological Research*, 101/1 (2020), 220–9, p. 226.

27. Thank you to Nadav Berman, Clare Chambers, Megha Chawla, Matthew Cull, Robin Dembroff, David Edmonds, Moya Mapps, Leah McCaskill, Peter Momtchiloff, Joan Ongchoco, and Lori Watson for helpful feedback on an earlier draft.

5

The Future of Friendship

Rebecca Roache

I'm writing this five months into lockdown in response to the COVID-19 pandemic. Until a few weeks ago, my children and I hadn't seen anyone else since March. No face-to-face conversations. No play-dates. No visiting friends. If the lockdown had happened a couple of decades earlier, any contact with people we don't live with would have taken place via phone calls or letter-writing. But now things are different. My daughter and her friends play a game on their phones while discussing their strategy in a WhatsApp group. My son, who is yet to reach the developmental milestone of smartphone ownership, chats with his classmates via Google Classroom. Both kids grew noticeably shy during lockdown, but their nervousness about speaking to friends they hadn't seen for a while was cured by using video-calling platforms with built-in games: after a few minutes of wordless, giggling competition in which they became unicorns and caught donuts on their virtual nose-horns, they had loosened up enough to discuss serious matters like Pokémon and Mario Kart.

None of this technology existed a generation ago. When I was their age, non-face-to-face, real-time interactions with friends would take place over the phone in the downstairs hallway at home, where everyone could hear what I was saying and where I could talk for no longer than ten minutes before an agitated parent started muttering about phone bills and 'blocking the line'. There were no donut-catching unicorns, although I was free to challenge my wits by attempting to untangle the spiral cable that linked the phone to the handset. Phone calls with friends were an occasional treat, not an everyday occurrence. Lockdown in my childhood would have been a very different social experience.

How different, though? Are the differences in the ways we interact with our friends today versus a generation ago merely superficial, comparable to the difference between writing a letter to a friend on lined versus unlined paper? Or is there something about contemporary friendships that is fundamentally different to the friendships of yesteryear—and if so, how might friendship continue to change in the future?

It's common these days to complain that friendships aren't what they used to be. That restaurants are filled with people staring at their phones instead of talking. That selfie culture has turned us into narcissists who care more about managing our own PR than about being present with each other. That social media enables people to present a deceptively polished version of their lives, leaving us feeling that real life is a poor imitation of Instagram life. That today's friendships are somehow more conditional than they were in the past, as we organise ourselves online into 'echo chambers' of like-minded individuals and reject those whose views differ from our own, narrowing our view of the world in the process and leaving us unable to get along with diverse people. Even the word 'friend' has been transformed by social media: there's a new sense in which *being friends with* someone just means having clicked 'accept' on their friend request, which we can do without ever saying hello. The pessimists among us might wonder where this is all going to end. Perhaps we'll find ourselves in a cynical world where we interact only with people who serve us, where we don't recognise our friends without their Snapchat filters, and where we don't form genuine connections with anyone.

I think these concerns are overblown. The changing world we live in isn't changing friendship for the worse, and there's no reason to believe that the future of friendship will be fundamentally different from how friendship has been in the past.

Friendship through a Screen

There's a pervasive anxiety that true friendship is in decline, and that technology is to blame. Headlines like 'The Era of Antisocial Social

Media' and 'Your Smartphone is Making You Stupid, Antisocial and Unhealthy' are familiar fare.[1] A Bizarro Comics cartoon from 2011 shows a couple sitting at a table in a coffee shop, with one staring at a phone and the other saying, 'Do you mind if I strap your phone to my forehead so I can pretend you're looking at me when I talk?'[2] It's tempting to conclude that we've entered a friendship apocalypse. But such concerns are nothing new.

Anxiety about the dystopic effects of new technology on friendship is as old as the written word. Older, in fact: for Socrates, the written word was itself part of the problem. Well over 2,000 years ago, in Plato's *Phaedrus*, Socrates relates an ancient (even for him) legend in which the Egyptian king Thamus addressed the god Theuth, the inventor of letters. According to Socrates, Theuth claimed that letters 'will make the Egyptians wiser and give them better memories.' Socrates approvingly paraphrases Thamus's unenthusiastic response:

> [T]his discovery of yours will create forgetfulness in the learners' souls, because they will not use their memories; they will trust to the external written characters and not remember of themselves. The specific which you have discovered is an aid not to memory, but to reminiscence, and you give your disciples not truth, but only the semblance of truth; they will be hearers of many things and will have learned nothing; they will appear to be omniscient and will generally know nothing; they will be tiresome company, having the show of wisdom without the reality.[3]

From our contemporary perspective, in which land-line telephones and the written word are about as benign as it's possible for technology to get, these concerns strike us as quaint. Of *course* telephones and writing don't undermine friendship. On the contrary, they promote it: phone calls and letters between distant friends are exactly the sorts of wholesome institutions that hand-wringers about social media are afraid will die out.

Perhaps social media, like these more established technologies, also promotes friendship—or, at least, perhaps it doesn't threaten it in the way that many people fear. In a 2012 paper, Shannon Vallor considers whether the sorts of friendships we have on Facebook can be *real* friendships, and she concludes that yes, they can.[4] Her argument does not rest upon new-fangled ideas about friendship; rather, she uses Aristotle's conception of friendship, which is over 2,000 years old.

I have previously argued that scepticism about the ability of social media to support friendship is likely biased: it is usually expressed by people whose early friendships were not formed around social media, which makes such people more likely to focus on the negatives of social media and ignore the positives.[5] In any case, it's looking probable that the encroachment of social media into our relationships isn't as inexorable as many have feared. A 2019 report from Edison Research reveals that social media use has peaked or is flattening out.[6] Similar results are reported by Global Web Index.[7]

People Like Us

Even if interacting through a screen is not destroying friendships, many people fear that the way in which we use digital technology to choose and nurture our friends encourages lower-quality social connections than we've seen in the past. One such fear relates to 'echo chambers': those groups of like-minded individuals into which we sort ourselves, with the result that cross-fertilisation of ideas is reduced and people become more polarised and entrenched in their views. Some scholars claim that online echo chambers have serious implications for liberal democracy.[8] But from a friendship point of view, they are nothing new. Long before the internet, people's social interactions were largely confined to communities of like-minded others. Communities would spring up around places of religious worship, the marketplace, sports teams, workplaces, and educational establishments, and along class, gender, and ethnic lines. There have always been venues that are closed to members of certain groups, either through explicit policies like the apartheid system adopted in South Africa in the last century, or through less formal norms, like those that ensured that women of my mother's generation would never dream of going for a drink in a pub unaccompanied. We may have internet echo chambers now, but many of these other groupings are defunct.

It's simply not true, then, that in the days before digitally mediated friendship, people drew their friends from all walks of life. Perhaps we are all missing out as a result. But even if we are, the fact that the internet enables us to connect with similar people has some great benefits for friendship. It enables us to tap into support and solidarity that might not otherwise be available, either because people with the right sort of shared experiences would be difficult to find offline, or because the shared experiences in question are so intimate that we're reluctant to discuss them—a reluctance that is eased by interacting online.[9] I rely heavily on this sort of community myself: for several years I've belonged to a private Facebook group of single mothers working in academia. The friendships I've made—which are spread across the world—along with the support I've given and received, have been hugely positive additions to my life.

It seems plausible that the view that echo chambers are bad for friendship is based partly on a view that friendship is—or ought to be—deeper than shared interests and experiences. We have long been moved by stories of friendships and romances between people from diverse, often conflicting, groups. Perhaps the most iconic romantic couple, William Shakespeare's Romeo and Juliet, belonged to feuding families. The friendship between Nelson Mandela, while imprisoned for conspiring to overthrow South Africa's apartheid government, and a young, initially pro-apartheid, white prison guard captured the public's attention and was the focus of a film, *Goodbye Bafana*.[10] In 2014, Arab-American journalist Sulome Anderson tweeted a photo of herself kissing her Jewish boyfriend, Jeremy, while holding a sign reading 'Jews and Arabs REFUSE to be ENEMIES'. The photo went viral.

These examples illustrate that we are captivated by the idea of looking beyond our friends' (perhaps unpalatable) views and interests, and loving the person behind them. It's certainly true that the best friendships don't stand or fall with shared interests. If you initially connected with your oldest friend over your shared love of 90s American boy bands but part ways when one of you loses interest in Boyz II Men, it would be hard not to conclude that your friendship didn't run very deep. But this doesn't entail that there is anything wrong with *seeking out* connections based on shared interests. A deep, loving, supportive friendship of many years is not made any less deep, loving, and supportive because the friends in question initially connected through their boy band obsession.

Friendships, Friendships, Everywhere . . .

What about the idea that we now live in a world in which friendship is debased? In which social media encourages us to value quantity over quality, and to project images of glossy perfection at the expense of forming deep, intimate connections?

The concern that quantity of friendships comes at the expense of quality is—like the other concerns we've discussed so far—not at all new. In an essay entitled 'On Having Many Friends', the 1st-century Greek philosopher Plutarch wrote:

> What then is the coin of friendship? It is goodwill and graciousness combined with virtue, than which nature has nothing more rare. It follows, then, that a strong mutual friendship with many persons is impossible, but, just as rivers whose waters are divided among branches and channels flow weak and thin, so affection, naturally strong in a soul, if portioned out among many persons become utterly enfeebled.[11]

A couple of millennia later, Abba sang, 'Facing twenty thousand of your friends / How can anyone be so lonely?' in their 1980 single, 'Super Trouper'. And in 2009, former *X Factor* contestant Eoghan Quigg released a single, '28,000 Friends', with the lines, 'You and your 28,000 friends / YouTube, Facebook, Myspace, IM' and 'How does it feel to be alone? / So many friends that you don't know'.

According to our digital timescales, Quigg's reference to Myspace is its own brand of ancient—but we might wonder whether the technology that has emerged over the past couple of decades encourages us to spread our friendships more thinly than ever. Does Quigg have more reason to gripe about this than Plutarch did? The answer is that, while empirical evidence supports the claim that we are incapable of having a great many close friendships, it's far from clear that social media's capacity to multiply our social connections is reducing the quality of our friendships. The anthropologist Robin Dunbar studied social groups over the centuries and found that the number of stable social connections that individuals can maintain has remained fairly constant, at roughly 150. This figure—which has come to be known as Dunbar's Number—denotes, more or less, 'the number of people you would not feel embarrassed about joining uninvited for a drink if you happened to bump into them in a bar'.[12] There are subdivisions within this. We each tend to have three to five people who constitute 'the small nucleus of really good friends to whom you go in times of trouble', and a 'sympathy group' of twelve to fifteen people 'whose death tomorrow would leave you distraught'—but, Dunbar argues, we simply lack the cognitive capacity to inflate these groups. '[I]f a new person comes into your life', Dunbar explains, 'someone has to drop down into the next level to make room for them'.[13] Since the number of friends we can have is limited by our cognitive capacity, not even the ease of making online connections can enable us to expand it. Commenting on social media, Dunbar remarks that 'there is an issue about what really counts as a friend. Those who have very large numbers—that's to say, larger than about two hundred—invariably know little or nothing about the individuals on their list.'[14]

The fact that Dunbar's Number is—as Dunbar sees it—limited by our *cognitive* capacities, points to a possible way in which friendship might look different in the future. Cognitive capacities—including attention, memory, perception, and decision-making—relate to the mental processing of information. We use various strategies and tools to help us improve these capacities. We drink coffee to help us focus, wear glasses to improve our vision, write lists to help us remember things, and so on. The improvements we make as a result are relatively modest, and often short-lived. However, many believe that, in the near future, we will be able to make far more drastic improvements to our cognitive capacities using technologies like drugs, transcranial electrical stimulation, brain implants, and genetic engineering. The results could see human cognitive capacities far exceed anything we've seen before.[15] In that case, perhaps we might be able to maintain close friendships with significantly more people. But given that even cognitively enhanced versions of ourselves would be constrained by the number of hours we have for socialising, increasing our number of close friends would need to involve wringing more intimacy from the time we spend with each friend. Or, it could be that a cognitively enhanced world would go hand in hand with other changes, such as a reduction in working hours, which could free up more time for friends. On the other hand, even with the cognitive capacity to have more close friendships, perhaps many would value having fewer friends. The world of romantic relationships provides an analogy: while some people choose a non-monogamous lifestyle with multiple romantic partners, many others value monogamy. Having the capacity to maintain multiple romantic relationships apparently does not result in most people wanting to live non-monogamously.[16] Similarly, attaining the increased cognitive capacity that Dunbar views as necessary to maintain significantly more close friendships does not entail that people would in general increase their friendship circles. A cognitively enhanced future of friendship *might* end up looking different to the way friendship looks now—but equally, it might not.

What We Owe to Our Friends

It might seem that, by encouraging us to use the term 'friend' to refer to hundreds or even thousands of people with whom we have only very superficial connections, social media is (to use Plutarch's metaphor) devaluing the coin of friendship. Facebook friends are, after all, often friends in name only—especially for those users whose friends run into the hundreds or thousands. But using 'friend' to refer to people one does not know particularly well is nothing new. In her study of social connections in 18th-century England, Naomi Tadmor explains that a few centuries ago, a person would count as friends not only those with whom they had relatively intimate emotional relationships, but also family, household staff, employers, and so on. She points to the term 'Society of Friends'—still used today as a term for Quakers—as an example of this wider use of the term.[17]

Despite changes over the years in whether certain people with whom we have relatively loose social connections count as friends, there has remained a stable core. The handful of people who constitute Dunbar's 'small nucleus' and the dozen or so who make up the 'sympathy group' have always counted as friends. But changes in our views about what we owe our friends hint at what might become of these smaller, intimate groups. Consider our views about loyalty. It's good to be loyal to our friends—but in professional contexts, we use terms like 'cronyism' and 'nepotism' to condemn loyalty to friends. Tadmor explains that things were different in the past. In the 18th century, serving one's friends was viewed as a virtue, even in politics.[18] Just as giving one's friends a shoo-in for a job in politics was virtuous three centuries ago but is objectionable today, perhaps some practices that today count as virtuous will one day be viewed as objectionable. Today, nobody raises an eyebrow at a lawyer who gives out free advice to friends (but not strangers) or a hairdresser who styles his friends' hair (but not strangers' hair) for free. Providing strangers, free of charge, with the sort of help that they would otherwise have to pay for is kind, but not expected or required. Things might change in the future. Perhaps giving friends the benefit of one's skills while denying it to strangers will be viewed as cronyism in the centuries to come.

What would a future world with different ideas about what we owe to our friends look like? Well, probably not *that* different to today's world. I've written here about contemporary friendship as if it's the same thing all over the world. It's not, of course—I'm writing from the perspective of a Western, European, English-speaking culture. The differences between friendships in different cultures, and between different individuals in different cultures, are as marked as any of the differences I've written about here. Friendships in individualist cultures—typical of English-speaking countries and much of Western Europe—differ in several important ways from friendships in Arab, East Asian, African, and Latin American countries where there is a more collectivist culture. For example, reciprocity between friends is typically valued more in individualist than in collectivist cultures. Individualists don't like to be indebted to friends by not returning favours; collectivists don't view such interactions in terms of favours and instead view those who resist accepting help from friends as aloof and egotistical. Behaviour between friends that, in individualist cultures, is seen as inappropriately interfering—like correcting a friend's class notes—is deemed considerate and caring in collectivist cultures. Those in collectivist cultures tend to be confident that their close friendships will endure without nurturing by saying positive things; as a result, they speak to their friends with a frankness that would be viewed as cold in individualist cultures. As Roger Baumgarte—from whose survey of cross-cultural friendship research I've drawn these observations—remarks, these cultural differences reveal that even what it *means* to be a close friend varies by culture.[19]

Conclusion

Despite cross-cultural differences, Dunbar's Number remains constant and people with different friendship styles enjoy roughly the same health and emotional benefits from their friendships. Barring drastic change, we can probably be confident that the future of friendship is not going to be markedly different from the past and the present of friendship. The sorts of things that are commonly viewed as threats to friendship—like social media and echo chambers—turn out to be less ominous on closer examination. An example of the sort of drastic change that could make a significant difference to friendship is cognitive enhancement; this would enable us to increase the number of close friendships that we are able to sustain. But even so, time constraints, established social norms, and personal and cultural preferences are likely to apply brakes to the speed at which friendship transforms over time even among cognitively enhanced future populations. Friendship, more or less as we know it, is here to stay.

Further Reading

Dixon, T., Five hundred years of friendship, *BBC Radio 4* (2014). Available at https://www.bbc.co.uk/programmes/b03yzn9h.

Notes

1. S. Wilson, The era of antisocial social media, *Harvard Business Review*, 5 February 2020. Available at https://hbr.org/2020/02/the-era-of-antisocial-social-media; E. A. Gee, Your smartphone is making you stupid, antisocial and unhealthy, *The Globe and Mail*, 6 January 2018. Available at https://www.theglobeandmail.com/technology/your-smartphone-is-making-you-stupid/article37511900/.
2. D. Piraro, Daily Cartoon, *Bizarro Comics*, 25 October 2011.
3. Plato, *Phaedrus*, tr. B. Jowett (The Internet Classics Archive, 360 BCE). Available at http://classics.mit.edu/Plato/phaedrus.html.
4. S. Vallor, Flourishing on Facebook: Virtue friendship and new social media, *Ethics and Information Technology*, 14 (2012), 185–99.
5. R. Roache, Social media and friendship. In D. Edmonds (ed.), *Ethics and the Contemporary World* (Routledge, 2019), pp. 135–48.
6. Edison Research, *The Social Habit 2019* (2019). Available at http://www.edisonresearch.com/wp-content/uploads/2019/05/The-Social-Habit-2019-from-Edison-Research.pdf.
7. Global Web Index, *Social Media by Generation* (2019). Available at https://www.visualcapitalist.com/visualizing-social-media-use-by-generation/.
8. E.g., C. Sunstein, *Republic.com* (Princeton University Press, 2001); C. Sunstein, *#republic: Divided Democracy in the Age of Social Media* (Princeton University Press, 2017).

9. N. Lapidot-Lefler and A. Barak, 'The benign online disinhibition effect: Could situational factors induce self-disclosure and prosocial behaviours?', *Cyberpsychology: Journal of Psychosocial Research on Cyberspace*, 9/2 (2015), article 3.

10. There is controversy about *which* young, initially pro-apartheid, white prison guard enjoyed a close friendship with Mandela. *Goodbye Bafana* was based on a book by Mandela's former guard, James Gregory. However, Anthony Sampson, Mandela's friend and author of his authorised biography, claimed that Gregory's account of his friendship with Mandela was largely fantasy, and that Mandela was in fact close friends with a different young, initially pro-apartheid, white prison guard, Christo Brand (A. Sampson, *Nelson Mandela: The Authorised Biography* (Vintage, 2000)).

11. Plutarch, On having many friends. In *Moralia*, vol. II (Loeb Classical Library, 1928), 45–69; quotation from p. 51.

12. R. Dunbar, *Grooming, Gossip, and the Evolution of Language* (Harvard University Press, 1998), p. 77.

13. R. Dunbar, *How Many Friends Does One Person Need?: Dunbar's Number and Other Evolutionary Quirks* (Harvard University Press, 2010), quotations from pp. 32–4.

14. Dunbar (2010), p. 22.

15. For further discussion, see the essays in part II of J. Savulescu, R. ter Muelen, and G. Kahane (eds.), *Enhancing Human Capacities* (Wiley-Blackwell, 2011).

16. Social norms play a part here, of course—it's likely that many people are monogamous because that's the cultural norm, and that if the norms were different, more would choose non-monogamy. Even so, others choose monogamy for other reasons. For more on this topic, see C. Jenkins, *What Love Is and What it Could Be* (Basic Books, 2017).

17. N. Tadmor, *Family and Friends in Eighteenth-Century England: Household, Kinship and Patronage* (Cambridge University Press, 2001).

18. Interview with Tadmor in T. Dixon, Five hundred years of friendship, *BBC Radio 4* (2014), episode 1. Available at https://www.bbc.co.uk/programmes/b03yzn9h.

19. R. Baumgarte, Conceptualizing cultural variations in close friendships, *Online Readings in Psychology and Culture*, 5/4 (2016), article 3.

6

Avatars

Erica L. Neely

In many ways, Naoko's life seems mundane. During the day she works on projects, attends teleconference meetings, and occasionally sits through training sessions for her job. After work she might go shopping or watch a dance troupe perform. Since her father died, she also has regular group therapy sessions, although sometimes she just wants to meet up with a friend and vent. She's even reached a point where she is dating again, which was difficult for several months after her loss. What makes Naoko's life different from yours or mine is that she does all these things without leaving her home—working, entertainment, socializing. In fact, her entire life is taking place inside virtual worlds.

So what exactly *is* a "virtual world"? There are three main aspects to it. First, as the name suggests, it is a computer-implemented simulation (this is the "virtual" part) of an environment (the "world" part). Second, individual people control at least some of the entities it contains, and multiple people can affect the environment at the same time. In other words, the world is shared and responds to the actions of its users. Third, the world is persistent, meaning that it exists even when nobody is interacting with it. This is different to, say, a single-player video game, where the game world essentially exists only while the user is playing the game. The best-known virtual world is probably *Second Life*, although some massively multiplayer online role-playing games such as *World of Warcraft* also count as virtual worlds.

In order to interact with the virtual world a user usually controls an avatar, which is a representation of the user inside the world. In this chapter we will look at ethical issues pertaining to avatars and their users.

Many of the ethical issues involve questions of customization: how much should a user be able to customize their avatar? While I do not suggest legal constraints on avatars, I argue that the designers of virtual worlds have an ethical obligation to afford all users the same range of customization options.

Historically avatars (and virtual worlds themselves) could be entirely text-based, but nowadays most are visual. Thus, an avatar can be thought of as a visual representation of the person using the world. This representation could, in theory, be almost anything: a human, a frog, a ray of light. In practice, however, most avatars are humanoid. They may not be actually human; there are many games, for instance, in which players create dwarves or elves or cat-people and use those as their avatars. Virtual worlds which are not games (generally referred to as "social worlds") contain a wide variety of humanoid representations as well. Even the human avatars may not look much like their users; when given the chance to customize their avatars, it is perhaps unsurprising that people tend to create avatars similar to themselves, but more attractive. Thus, avatars are frequently idealizations of who we are, rather than exact copies.

Avatars and Ethics

Despite their virtual nature, people can become emotionally attached to virtual worlds and the avatars that populate them. Sociologists often discuss "third places", places in which people spend time besides their home and where they work; they are where we build relationships and enjoy ourselves. Traditionally these have been physical places, such as churches or coffee shops, but virtual worlds have also begun to fill that need. And people can get attached to virtual spaces just as they can to their favourite coffee shop.

Avatars are also subject to this sort of attachment. In one sense they are tools: in order to move around a virtual world and interact with it, a user needs a body—that is what the avatar provides. But many people also identify with their avatars. Since an avatar is under the user's control, there is a sense of ownership; it is not simply a character moving on the screen, it is *my* character. It is how I represent myself in the virtual world.

This connection between avatars and ourselves generates a number of ethical issues. Avatars vary greatly in terms of how much customization is available to them. At one extreme, there could be no customization—a user has no choice and is represented by a pre-designed avatar. This is usually less than ideal; people tend to prefer customization options, and it would be terribly confusing to have multiple people wandering around a virtual world who all looked exactly the same. Next along the customization spectrum is having to choose from a number of pre-designed avatars; in this case a user cannot customize the avatar per se, but she at least has some choice about how to represent herself.

In most popular virtual worlds, customization goes a bit further and they allow users to customize specific parts of the avatar in order to create a more personalized representation. Users might choose their hair style and colour, particular facial features, skin tone, and so forth, usually selecting from a number of options. In some cases, users are even permitted to create their own customizations. In *Second Life*, for instance, there is a booming market for avatar customization options, so one can actually make money selling features, like customized eyes, to other users. At the far end of the customization spectrum, it is possible to create three-dimensional avatars from photographs or scans of people, which allows users to create virtual copies of themselves.

Putting that last case aside for now, customization raises ethical concerns about what options are available. In many video games, for instance, it is very difficult to create a character with non-white features; while it may be possible to alter the skin tone, it is not usually possible to alter eye shape, bone structure, hair texture, or many other features necessary for creating diverse representations. In terms of social virtual worlds, *Second Life* provides a number of default avatars as a starting place, at which point the user is free to acquire customizations from what's called the Marketplace, or change their avatar themselves in various ways. The availability of user-created content broadens the customization options available, but the default avatars remain limited; there are no avatars with visible disabilities, for instance. A user who wishes to represent themselves in such a way would have to purchase items in the Marketplace.

Customization design choices in virtual worlds are just that: choices. Creating a virtual world and an avatar customization process involves choosing what options to offer. Some limits will have to exist—designers have to make trade-offs about how to spend their time. However, those choices need to be made thoughtfully. Research has shown that users have greater identification and more satisfaction with avatars that they can customize.[1] And, of course, the type of customization matters. Having to settle for a hairstyle that isn't quite right is not on a par with being unable to represent oneself as Japanese or as disabled, particularly in social virtual worlds where most people are creating representations that (at least somewhat) resemble themselves.

So one ethical question will be what options to provide to users when they create their avatars. Turning that around, a related question is whether users will (or should) feel restrictions on how they represent themselves. In certain situations, it will be to the user's advantage to create an avatar that is as much like their physical body as possible. For instance, when Naoko goes clothes shopping, she will likely want to use an avatar that is a virtual projection of herself; trying on clothes virtually is not very useful unless the avatar trying them on reflects the person who will be wearing them! But in many cases this sort of direct correlation is unnecessary—in a virtual world where some people are choosing anthropomorphic pandas as their avatars, there's unlikely to be much protest if your avatar is a shade more attractive than you are in real life.

There could be times and places in the virtual world where social pressure exists to choose an avatar that more accurately represents yourself. In a game there's not normally an expectation that avatars bear a strong resemblance to their users, but in other social virtual worlds there might be. We can imagine a virtual space used for dating where there was pressure to represent yourself accurately (though perhaps slightly idealized, much as people use the best photo of themselves on dating websites). If the users never expected to meet up outside of the world it might be impossible to enforce any kind of accuracy requirements. However, if the virtual dates were considered as precursors to, or occasional substitutions for, in-person dates, then the threat of being shamed—or in worse cases, ostracized—by other users could affect users' behaviour as well as the avatars they create.

Beyond accuracy, there is an interesting further question over whether we should worry about uniqueness. In the dating case we might mostly care about accuracy and authenticity: is the avatar a good representation of the real-world person? But in other settings it might matter whether the avatar were uniquely linked to a particular person. At a virtual trade show it could be necessary to link avatars to specific people who are authorized to give demonstrations or discuss sales issues; the company would not want to risk an imposter tarnishing their reputation. This could require some kind of verification process or symbol of uniqueness for avatars; current research focuses on watermarking, which would be akin to a virtual fingerprint.[2]

The prospect of having an avatar that is directly linked to your physical person raises privacy concerns; we are used to a certain degree of anonymity online, which this would seem to threaten. On the other hand, it could also force people to consider their online behaviour more carefully, since it could be more difficult to avoid the consequences of that behaviour. Of course, even in the physical world (where all of our interactions are tied to one physical body) we do not present ourselves the same in all situations. For instance, we usually dress and act somewhat differently in a work setting than when socializing with friends. So perhaps we would prefer to have different avatars for different settings. At the very least, a business might mandate their employees to represent themselves in particular ways when acting on behalf of the company in a virtual world. In the physical world we might enforce this through a dress code, but in the virtual world we could require an entirely different avatar.

At the moment, this worry is somewhat diminished because avatars lack portability; it is not generally possible to take an avatar from one virtual world and use it in a different one. But if we spent more time in virtual worlds this might change. Just as people do not reinvent themselves each time they enter a new store or bar in the physical world, so too we might grow tired of having to create separate avatars for every virtual space. There are thus two likely futures for virtual worlds: in the first, people converge on a small number of worlds, so it is feasible to create a separate avatar for each, and in the second, avatars become portable across social virtual worlds, alleviating the need to create multiple avatars. In the latter scenario, users may have a default avatar they use much of the time, only creating new ones for specific purposes, such as to play a game.

Customization options become increasingly important if we converge on a small number of worlds or even have a sole avatar that we use in all virtual worlds. In such a future, it would be more difficult to find a different world (with a different designer, who has made a different set of customization choices). Since avatars affect how invested we become in a virtual world, we would run the risk of alienating potential users by curtailing their ability to create a virtual self that reflects their physical body. One simple solution would be to use some sort of scanning technique that would build the avatar from photos or images of the user. Yet, I do not think this is the best answer in most situations.

It is true that in some limited situations having an exact virtual duplicate of our bodies could be useful, such as in the case of clothes shopping. But one of the powerful features of virtual space is that it is not a perfect copy of physical space and that we have more control over our representations. This can allow for identity exploration—a person can try presenting themselves in different ways and see what happens. It can also allow a user to control visible aspects of their identity that they usually cannot. People with visible disabilities are often treated differently than able-bodied people; perhaps Naoko doesn't want to be known as "the woman in the wheelchair" and would prefer to represent herself without it.

Of course, while I have stressed the identity aspects of avatars, for many people the main point of avatars is simply that they allow the user to do things in virtual worlds. Naoko may not care if her avatar for a virtual meeting isn't a perfect representation, because her main focus is the discussion in the meeting. Similarly, if she is exploring a recreation of an Egyptian tomb, then the accuracy of the tomb may matter more than the avatar itself. And part of the appeal of virtual worlds is their difference from physical space—it allows us to do things we couldn't do in our usual surroundings. We can explore ancient cities or choreograph dances that involve floating in mid-air (since the laws of physics can be more flexible in virtual worlds). We can provide opportunities for people with limited mobility to socialize or even pursue therapeutic endeavours such as attending a support group.

And we can do so when we are ill or injured or simply stuck in quarantine during a global pandemic.

Avatar Harms

For all of the promise virtual worlds hold, however, there are potential downsides to Naoko's virtual life. She could still be harmed in these spaces; it is sometimes too easy for people to treat others badly online, forgetting that there is a real person behind the avatar. Problems may also be caused by differences in how we interact online. Avatars don't have natural body language; we have to consciously choose an action. In a typical therapy session, it can be revealing to see how a patient sits; is she curled up, with her arms hugged tightly to her body? But in an online space, a user would actively have to decide to present her avatar that way. The therapist thus has less information in a virtual setting.

Virtual spaces are also not free of social pressures or biases. Even if perfect customization options existed, a person might feel pressure to present themselves in ways that live up to others' expectations; they may choose to make themselves thinner or sexier, not because they prefer it, but because they fear being less popular, even ostracized, if they do not. This happens in physical spaces as well, but with so much more under our control online, it may be tempting to conform in ways that are harder to do outside the virtual world. In much of the world there is a bias in favour of lighter-coloured skin; this leads people to engage in numerous harmful behaviours, such as skin bleaching, in pursuit of lighter colouration. In the virtual world this can be achieved by a few clicks of a mouse button—but while that might avoid the harmful physical effects on the user, the mental ones remain. It is easier to pass online as something you are not, but there is evidence that feeling like the only person of colour in a sea of white avatars could take a toll.[3]

There was a period of time after *Second Life* was released in 2003 when virtual worlds were heralded as the wave of the future—we would be doing everything in them. This furore died down, but perhaps *Second Life* was simply ahead of its time. The 2020 pandemic caused a resurgence of interest in moving life online, because so many people were forced to physically separate. While I suspect that few people would choose to live their lives quite as fully online as Naoko, elements of her life will resonate with many. Some people may use virtual worlds for work or educational purposes, holding meetings or classes with avatars that can move around and interact much as we do in physical space. They may engage in training of various sorts, perhaps creating a simulation of a situation and working through how to handle it—a kind of virtual role play. The virtual setting may even enrich and deepen certain interactions; perhaps the relative anonymity would make it easier to attend a support group for addiction, say. And many people may dip their toes in for leisure purposes, whether attending a virtual performance, walking around a virtual store, or simply hanging out in a virtual coffee shop.

Ultimately, one of the key ethical issues related to avatars is customization, understood broadly. Designers need to walk a delicate line here. Users should have the *option* to create avatar: that reflect themselves, but in most situations they should not be *required* to do so. The tools to create an accurate avatar should be provided, but users should not be compelled to use them. Controlling an avatar in a virtual world allows us to be ourselves, but it also provides us with opportunities to choose our representations in ways we generally cannot. This can be for serious reasons such as removing an appearance that causes bad reactions, or even for frivolous ones such as trying a new hair colour. The power of identity exploration is strong. And let's be honest: one sure way of improving a boring meeting is to have it chaired by a giant panda.

Further Reading

Yee, N., *The Proteus Paradox* (Yale University Press, 2014).

Notes

1. S. Turkay and S. Adinolf, The effects of customization on motivation in an extended study with a massively multiplayer online roleplaying game, *Cyberpsychology: Journal of Psychosocial Research on Cyberspace*, 9/3 (2015), article 2.
2. S. Bader, R. Chaaba, and N. E. Ben Amara, *Robust and Blind Watermarking of Avatar Faces* (Information and Communication Technologies Innovation and Application, Sousse, Tunisia, 2014).

3. For discussion of how racial cues shape users' views of virtual worlds, see J. E. Lee and S. G. Park, "Whose second life is this?" How avatar-based racial cues shape ethno-racial minorities' perception of virtual worlds, *Cyberpsychology, Behavior, and Social Networking*, 14/11 (2011), 637–42. For discussion of how this discomfort leads non-white users to conceal their race by choosing white avatars, see J.-E. R. Lee, Does virtual diversity matter?: Effects of avatar-based diversity representation on willingness to express offline racial identity and avatar customization, *Computers in Human Behavior*, 36 (2014), 190–7.

Future Machines

7

Predictive Policing

Seumas Miller

Predictive policing (PP) is a term that refers to a range of crime-fighting approaches that use crime mapping data and analysis, and, more recently, social network analysis, big data, and predictive algorithms.

Historically, police services have used statistical information to target specific locations in relation to particular types of crime, i.e. they have utilised various methods of crime mapping data and analysis.[1] For instance, police resources have been directed to crime hotspots identified not simply on the basis of past crimes committed at that location, but also based on the location in question having features correlated with crimes of the relevant type, such as high incidences of theft at locations in which there are a number of tourist attractions and good escape routes for thieves. In doing so police are, in effect, predicting the crime of theft at the location in question and acting to prevent it. Moreover, police services have also had the practice of targeting known offenders as opposed to merely reactively investigating crimes; for example, if there is a spate of burglaries involving the same modus operandi, they might target a recently released offender known to burgle using that method. In doing so police are, in effect, predicting that a past offender will continue to offend and acting to prevent him or her doing so.

PP is in many ways simply an extension of these historical police practices. However, it has introduced some new methods.[2] In relation to high-volume crimes, such as burglary and car theft, it has utilised big data analytics, including the use of predictive algorithms, to establish a wider set of statistically-based correlations that rely on much larger data sets. For example, big data analysis has revealed that a burglary in a given location often generates additional burglaries in that area (burglary is 'self-exciting' to use the jargon), leading to a crime 'hotspot' in an analogous manner to the spread of an infectious disease such as COVID-19 in a so-called Covid 'hotspot'. In relation to offenders, notably violent offenders, PP has used social network analysis (as well as statistically-based correlations). This involves first identifying offenders, then tracing their associates, then the associates of their associates, and so on. Social media analysis is used to identify and track links in the network.

The rise of PP, especially in many police jurisdictions in large cities in the USA, such as Los Angeles, Chicago, New York, and New Orleans, has raised the spectre of the surveillance society, depicted in the film *Minority Report*, in which citizens can be arrested by police for crimes they have not yet committed (and have no intention of committing at the time of arrest) on the basis of (supposedly reliable) evidence that they will commit them. By analogy, police utilising PP in a city somewhere in the world today might, let us suppose, arrest a citizen, John Smith, for a violent crime, even though he is yet to commit this crime and has no intention of doing so. However, Smith is found 'loitering' in a violent crime hotspot in the neighbourhood where he lives and he is a known associate of members of the local violent youth gang.

But how realistic is this scenario?

Let us consider a pioneering example of predictive policing, the Los Angeles LASER programme (Los Angeles Strategic Extraction and Restoration Programme). The programme began in 2011 with the aim of reducing violent, gang-related crime in LA. It comprised a location-based 'hotspot' component and an offender-based component.[3] The offender-based component involved identifying chronic offenders based on criteria such as gang membership, past violent crime offences, and prior arrests with a handgun. Chronic offenders were then contacted, but not with a view to arresting them since, for one thing, there was, at least at this stage, not enough evidence to do this. Rather, the purpose of this intervention was deterrence (and crime reduction as a result of deterrence). The offenders were told about available programmes and services designed to reduce their risk of recidivism.

However, this served, in effect, as a deterrent since they were also put on notice that they were being watched and that, if arrested, their failure to avail themselves of these programmes and services would count against them in future sentencing, e.g. other things being equal, it would result in longer prison terms. The location-based component involved identifying quite specific spatio-temporal locations (e.g. 500 square metre locations during a six-hour period on certain days of the week) for intervention by police officers. These 'hotspot' locations were selected based on a historical analysis of gun-related crime data. This was followed by an analysis to try to determine the causes of the high level of gun-related crime in a given location—e.g. it was a border-area between rival gangs who were most active on weekend evenings—and to develop an appropriate crime prevention strategy for that location, e.g. high police visibility. The effect of the strategy in terms of statistical levels of gun violence in a given location was continuously monitored and the strategy adjusted as required.

According to the official review by the Inspector General of the Los Angeles Police Commissioner, the LASER programme met with considerable success in reducing violent gang-related crime in a number of high-crime neighbourhoods, at least initially.[4] However, the programme was discontinued in 2019, partly on the grounds that police were failing to comply with its protocols and unfairly targeting some community members including some who had not previously been arrested. Nonetheless, police in Los Angeles and in other US cities have continued to use predictive policing models in one form or another.[5]

Problems

While collecting and analysing location-based crime data of the kind in question is not morally problematic per se, moral problems might arise with some of the crime prevention strategies employed in response to that data. For instance, possession of data indicating a crime hotspot would not in and of itself justify stopping and searching or arresting a person merely because s/he happened to be at that location. The data would not justify this since it would not reach the threshold of reasonable suspicion of a *particular* person. Accordingly, if such a person was to be stopped and searched or arrested there would need to be additional evidential facts about that person based on, presumably, real-time observation of her/him, such as visual evidence that s/he was carrying a gun.

Of course, this is not to say that police in the US and elsewhere always comply with this understanding of the principle of reasonable suspicion—a principle enshrined in the law in most liberal democracies, including the US. Indeed, there are many instances in which they do not, notably in black neighbourhoods in the US. To this extent the John Smith scenario is not unrealistic.

Nor would collecting and analysing offender-based data be in and of itself morally concerning. After all, the individuals in question are known to be violent offenders by virtue of their past convictions for violent crime. However, if predictive policing was applied to those without a record, the level of intrusive attention might well be morally problematic. Individuals have a moral right to freedom from state interference absent prior evidence of violation of its laws.[6] Accordingly, the level of intrusive police attention to John Smith in our fictitious scenario is not morally or (in most liberal democracies) legally justified. This, once again, is not to say that it does not happen—surely it does and, again, notably in black neighbourhoods in the US—and, to the extent that it does, the John Smith scenario is, again, realistic.

It might be suggested that there are certain categories of legitimately targeted putative offenders for which this is not the case. One category might be members of a terrorist organisation who have not themselves been convicted or even performed a terrorist act. But usually, in such circumstances, a justifiable law will in fact have been broken, namely, membership of a terrorist organisation. This is, of course, not to say that membership of a violent youth gang should be a criminal offence. And certainly, associating with members of such a gang, as John Smith does, should not be a criminal offence (and it is not in liberal democracies)—after all, gang members have parents, brothers and sisters etc. who are not gang members.

Arguably, a second category of legitimately targeted putative offenders are the police themselves. Consider police officers who are not known to have committed any crime. Is there a justification for monitoring their behaviour, other than for ordinary work performance purposes? Are police any different from ordinary citizens in this regard? It might be claimed that, given their position of trust and the fact that they have extensive powers of arrest and use of lethal force not possessed by ordinary citizens, such monitoring is morally justified.[7] Moreover, their occupational role as a police officer is one freely chosen.

Speaking generally, predictive policing faces several problems. Some of these are problems for predictive policing even in its own terms of contributing to crime reduction. Others are moral problems, about whether PP violates moral rights or is unjust. These two types of problems are interconnected. For example, when a form of predictive policing is regarded as unjust, it may also become less effective. Aggressive policing tactics, such as so-called saturation policing, have often created more problems than they've solved. In the 1980s, they stoked the riots in the London neighbourhood of Brixton—home to a large black population.

So what, in more detail, might the problems of predictive policing be?

First, there can be issues with the data, e.g. false data input. To return to our scenario, perhaps the arrest of John Smith is an instance of mistaken identity; after all there are many citizens with the name John Smith, and the data concerning John Smith the associate of the violent youth gang might have been wrongly interlinked in the police database to the photo of John Smith the mild-mannered visitor to the city who has had no contact with any gang members but who took a wrong turn and found himself in the crime hotspot. At any rate, false data input leads to false positives (targeting the innocent) and false negatives (failure to target the guilty). Nor is error always easy to correct, given the bureaucratic processes involved in changing data in large police databases.

Second, for some serious crimes, such as murder and terrorism, the databases are comparatively small. This impedes predictive techniques such as machine learning that are dependent on big data. It makes it difficult to generate accurate profiles of 'typical terrorists'.

Third, the prediction of future crime, and the use of machine-learning techniques in particular, are based on past reported crimes, arrests, prosecutions, police incident reports, lists of offenders and so on. Thus, if law enforcement agencies rely on machine learning then (other things being equal) offenders and offence types that have escaped detection in the past (e.g. child sexual abuse) are less likely than those which have not (e.g. grievous bodily harm) to be targeted by police. (Naturally, other things might not be equal and police might choose to target offence types that are now known to have gone undetected in the past, as has recently happened in the case of child sexual abuse.) For the same reason, communities that have been over-policed in the past are likely to continue to be over-policed, relative to other communities. This is especially the case if predictive policing techniques utilise socio-economic indicators that statistically correlate with crime indicators—which, for example, might indicate a greater risk of crime in poor black neighbourhoods in the United States.[8]

Fourth, and related to this last point, one of the more controversial predictive policing techniques is profiling, which can take the form of morally problematic racial profiling. A famous case in the US is that of Andrew Sokolow who was searched by airport customs officials and found to possess drugs. He was searched because he fitted the profile of a drug courier and this was taken to constitute reasonable grounds for suspicion. Sokolow argued in court that fitting a profile did not constitute reasonable grounds for suspicion. He lost the case because it was held that whereas fitting a profile did not of itself constitute reasonable suspicion, the evidence that constituted the profile in his particular case did.[9] However, there are dangers in the practice of profiling, including profiling that uses machine learning. Specifically, there is the risk of discriminatory algorithms, e.g. an algorithm that relies on a past data set comprising an unjustifiably disproportionate number of 'stop and frisk' searches of black citizens. Profiling algorithms can thus end up generating morally unjustified, racially-based profiles of offenders and, thereby, entrench existing racist attitudes among police officers and others.

Fifth, there is an issue of privacy or confidentiality. Specifically, do some of the databases upon which PP techniques rely consist of personal or confidential information to which the police do not have a moral or legal right? There are, of course, complications about what counts as personal information. The content of telephone calls, emails etc. is typically regarded as personal or confidential, but what of meta-data such as the duration of the call, or the name of the caller and person called? Some argue that this is not personal or confidential any more than the sender's and receiver's name on a parcel sent through the postal service are items of personal data. However, a large bank of metadata extracted from, for example, a person's phone calls and emails can enable a detailed picture of that person's associates and movements; a picture sufficiently detailed to count as an infringement of their privacy.

Sixth, the existence of large police databases of personal and confidential information pertaining to offenders and other citizens raises data security concerns. Data security consists in ensuring that such information is protected from illegitimate accessing. Clearly data security is critical. If databases, such as those of informants and undercover operatives, were hacked by criminal organisations, lives might even be at risk. A hacking of biometric facial images compromises the identity security of citizens thereby enabling credit card fraud, passport fraud etc.

Seventh, there are additional moral problems inherent in some of the new techniques used in predictive policing, such as the so-called 'black box' issue in machine learning. If offender profiles are generated by machine learning the algorithmic-based correlations may not be known or understood by law enforcement, let alone putative offenders or ordinary citizens. So citizen John Smith might be being monitored without either John Smith or the police monitoring him knowing at any point what a key part of the justification for this monitoring is, i.e. what features he possesses, additional to those that are understood, such as, say, his convictions in the distant past, that make him a current object of suspicion or, at least, a person of interest.

Finally, there is the general problem of the effectiveness of PP in criminal justice contexts in which offenders can themselves predict the results of PP predictive processes and, thereby, thwart them. If, for example, criminals become aware of the profiles used by police they can adjust their methods so as to escape detection. If, for example, criminals know that police are targeting resources in a particular hotspot, they can simply direct their criminal activities elsewhere.

New Technologies

Thus far we have focused on predictive policing as it is currently practised, at least for the most part, in liberal democracies, such as the USA, the UK, and Australia. But predictive policing is constantly changing and is doing so utilising new technologies. Fingerprint recognition and DNA identification have a long history of successful use in the investigation of serious crime. However, new biometric identification technologies, such as facial recognition, gait analysis, voice recognition, and vein recognition are rapidly evolving. Recently, biometric databases have been established by government and the private sector; for example, automated facial recognition is now a key part of passports and border security in many countries. Automated facial recognition is a powerful technology with the potential to identify a face in a large crowd, through integration with CCTV systems, enabling real-time surveillance, identification, and tracking of individuals through public places by police. Further notable applications of facial recognition include the analysis of images taken from the internet, particularly from social media, such as Facebook. Facebook alone holds several hundred billion photographs in its database and uses automated facial recognition software to identify or 'tag' users in photographs.

The use of these technologies raises pressing ethical concerns. The capacity to integrate databases of biometric and non-biometric information—such as smartphone and email metadata, financial, medical, and tax records—adds to these concerns. For instance, biometric facial image templates can be used in conjunction with digital images sourced from CCTV, phone GPS data, and internet history, to provide an increasingly complete picture of an individual's movements and lifestyle. Privacy and confidentiality in relation to personal data consists in large part in the right to control access to, and use of, that data. As such, it is a component of individual autonomy, a cornerstone of liberal democracy.

China provides an insight into potential developments in the use of integrated databases by government and police. In public places in China, the government is combining CCTV with biometric facial recognition and gait analysis systems to identify suspects of minor crimes, such as jaywalking. Biometric facial recognition systems now play a role in China's 'social credit' system, which rewards and punishes citizens on the basis of their norm-following behaviour, honesty and courtesy, in concert with other big data analysis capabilities that facilitate tracking, such as GPS data, internet use, and financial transaction history. The implications of a low social credit score for Chinese citizens are serious: they include travel bans, and exclusion from private schools and higher status professions. In Xinjiang, in particular, the Uighur population has been subjected to what is, in effect, a surveillance society.

Accordingly, the establishment of comprehensive, integrated biometric and non-biometric databases of the personal information of citizens by governments, and the utilisation of these new technologies in the service of law enforcement, under the banner of PP, has the potential to undermine individual autonomy. And it is not simply that a single individual, such as John Smith in our scenario, suffers an injustice or rights violation; rather there is widespread rights violation of the citizenry and, as a result, a power imbalance is created between government and the citizenry as a whole.

Conclusion

The expanding use of biometric facial recognition databases and other emerging technologies in law enforcement as part of PP should be clearly and demonstrably justified in terms of efficiency and effectiveness in the service of *specific* law enforcement purposes rather than by general appeals to community security or safety. Moreover, it should comply with moral principles constitutive of liberal democracy, such as the principle that individuals have a moral right to freedom from state interference absent prior evidence of violation of its laws.

In so far as the use of these technologies and databases can be justified for specific security and safety purposes it is, nevertheless, imperative that they be subject to accountability mechanisms to guard against misuse. Further, the citizenry should be well informed about these systems and should have consented to their use for the specific, justified purposes in question: they should be publicly debated, backed by legislation, and their operation subject to judicial review.

Further Reading

Ferguson, A. G., *The Rise of Big Data Policing* (New York University Press, 2017).
Miller, S. and Gordon, I., *Investigative Ethics: Ethics for Police Detectives and Criminal Investigators* (Wiley-Blackwell, 2014).

Notes

1. See, for instance, S. Miller and I. Gordon, *Investigative Ethics: Ethics for Police Detectives and Criminal Investigators* (Wiley-Blackwell, 2014), chapters 2, 3, and 10.
2. For an overview see A. G. Ferguson, *The Rise of Big Data Policing* (New York University Press, 2017).
3. M. P. Smith (Inspector General, Los Angeles Police Commission), *Review of Selected Los Angeles Police Department Data-Driven Policing Strategies* (Los Angeles Police Commission, 2019).
4. Smith (2019).
5. A. G. Ferguson, Predictive policing theory. In T. Rice Lave and E. J. Miller (eds.), *Cambridge Handbook of Policing in the United States* (Cambridge University Press, 2020), pp. 491–510.
6. S. Miller, Machine learning, ethics and law, *Australian Journal of Information Systems*, 22 (2018), 1–13.
7. Miller and Gordon (2014), pp. 201–23.
8. See Ferguson (2017) for an extended discussion of this latter point.
9. United States vs Sokolow (1989), https://caselaw.findlaw.com/us-supreme-court/490/1.html.

8

AI in Medicine

Angeliki Kerasidou and Xaroula (Charalampia) Kerasidou

Case study: Grace's Future

After several weeks of experiencing abdominal pain, Grace pays a visit to her doctor. There, a number of samples, including blood samples, are collected, and an MRI is performed. The examination data is then combined with her health records—collected both during medical visits and in real time through her smartphone. The doctor informs Grace that the results will be ready in 72 hours and the diagnosis will be promptly communicated to her, along with an action plan.

In the three days she awaits the results, Grace reflects on how things have changed since she was young. Although she still describes these medical visits as 'going to the doctor', she didn't see a doctor in the flesh. From the virtual receptionist, who always greets her a little too cheerfully, to the polite but slightly bossy-sounding bot taking her medical history, to the MRI scanner barking instructions, the majority of tasks are now performed by intelligent machines. The only role left for humans is the delicate procedure of taking intravenous blood samples. Grace is thankful that phlebotomists have survived the introduction of AI in medicine because she has always been afraid of needles and is reassured by a human presence. She tries to start a conversation; "How's your day been?"—"Busy! I have twenty more samples to take before the end of my shift", replies the nurse without lifting his eyes.

The results duly appear on Grace's smartphone within the promised period. It's not good news. There's a cancer diagnosis accompanied by an action plan. "Based on your individual results and the latest system upgrade", reads the message, "the recommendation is for chemotherapy to commence immediately. Click *here* and *here* for more information about what this means for you. Click *Yes* if you consent." The message explains that, following consent, appropriate healthcare facilities (hospital and pharmacy) will be informed and that details of the dates and times for treatment will follow.

Grace wonders how good the latest upgrade is. Even after all these years, data on some ethnic groups are incomplete and misdiagnoses common. She once heard the Secretary of Health proclaiming: "AI will benefit all of us! It will deliver a truly personalised and efficient healthcare system, saving tax-payer money." Grace is not so sure. She could request to see a specialist for a face-to-face consultation, but the waiting list is long, and she cannot afford to pay out-of-pocket for such a 'luxury'. She clicks *Yes*, and heads back to work.

Augmented Patient-Centred Care

In recent decades, the doctor–patient relationship has undergone a transformation—from medical paternalism, where decisions are taken by the doctor with minimal, if any, involvement from the patient, to a model of care that places the patient at its centre.[1] Once, healthcare professionals were perceived as the unchallenged authority and patients as the ill or broken bodies that required fixing. Today, patients are seen as partners in the therapeutic encounter, contributing not only their own knowledge and expertise about their condition, but also their values that might bear upon the care plan. In the patient-centred model of care, effective communication and empathy, and recognition that different people might hold different values and priorities regarding their health, are the new professional and ethical norms.

The introduction of artificial intelligence (AI) into healthcare has the potential to disrupt this model by augmenting some aspects of it and challenging others. AI is often described as being more rational and reliable than humans. The judgement and reasoning of humans can be affected by an array of irrelevant factors, such as the amount of glucose in their bloodstream or the time of the day.[2] In healthcare, where decisions can be, literally, a matter of life or death, augmented rationality and impartiality could prove invaluable qualities. AI systems also have the potential to improve the personalised character of patient-centred care. Through the use of devices such as smartphones and wearables, AI tools could track our movements, our interactions with others, our eating habits and sleeping patterns. This could lead to highly-tailored health advice and treatment without the need for a consultation with a human doctor. Individual values and preferences could be directly entered into the system, and patients could be empowered to take active ownership and control of their health.

That, at least, is the promise. But studies show that the effectiveness of AI to date has been exaggerated.[3,4] Hopes that machine learning algorithms could overcome the limitations of humans by being more rational, neutral, and objective have been undermined by evidence that such systems can perpetuate human prejudices, amplify bias, and make inaccurate predictions.[5,6] Consider, for example, the app which, when presented with exactly the same set of symptoms, was found to suggest a heart attack as a possible diagnosis if the user was a man, but merely a panic attack if was a woman. This discrepancy was explained by the "heart attack gender gap": the unsettling finding that the overrepresentation of men in the medical and research data means that women are up to 50 percent more at risk of receiving a misdiagnosis for a heart attack than men.[7] Yet, faced with a technology that cannot be interrogated and yet is touted to exhibit superior decision-making abilities, there is a danger that doctors, nurses, and patients will be reluctant to challenge its recommendations.

AI developers are seeking technological solutions that could diagnose and mitigate bias; algorithms, it is said, can be improved by utilising more and 'better' data. However, the implication that social, political, and ethical problems are just mathematical riddles to be computed out, seems naive. Even though reliable data are crucial for safe healthcare, equally important is understanding the social context in which these health data are collected. Consider, for example, the US case of a medical algorithm designed to identify "high risk" patients in need of extra care based on healthcare expenditure data—this was found to dramatically underestimate the health needs of the sickest black patients. While race-blind, the algorithm, which guided the decision-making for millions of Americans, failed to take into account the long-standing health inequalities that black patients face because of barriers to accessing care, lack of insurance, mistrust of the medical system, etc.[8] For these reasons, black patients tend to spend less of their income on healthcare; it does not follow that their need for care is less acute. There are now increasing calls for a more inclusive and engaged agenda around health and AI which could see the patient-centred model of care expand in two ways: first, by establishing healthcare professionals as gatekeepers or mediators between patients and AI systems in order to ensure not only accessibility, but also safety, quality, and fairness of care;[9] second, by enlisting diverse voices and expertise from patient groups, community health workers, nurses, carers, and others in order to better understand the impact of AI technologies on the ground.[10]

Trust

Since Grace has consented to the recommended treatment plan, we might be tempted to say that she trusts her doctor to make the right decision for her. But does she? Is her attitude truly one of trust?

If we trust someone to do something for us, we believe they have the skill and knowledge to perform the entrusted action, and goodwill towards us, meaning that they will not try to wrong or hurt us. Trust takes time to establish and can easily be broken, which makes it important that beliefs in skill and goodwill are regularly reinforced through new, positive experiences. In a purely trust relationship, the trustor does not have guarantees, only her justified belief, that the trusted person will confirm her trust. Effectively, a trust relationship is a relationship of vulnerability, in which the trustor becomes vulnerable towards the trustee.

Grace seems to trust her doctor and this seems unsurprising. Medicine is one of the most trusted professions. We allow doctors to poke and prod us, to cut us open and stitch us up, we tell them our private thoughts, concerns, and even dark secrets. We trust doctors and nurses because we believe they know how to care for us; they have the specialist skill and knowledge, but also goodwill. And by trusting them to care for us, we make ourselves vulnerable to them. Patients invariably find themselves in a position of vulnerability towards their doctors, not least because of the knowledge and power imbalance between them.

Some claim that AI will make trust redundant. The increased accuracy, efficiency, and patient empowerment it promises could remove vulnerability from the doctor–patient relationship. And without vulnerability there is no reason for trust. People will be able to rely on their healthcare professionals and healthcare systems to always deliver what has been agreed. The institutional organisation of the medical and nursing professions with accreditation systems, professional governance structures, and treatment protocols has gone some way to remove vulnerability and establish more of a relationship of reliance between doctors and patients. AI could accelerate this process. But the downside of this operationalisation and subsequent loss of trust has been the increase in the litigation culture. Patients are treated more like customers expecting a certain service. When patients feel that the service promised has not been delivered, they use legal means to complain and demand compensation (as opposed to feeling gratitude when things go well, or betrayal when things go wrong, as in trust relationships). AI, with its promises for augmented rationality and reliability, is likely to accelerate this trend too. If patients are promised augmented care, they will expect augmented care, and will feel within their rights to complain when their expectations are not fully met.

There is another way that AI in medicine could reduce trust. Technological advances in machine learning and cloud computing have resulted in the *datafication* of our lives and bodies, rendering our every action and activity—how many steps we take, or what we post on social media—as "actionable" health data, which can be collected and deployed in addressing health challenges such as diabetes or mental health problems. This has opened up the clinical space to new actors and created a fertile ground for new clinical-corporate alliances—the former eager to find solutions in an environment in which money is short, the latter eager to get hold of valuable personal healthcare data to train their AI models. Importantly, these new actors are not bound by the same moral commitments and fiduciary duties as traditional healthcare providers, nor by the same legal and regulatory frameworks.[11] Although people seem to understand the need for public–private partnerships, they remain wary about what they regard as unaccountable private companies profiteering from the use of their health data; data that were entrusted to their doctors to be used in their own care and for the common good.[12,13] A strong legal and regulatory framework could redress these issues and help establish a successful relationship with these new actors. What is needed, beyond that, is the development of a new moral attitude and culture that would allow AI developers to be ethically and socially reflexive about their work and its real world impact.

Empathy

Grace read the diagnosis and treatment plan on her smartphone. There was no standard consultation with a doctor. She could have asked for one, if she had the time to wait, or the money to pay for it. She chose not to. What more would the doctor say to her, anyway? All she needed to know was in that text.

Efficiency, in the use of time and other resources, is important in healthcare and, with our ageing population, is likely to become more so. By using AI tools to triage, diagnose, and treat patients, healthcare systems could use resources more prudently without, theoretically, compromising accuracy and effectiveness.

However, the quest for greater efficiency might have a negative effect on other fundamental healthcare values, such as empathy.[14] When every minute counts, and resources cannot stretch to cover all needs, holding someone's hand, and listening to their worries and concerns, are the things health services are tempted to leave out. Although the patient-centred model of care put empathy back on the professional map, economic imperatives have curtailed the ability of healthcare professionals to engage with their patients in an empathetic way. Indeed, it is an interesting observation that, on the one hand, we try to develop more personalised, even empathetic machines, attentive to our individual needs, whilst, on the other, healthcare professionals are left to operate in time- and resource-austere environments, forcing them to become more detached and mechanical in their dealings with patients.

Some proponents of AI argue, however, that employing AI systems could actually help healthcare professionals exercise empathy. Such systems will free up time, they maintain, for doctors and nurses to sit by the patient, engage with them, and care for them in a more humane way than has been possible so far.[15] This optimistic vision should not be discounted. Such a future is indeed possible. But its actualisation depends less on AI and more on those making healthcare decisions valuing empathy enough to adequately fund it.

Whatever side one takes, the constructed and oft-repeated dichotomy between a caring human and a cold impersonal machine is, well, artificial. Humans have always been shaped by and with technology and this is as true in the healthcare sector as any other. Empathy and caring manifest themselves with, and through, technology. From warming the stethoscope so as not to chill a naked body, to pain relief, to a well-designed prosthesis, to an efficient AI logistics system that won't leave an A&E patient without a much needed bed, caring is a combined achievement of humans and nonhumans. It is a choreography of practices between doctors, patients, nurses, cleaners, machines, algorithms, drugs, needles, institutions, regulations—to mention only a few—requiring constant rebalancing of complex needs and shifting tensions.[16] Finding the right balance is not a technological problem—it is an ethical, social, and political one, that societies will have to negotiate for themselves.

Conclusion

Grace's story is neither the worst nor the most exciting future one can imagine for healthcare. It sounds pretty mundane, believable, and almost inevitable. In most economically advanced countries, there will still be a functioning healthcare system, people will still be able to access services one way or another, get treatment and hopefully get better as a result. Maybe there won't be enough 'human touch' or empathy in the system, nurses and other professionals will often be overworked, specialist services will be difficult to access unless one can afford to pay, and AI will occasionally get things wrong—perhaps more often for some groups than others.

But even though Grace's story might sound inevitable, the future is never determined. So, is this the best possible outlook we can imagine?

AI promises major benefits for healthcare. But along with the benefits come risks. Not so much the risk of powerful super-intelligent machines taking over, but the risk of structural injustices, biases, and inequalities being perpetuated in a system that cannot be challenged because nobody actually knows how the algorithms work. Or the risk that there might be no doctor or nurse present to hold your hand and reassure you when you are at your most vulnerable. There are many initiatives to come up with ethical or trustworthy AI and these efforts are important. Yet we should demand more than this. Technological solutionism and the urge to "move fast and break things" often dominate the tech industry but are inappropriate for the healthcare context and incompatible with basic healthcare values of empathy, solidarity, and trust.

So how can such socio-political and ethical issues get resolved?

It is at this juncture that we have the opportunity to imagine different futures. We, the patients, doctors, nurses, carers—not merely figured as a group of users, consumers, or clients but as a collective of active citizens who are essential in the shaping of these technological futures—need to claim our place at the forefront of this process. Technology workers, researchers, medical professionals and activists, civil society and patient groups, need to form coalitions that push for accountability, for ongoing monitoring of AI systems, for the termination of AI projects that prove not to be good enough for those with the least power to protest, and even for the opportunity to say no to some of these technologies at the design stage and before their implementation.

To shape the future of healthcare we need to decide whether, to what extent, and how—under what regulatory frameworks and safeguards—these technologies could and should play a part in this future. AI can indeed improve healthcare but, instead of casting ourselves loose and at the mercy of this seemingly inevitable technological drift, we should be actively paddling towards a future of our choice.

In many respects "Grace's future" mirrors our present reality. She lives in a world with increased technology but the fundamental socio-political and ethical issues that characterise our present remain unresolved. Surely Grace deserves a better future—as do we.

Further Reading

D'Ignazio, C. and Klein, L. F., *Data Feminism* (MIT Press, 2020).

Eubanks, V., *Automating Inequality: How High-tech Tools Profile, Police, and Punish the Poor* (St Martin's Press, 2018).

Noble, S. U., *Algorithms of Oppression: How Search Engines Reinforce Racism* (NYU Press, 2018).

Topol, E., *Deep Medicine: How Artificial Intelligence Can Make Healthcare Human Again* (Basic Books, 2019).

Notes

1. R. Kaba and P. Sooriakumaran, The evolution of the doctor–patient relationship, *International Journal of Surgery*, 5/1 (2007).

2. S. Danziger, J. Levav, and L. Avnaim-Pesso, Extraneous factors in judicial decisions, *Proceedings of the National Academy of Sciences*, 108/17 (2011).

3. M. Nagendran, Y. Chen, C. A. Lovejoy, A. C. Gordon, M. Komorowski, H. Harvey, E. J. Topol, J. P. A. Ioannidis, G. S. Collins, and M. Maruthappu, Artificial intelligence versus clinicians: Systematic review of design, reporting standards, and claims of deep learning studies, *BMJ* (2020), 368: m689.

4. H. Salisbury, Prestidigitation, *BMJ* (2020), 368: m648.

5. Z. Obermeyer, B. Powers, C. Vogeli, and S. Mullainathan, Dissecting racial bias in an algorithm used to manage the health of populations, *Science*, 366/6464 (October 2019), 447–53.

6. T. C. Veinot, H. Mitchell, and J. S. Ancker, Good intentions are not enough: How informatics interventions can worsen inequality, *Journal of the American Medical Informatics Association*, 25/8 (August 2018), 1080–8, https://doi.org/10.1093/jamia/ocy052.

7. S. Das, It's hysteria, not a heart attack, GP app Babylon tells women, *Sunday Times*, 13 October 2019, available at: https://www.thetimes.co.uk/article/its-hysteria-not-a-heart-attack-gp-app-tells-women-gm2vxbrqk.

8. C. Y. Johnson, Racial bias in a medical algorithm favours white patients over sicker black patients, *The Washington Post*, 24 October 2019, available at: https://www.washingtonpost.com/health/2019/10/24/racial-bias-medical-algorithm-favors-white-patients-over-sicker-black-patients/.

9. Academy of Medical Royal Colleges, Artificial intelligence in healthcare, January 2019, available at: https://www.aomrc.org.uk/wp-content/uploads/2019/01/Artificial_intelligence_in_healthcare_0119.pdf.

10. K. Crawford, R. Dobbe, T. Dryer, G. Fried, B. Green, E. Kaziunas, et al., *AI Now 2019 Report* (AI Now Institute, 2019), available at: https://ainowinstitute.org/AI_Now_2019_Report.html.

11. B. Mittelstadt, Principles alone cannot guarantee ethical AI, *Nature Machine Intelligence* (2019), 1–7.

12. Ipsos Mori, The one-way mirror: public attitudes to commercial access to health data (Wellcome Trust, March 2016), available at: https://wellcome.ac.uk/sites/default/files/public-attitudes-to-commercial-access-to-health-data-wellcome-mar16.pdf.

13. H. Van Mil, Foundations of fairness: Views on uses of NHS patient data and NHS operational data (February 2020), *Understanding Patient Data*, available at: https://understandingpatientdata.org.uk/news/accountability-transparency-and-public-participation-must-be-established-third-party-use-nhs.

14. A. Kerasidou, Empathy and efficiency in healthcare at times of austerity, *Health Care Analysis*, 27/3 (2019).

15. E. Topol, The Topol Review: Preparing the healthcare workforce to deliver the digital future (National Health Service, 2019).

16. A. Mol, I. Moser, and J. Pols, Care: putting practice into theory. In A. Mol, I. Moser, and J. Pols (eds), *Care in Practice: On Tinkering in Clinics, Homes and Farms* (transcript Verlag, 2010), pp. 7–27.

9

Robots and the Future of Retribution

John Danaher

The *Bouphonia* was a strange ritual performed in Ancient Greece. It took place every midsummer. A group of oxen would be driven into the Acropolis and pushed forward to the altar of the temple. Once there, they would find sacred grain spread out as an offering to Zeus. Inevitably, one ox would step forward and start eating the grain. By doing this, it selected itself for sacrifice. A person would step forward and kill the ox with a knife. This person would then flee. Why? Because killing a working animal was considered a terrible crime.

This chapter is about the future of retribution and, in particular, the role that robots will play in shaping that future. But let us first return to the past—and the *Bouphonia* ritual of 2500 years ago.

The *Bouphonia*

Ritual sacrifices were common in the ancient world. But the *Bouphonia* ritual contained some unusual aspects. With the guilty party having fled the scene of the crime, those remaining in the temple would conduct a trial to determine who was guilty. Anyone who had a hand in the deed would be called to give an account of themselves. First up were the people who fetched the water used to sharpen the knife. They would plead innocence and say they were not to blame: they pointed the finger at the person who did the sharpening. The person who sharpened the knife would say it was not his fault: the knife itself was the only one directly involved in the crime. The knife, with no voice of its own, would be found guilty and cast into the sea as punishment.[1]

That's pretty strange, right? But there is some logic to it. The people felt the sacrifice of the ox had to take place to appease the gods, but they also felt strongly that it was a crime. Someone had to take the blame. The ritual trial was a way of absolving any human party of guilt while still making sure that someone—or, rather, some *thing*—took the blame.

For all its oddities, the *Bouphonia* speaks to two important features of the human condition. First, it says something about the enduring significance of practices of blame and punishment in human life. Even through the haze of 2500 years of cultural and technical innovation, there is something very familiar about the ritual. We follow similar rituals today, day in, day out, in criminal courts and tribunals all over the world. The desire to find someone responsible whenever some wrongdoing has occurred is a powerful one, and something we can all appreciate. Second, the ritual highlights the occasional absurdity of this desire. Our rituals of blame and punishment often assume that we are isolated and self-determined agents, capable of controlling our own lives. The reality is that each of us is embedded in complex causal webs. We influence one another and we are influenced and shaped by our cultures, societies, and technologies. Absurd though it may seem, the knife really did have a part to play in the crime. Technology often has a part to play by making crimes possible.

The question I want to consider in the remainder of this chapter is this: what happens when robots—or other sophisticated artificially intelligent (AI) machines—get embedded in our societies and have a part to play in criminal acts? Should they, like the knife in the *Bouphonia* ritual, be blamed for their contribution? Or should something else happen, something a little more radical? I am going to make the case for radicalism. In particular, I'm going to suggest that the rise of the robots should lead us to reconsider the wisdom of our traditional practices of punishment and blame.

The Importance of Punishment and Blame

Before I make the case for that radical future, I will say a few words in defence of the past. The rituals of punishment and blame play a very important role in human life. If we cast them off, we risk losing something of great value.

One reason for this is that punishment and blame are the foundation upon which human morality is built. If we did away with them, we would be doing away with morality itself. This is a view that is endorsed by several philosophers and psychologists.[2] One version of this thesis holds that morality got started with cooperative hunting.[3] When our ancestors began hunting big game, they faced a unique challenge. It was all but impossible for a single person to take down a deer or bison. They had to work in teams where one person might chase the animal into a clearing while another might fell it with a spear. To cooperate effectively, these human hunting teams had to develop a special psychological toolkit. They had to understand that they were working together toward a common goal, developing what philosophers would call a capacity for *collective intentionality* (i.e. their beliefs, desires, and intentions had to have a common object or focus). They then had to understand that they each had different roles to play in relation to that common goal. In other words, in order for them to succeed, one person had to do one thing right and another person had to do another thing right: if they failed to do so the goal would not be attained. This created *norms* for cooperation. Finally, they had to understand that the failure to abide by the norms would let the team down. When this happened, other team members could rightly hold this individual to account, criticising them for failing to do their part, and *punishing* them for not doing so. The idea, then, is that the psychological necessities of cooperative hunting drove the development of our distinctive moral beliefs and practices: morality arose when we started to see society as a common endeavour, in which we all have our part to play, and in which we can be blamed if we fail to play that part correctly.

Related to this, there is the importance of reactive attitudes in our moral lives. Reactive attitudes are emotional responses to events that occur in interpersonal relationships. They underpin our social morality. Reactive attitudes include anger, resentment, indignation, gratitude, and forgiveness. These attitudes tell us something about the moral flavour of our experiences. If your partner has an affair, you might feel angry and resentful. If they buy you an ice-cream, you might feel grateful and forgiving. Reactive attitudes of this sort can be more or less appropriate. Some people tend to overreact to the slightest misdeed; some people are too kind-hearted. Either way, reactive attitudes are tied to perceptions of responsibility, blame, and praise. It is because we perceive others to be responsible for our experiences that we react to them in a particular way. A well-calibrated repertoire of reactive attitudes is important for our practices of punishment and blame. It is also important for another reason. According to some accounts, reactive attitudes tell us something about how attached we are to one another. If we did not genuinely care about our interpersonal relationships, if we were cool or indifferent to everything that other people did, then we wouldn't be capable of loving and caring for others. It is only because we care that we tend to slip into anger, blame, and indignation. We cannot have the highs of love and gratitude without running the risk of anger and resentment. Consequently, without punishment and blame, and the reactive attitudes they entail, we wouldn't be able to have one of the most valuable of all human experiences: love.

Finally, there is another sense in which punishment and blame are important. Moral philosophers often rest a lot of weight on intuitions in their arguments. Most people have a strong intuition that punishment is morally necessary. This intuition seems to track perceptions of wrongdoing more than it tracks perceptions of the consequential benefit of punishment. To put that in less obscure terms: when people intuit that another person should be punished, they base this assessment on whether the person is responsible for some wrongdoing and not whether punishing them will deter future wrongdoers or have some other future benefit. This intuition has been tested, repeatedly, in experiments in which people have to react to real or hypothetical events.[4] We can run a test right now with an example.

Example: Jim has just committed the brutal and intentional murder of his wife and child. When asked if he feels any remorse, he says no. You are on a jury tasked with deciding what should be done. You are given two options: (i) send Jim to jail for the rest of his life without the possibility of parole or (ii) send him to a luxurious villa on a tropical island to live out the rest of his days in bliss. Suppose you are told that both options will deter the same number of future criminals. You know this to a high degree of probability. The government assures you that they can keep Jim's presence on the tropical island a secret and convince others that he was punished in the ordinary way.

If, under these conditions, you think there would be something wrong with option (ii)—that Jim can't be treated so kindly whatever the social benefits might be—then you are like most people. You are an intuitive retributivist. You think that if someone does something wrong then they ought to be punished for it. To the extent that intuitions like this should play any part in how we rank the moral value of human practices, it seems plausible to suggest that our practices of punishment and blame are morally important. If we lost them, we would lose something that many people intuit to be of great value.

The Disruption of Robots

How might robots disrupt our practices of punishment and blame? Well, consider another story, more recent in origin.

In 2014, a group of Swiss artists created a novel art installation.[5] Instead of boring people with severed cows and unmade beds,[6] they decided to create an AI criminal. More precisely, they created an algorithm that could shop for illegal goods online. The Random Darknet Shopper, as it was called, was given a budget of bitcoin to make purchases—approximately $100 per week—on the darknet. The algorithm purchased all manner of illicit goods, including knock-off Louis Vuitton handbags and, most controversially, some Ecstasy. The purchased items were then displayed at an art exhibition in St Galen, Switzerland.

The story doesn't end there. The local police force weren't too happy about the Random Darknet Shopper. They arrested it (or, rather, confiscated the software) and carried out an investigation. In the end, they decided that nothing criminal had taken place. The artistic value of the project was recognised and the software was released back to its creators.

The Random Darknet Shopper was not a particularly sophisticated AI. It was created by its programmers with a clear intent to purchase illegal items on the darknet. They couldn't know, in advance, what items it would purchase. So, in a strict sense, they did not have the intention to purchase the Ecstasy. But they knew this was a serious possibility. They could, rightly, have been held responsible for its actions as its human creators. They were like the knife-wielder in the *Bouphonia* ritual: they were using a tool to accomplish a goal.

But what happens if AIs and robots get a little bit more sophisticated and independent in their capacities? What happens as they learn and develop new strategies as a result of their experiences? What if they misinterpret a human instruction to "maximise profit" as a permission to engage in fraud? This is already something that is seriously worrying regulators and policy-makers in the world of high-tech AI-based financial trading. Similar worries have cropped up in relation to military robots and self-driving cars. So much so that there is now something of a scramble to create ethics codes that will ensure that robots follow our moral rules. There is, however, always a chance that they won't: that they will make mistakes and exploit ambiguities in the fuzzy logic of human morality.

If this happens, will we start to blame robots for their misdeeds? Will we be like the temple-goers in Ancient Greece, punishing the knife when we should really be punishing the person that wielded it?

The Three Futures

It seems that we face three possible futures when it comes to the impact of robots on our practices of punishment and blame.

The first future is the most familiar. We can resist the notion that robots are moral agents independent from their human creators. We can insist (by design or law) that they are mere tools, conforming themselves to our individual and collective wills. This means that we will always be able to trace the misdeeds of a robot back to at least one human agent. We can then exercise our retributive instincts on them and hold them responsible for what happened. In this future, the rise of the robots does not disrupt traditional human moral practices of punishment and blame.

The second future is more unusual. We can embrace the notion that robots are moral agents independent from their human creators. We can accept that they can be autonomous moral partners in our collective endeavours. We can form attachments to them and chastise them when they step out of line. Despite their inhuman origins and alien psychologies we might see nothing improper in the idea of punishing them if they commit a crime. This future will involve some revision of our moral practices—we will have to accept robots as moral partners—but, in the end, it is also a familiar future. Our practices of punishment and blame retain their central moral importance.

The third future is the radical one. Robots proliferate. They perform more actions in the world, but we never view them as full moral agents. We don't think it would be right to punish them for their misdeeds. We focus instead on mitigating and managing the risks that arise from their widescale deployment. Nevertheless, we don't think they are mere tools either, and we start to see more and more similarities between them and us. We see ourselves as little more than sophisticated robots, programmed in a different way, perhaps—by a combination of evolution, culture, and personal experience—but ultimately subject to the same basic causal processes. This leads us to question the propriety of our traditional practices of punishment and blame. We start to see something absurd in them. To throw a human (or robot) in jail starts to seem a lot like throwing the knife in the water. It may satisfy some primal urge, but it is illogical and unjustified.

This is the future I want to defend. Why? Well, there are two reasons to favour it. The first is that many (but not all) of our current practices of punishment and blame rest on a philosophical fiction: namely that we are independent, freely-willed agents capable of being wholly morally responsible for our actions. This seems to be false. None of us is truly independent and wholly self-determined: we are shaped by our biological, cultural, and personal histories. Even if we are not fully causally determined by those histories, to treat us as somehow independent from them, and therefore wholly responsible for what we do, seems unfair. This is, admittedly, a controversial position but I stand by it. The second reason is that, for all their merits, our practices of punishment and blame have a dark side. They encourage and justify practices of remarkable cruelty and violence, from state sanctioned killings to hard labour and solitary confinement. They can also induce destructive cycles of vengeance and violence.

What about the previously mentioned advantages of these practices? They are not as compelling as they first appear. Consider the role that punishment plays in social morality. It may well be true that social morality got started with retributive punishment at its foundation, but there is no reason this has to continue. We can view society as a collective endeavour. We can have responsibilities and obligations towards one another, without insisting upon punishing people for their past misdeeds. Instead of viewing responsibility as a backwards-looking phenomenon, we can view it as a forward-looking phenomenon. We can *take responsibility* for our collective future without holding one another responsible for the past. Consider, also, the positive role of reactive attitudes in our lives. Is it really true that we cannot love and care for one another without running the risk of anger and resentment? It seems plausible to think that we can have compassion for one another without getting too hot and bothered about it. Indeed, maybe some emotional coolness, particularly in relation to anger and resentment, would be a net gain for society. Finally, consider the importance of retributive intuitions. While many people have them, it is also possible to reconsider our intuitions in light of new evidence. Intuitively, it seems to many people that a feather should fall slower than an anvil (in a vacuum), but we now know that this is wrong.

Maybe something similar is true for our intuitive desire for retribution? In the future world of robots and advanced AIs, we can start to question its wisdom. After all, in the *Bouphonia* ritual, not only is there something absurd about blaming the knife, there is also something absurd about blaming the wielder of the knife.

Further Reading

Nyholm, S., *Humans and Robots: Ethics, Agency and Anthropomorphism* (Rowman & Littlefield, 2020).
Turner, J., *Robot Rules: Regulating Artificial Intelligence* (Palgrave Macmillan, 2018).

Notes

1. Classicists may not be happy with my description of the ritual. I have simplified some details in the interests of rhetorical brevity. For details, see W. Burkert, *Greek Religion* (Harvard University Press, 1985).
2. For example, C. Boehm, *Moral Origins: The Evolution of Virtue, Altruism, and Shame* (Basic Books, 2012).

3. M. Tomasello, *The Natural History of Human Morality* (Harvard University Press, 2016).
4. K. M. Carlsmith and J. M. Darley, Psychological aspects of retributive justice. In M. Zanna (ed.), *Advances in Experimental Social Psychology* (Elsevier, 2008).
5. Information about the exhibit and the criminal investigation comes from two articles in *The Guardian*, available at: https://www.theguardian.com/technology/2014/dec/05/software-bot-darknet-shopping-spree-random-shopper and https://www.theguardian.com/world/2015/apr/22/swiss-police-release-robot-random-darknet-shopper-ecstasy-deep-web.
6. Perhaps I'm showing my age? These were two infamous Turner Prize winning art exhibits from the 1990s by Damian Hirst and Tracey Emin, respectively.

10

AI and Decision-Making

Jess Whittlestone

Introduction

How can advances in artificial intelligence (AI) help us address the biggest global challenges we face today?

Psychology research has painted a pessimistic picture of human decision-making in recent decades, documenting a whole host of biases and irrationalities people are prone to.[1] These limitations seem to at least partly underpin our struggle to overcome our most pressing global challenges, such as mitigating climate change and threats from new technologies, and reducing global inequality. We find it difficult to be motivated by long-term, abstract, or statistical considerations; many global challenges are far too complex for a human brain to understand in their entirety; and we cannot predict far into the future with any degree of certainty.

At the same time, advances in AI are receiving increasing amounts of attention, raising the question: might we be able to leverage these AI developments to improve human decision-making on the problems that matter most for humanity's future? If so, how?

The Strengths and Limitations of Human Decision-Making

If anything, research in AI in recent decades has shown us that human capabilities are incredibly impressive—just not in ways we are accustomed to find impressive. Many aspects of human cognition which we take completely for granted have turned out to be difficult for machines to replicate. For example, we're able to recognise many different chairs or dogs as belonging to the same category, and to do so across a wide variety of images, with different lighting, context, and perspective. This comes to us easily, but it's a facility that has been surprisingly difficult to build into AI systems. By contrast, the game of chess, which we see as requiring a fair amount of intelligence, turned out to be relatively easy for a computer programme to master with brute force. The world chess champion was defeated by a computer as long ago as 1997.[2]

In general, human cognition has proved to be remarkably robust and flexible compared to machines.[3] When we consider how much complex and ambiguous information we have to process and the number of decisions we have to make every day, simple tasks like navigating our environment and picking up emotions in others' faces seem much more remarkable.

Because we're faced with this huge amount of complexity and uncertainty, we can't possibly optimise every decision. So we use heuristics, shortcuts: we take the route we've always taken in the past without thinking about it. We copy what others around us do much of the time. And we're constantly filtering out huge amounts of information that we don't immediately need. To understand both the strengths and limitations of human reasoning, it is important to understand that our capacity to take in and process information is severely limited, and we need heuristics to make sense of an incredibly complex and uncertain world. These heuristics work very well most of the time, but also limit us in some systematic ways.

When we take even the simplest decisions, such as what to have for dinner or what to buy a friend for their birthday, we have to decide what information to pay attention to and what to filter out. There are numerous different options you might consider, and even if you narrow it down to one idea—a new jumper, say—there are thousands of different brands and retailers online to choose from. Even if you only have 10 ingredients in your fridge, there are hundreds of different ways you might combine them.

All this can mean that we're prone to over-weigh information that's particularly emotionally compelling or immediately in front of us, relative to perhaps more important information that might be more abstract and uncertain. Rather than tackling the difficult question of what would actually improve my friend's life the most, I might just buy them the first jumper I see that I like. We're also much more motivated by immediate rewards—the desire for just one more scoop of ice cream—than longer-term, more probabilistic ones—such as the benefits of eating healthily.

Our use of rough heuristics in decision-making also means consistency is not a human strength. Ask me the same question on two different days, and I might give you different answers depending on how you frame the question, and what is on my mind at the time. The fact we have to use many shortcuts also makes us prone to learning 'illusory correlations' when faced with complex and ambiguous information: that is, convincing ourselves of patterns or relationships that don't really exist. Some have suggested that this tendency underpins how untrue and harmful stereotypes form and persist: if you believe that women are less competent than men, for example, then your brain may start paying attention to all the cases where this is true of individual men and women whilst ignoring all the cases where it isn't.

These limitations seem particularly likely to impact our ability to address global challenges, which require the kind of advance preparation and collective action that we struggle with. It is precisely the 'global' nature of these problems that makes them very difficult to fully understand and predict: our intuitions are not reliable guides when it comes to complex questions like what interventions are most effective at mitigating climate change, how large the threat from nuclear weapons is, or how fast a new pandemic might spread. It is easy for us to develop convincing-seeming but oversimplified theories to answer questions like these, and to waste time and resources acting upon them.

The biases and mistakes we see in human decision-making are often a consequence of our brains being overloaded with more information than we can possibly make sense of. In many ways, this overload is only increasing—there is more and more information at our fingertips online, and more options open to us than ever before—which therefore makes our limitations more pronounced.

But are there ways in which we could use global connectedness and the ready availability of information to tackle global challenges?

The Promise of AI

There are two quite different ways we might think about AI improving decision-making.

The first is to think of AI systems as *replacing* human decisions: increasingly outsourcing decisions to automated systems which can solve them more quickly, efficiently, and effectively. To give a simple example, Google maps is much better than my brain could ever be at knowing all the different routes in a city and calculating the quickest way to get from A to B, so much of the time I just outsource my routing decisions to Google maps and blindly follow what it tells me to do.

A second option is to think of AI systems as *complementing* human capabilities: they can help us to understand the world in new important ways, that are complementary to—rather than simply 'better than'—the way humans understand the world. There may well be things I know about my city, such as which routes are safest at night or most scenic during the day, that can't easily be captured by Google maps' software. Using Google maps can help me to identify the quickest route, saving me time and energy, but in many cases this will be best used in conjunction with other things I already know.

A lot of current discussion around AI and its application in society implicitly assumes the first model: that the aim is to replace human decisions with better, more efficient processes based on AI. This perspective also seems to underpin many of the concerns about the implications of AI for society and humanity: concerns about what increasing automation of jobs will mean for the economy, inequality, and people's sense of meaning;[4] concerns about bias being built into algorithmic decision-making;[5] and concerns about the safety and reliability of AI systems as they begin to replace humans in more and more areas of life.[6]

Given these concerns, an important question we should be asking as a society is whether we actually want, or need, to build AI systems that replace human capabilities. I want to suggest that we should be thinking more explicitly about combining the relative strengths of humans and machines, especially when it comes to solving the most critical problems we face as a society.

Since many limitations of human reasoning stem from our limited cognitive capacity, there's good reason to think AI systems can complement and help us overcome these specific limitations. AI systems tend to be much less flexible and efficient than humans when it comes to most day-to-day tasks such as getting around and interacting with other people, but they *can* help us make sense of large amounts of complex information with much greater reliability and precision. In a recent report from the United Nations (UN) on their activities in AI, the Food and Agriculture Organisation (FAO) stated that: "the most important role of AI . . . is the ability to predict unexpected events, threats, and crises. Challenges such as hunger, climate change, and migration could be addressed before they become crises through early detection, prevention, and mitigation."[7]

For example, an AI system designed by epidemiologists provided one of the first warnings of the SARS-CoV-2 virus outbreak in Wuhan.[8] On December 31, 2019, the BlueDot platform detected an unusual cluster of pneumonia cases in the Hubei province, based on analysis of patterns in thousands of online sources, including foreign-language news reports and posts from animal disease—this was nine days before the World Health Organisation officially flagged the virus. Subsequently, BlueDot used airline ticketing data to accurately anticipate the spread of the virus across East Asia and beyond. An AI-based model like BlueDot cannot by itself mitigate severe threats to global health: doing so requires human scientists and experts to take its warnings and predictions seriously, and take appropriate action. But such models can certainly provide vital and timely information for experts to make the best possible decisions. If Blue-Dot's predictions had been used sooner to identify countries and cities at greatest risk, perhaps the worldwide spread of SARS-CoV-2 could have been substantially slowed.

Another clear way that AI can complement human capabilities is by providing tools to *structure* decision-making processes more rigorously, leading to more consistent and systematic decisions.

There is evidence that even very simple algorithms can outperform expert judgement on simple prediction problems. For example, algorithms have proved more accurate than humans in predicting whether a prisoner released on parole will go on to commit another crime, or in predicting whether a potential candidate will perform well in a job in future. In over 100 studies across many different domains, half of all cases show simple formulas make better significant predictions than human experts, and the remainder (bar a very small handful), show a tie between the two.[9] When there are a lot of different factors involved and a situation is very uncertain, simple formulas can win out by focusing on the most important factors and being consistent, while human judgement is too easily swayed by particularly salient and perhaps irrelevant considerations. A similar idea is supported by further evidence that 'checklists' can improve the quality of expert decisions in a range of domains by ensuring that important steps or considerations aren't missed when people are feeling overloaded.[10] For example, treating patients in intensive care can require hundreds of small actions per day, and one small error could cost a life. Using checklists to ensure that no crucial steps are missed has proved to be remarkably effective in a range of medical contexts, from preventing live infections to reducing pneumonia.

Going beyond very simple algorithms, other AI-based tools hold out the promise of supporting better causal and probabilistic reasoning in complex domains. Humans have a natural ability to build causal models of the world—that is, to explain *why* things happen— that AI systems still largely lack. For example, while a doctor can explain to a patient why a treatment works, referring to the changes it causes in the body, a modern machine-learning system could only tell you that patients who are given this treatment tend, on average, to get better. However, human reasoning is still notoriously prone to confusion and error when causal questions become sufficiently complex, such as when it comes to assessing the impact of policy interventions across society. In these cases, supporting human reasoning with more structured AI-based tools may be helpful. Researchers have been exploring the use of Bayesian Networks—an AI technology that can be used to map out the causal relationships between events, and to represent degrees of uncertainty around different areas—for decision support, such as to enable more accurate risk assessment.[11] These may be particularly useful for assessing the threat of novel or rare threats, where little historical data is available, such as the risk of terrorist attacks and new ecological disasters.

What does this Mean for the Kind of AI Systems We Should be Building?

You might notice two things from these examples of where AI might support better decision-making. First, none of these cases involves having an algorithm or AI system entirely take over the decision process: instead, they are used to distill useful information and structure information in ways that help avoid some of the common pitfalls of human reasoning. Second, many of the examples do not involve remotely sophisticated machine learning methods, but instead relatively simple algorithms and tools for analysing data and structuring decisions—which, by most definitions, would not be classified as 'AI'.

Humans alone would struggle to collect and analyse the data needed to predict the spread of a virus or map population density in developing nations. However, the decisions that need to be made on the basis of this information—what public health interventions should be implemented, or how to prioritise scarce resources across a country—must still be taken by humans. Such decisions may end up being political or value-laden, requiring complex trade-offs on which people may reasonably disagree. For example, deciding how to effectively allocate resources across and between hospitals may require making trade-offs between prioritising the worst-off patients and those most likely to recover. To ensure these decisions are as fair and transparent as possible, they must be made by humans who understand the full context and can be held accountable.

Many of the problems that have recently arisen from the use of AI in society, in fact, stem from AI being used to automate decisions that are inherently value-laden: decisions about whether someone should be given parole, a job, or a loan. An algorithm can give us statistical information about how likely someone from a given demographic group is to reoffend, succeed in a job, or pay back their loan—but the question of who *should* be given what opportunities on the basis of this statistical information is still a normative one. Unquestioningly following the outputs of algorithms can end up reinforcing historical injustices: if ethnic minorities have historically been discriminated against in hiring, then the data will show them as less likely to succeed in jobs, which will lead to further discrimination in future.

If, instead, we considered the algorithms used in these contexts as just *one* piece of data analysis feeding into a broader decision, it might be much easier to notice and mitigate concerns about bias. We should not expect AI systems to understand the nuance and complexity of human values—and given the relative strengths of human and AI capabilities, this very clearly isn't where they can help us most right now.[12]

When it comes to these more contextual, value-laden decisions, algorithms *can* nonetheless sometimes help us to structure the problem more clearly, reducing cognitive effort: distilling key pieces of information, ensuring we do not neglect important factors, and helping us think more clearly about causal relationships in complex systems. Returning to the example of disease management, an AI system cannot tell a government how to save the most lives, but different tools can provide useful statistical information about possible spread and outcomes, help ensure that policymakers consider all important factors when making decisions, and provide decision support for thinking through the possible impact of implementing alternative policies.

Thinking about AI more as supporting and complementing human decisions, than as replacing them, we might find that what we most need is quite far from the most sophisticated machine learning capabilities that are the subject of hype and research attention today. For many important real-world problems, what is most needed is not necessarily better computer vision or natural language processing—humans are already pretty good at seeing and speaking!—but simpler ways to do large-scale data analysis, and practical tools for structuring reasoning and decision-making.

If we aimed explicitly to build AI to do the important things humans struggle with, the research field would look quite different.

Further Reading

Ord, T., *The Precipice* (Bloomsbury Publishing, 2020).
Russell, S., *Human Compatible* (Penguin, 2019).
Sapolsky, R., *Behave* (Penguin Random House, 2017).

Notes

1. D. Kahneman, *Thinking, Fast and Slow* (Farrar, Straus and Giroux, 2011).

2. IBM's supercomputer *Deep Blue* beat the then world chess champion, Garry Kasparov.

3. B. M. Lake, T. D. Ullman, J. B. Tenenbaum, and S. J. Gershman, Building machines that learn and think like people, *Behavioral and Brain Sciences*, 40 (2017).

4. T. Walsh, Expert and non-expert opinion about technological unemployment, *International Journal of Automation and Computing*, 15/5 (2018), 637–42.

5. S. Myers West, M. Whittaker, and K. Crawford, *Discriminating Systems: Gender, Race and Power in AI* (AI Now Institute, 2019).

6. D. Amodei, C. Olah, J. Steinhardt, P. Christiano, J. Schulman, and D. Mané, *Concrete Problems in AI Safety* (arXiv preprint arXiv:1606.06565, 2016).

7. *United Nations Activities on Artificial Intelligence* (AI) (2019), report available at: https://www.itu.int/dms_pub/itu-s/opb/gen/S-GEN-UNACT-2019-1-PDF-E.pdf.

8. E. Niller, An AI epidemiologist sent the first warnings of the Wuhan virus, *Wired Magazine*, https://www.wired.com/story/ai-epidemiologist-wuhan-public-health-warnings/.

9. W. M. Grove and P. E. Meehl, Comparative efficiency of informal (subjective, impressionistic) and formal (mechanical, algorithmic) prediction procedures: The clinical–statistical controversy, *Psychology, Public Policy, and Law*, 2 (1996), 293–323.

10. A. Gawande, *The Checklist Manifesto* (Henry Holt and Company, 2009).

11. N. Fenton and M. Neil, *Risk Assessment and Decision Analysis with Bayesian Networks* (CRC Press, 2012).

12. R. Nyrup, J. Whittlestone, and S. Cave, *Why Value Judgements Should Not Be Automated* (Evidence submitted to the Committee on Standards in Public Life, 2019).

11

The Future Car

David Edmonds

A few years ago, I was travelling by car in the British Midlands. I drove to the gym, then to work, before returning home. There was nothing exceptional about the journey, except for one thing—there was nobody behind the steering wheel.

The future of the driverless car exhibits something of a Zeno's paradox: for many years we've been told that its appearance on our streets is imminent, but that much-anticipated day, although it moves closer and closer, never seems to arrive.

I tested a driverless car on a specially built track—the car's satnav had various destinations programmed into it—marked 'gym', 'work', and 'home'. Reflecting on the experience later, I was struck by how quickly I'd adjusted to the experience. For the first few minutes I watched amazed and slightly alarmed as the car signalled on its own, stopped at junctions and traffic lights, navigated roundabouts. The steering wheel turned without human touch. The brakes applied themselves. But the excitement and anxiety soon passed. After a quarter of an hour, it already felt perfectly natural.

To my inexpert eyes, the car seemed almost ready for commercial production. Still, real road use poses challenges that engineers and designers are finding difficult to overcome. There are some interesting technical and legal problems. Some of these are particularly relevant for what might be merely a transition period, when human drivers coexist on the road alongside driverless vehicles. For example, driverless cars are law-abiding. This is fine if all cars obey the law, but if human-driven cars are zipping along well above the speed limit, then it may be safer for the driverless car, on occasion, to transgress the law too. But, there are all sorts of problems with programming driverless cars with what's been called 'naughty software'—adjusting their behaviour to accommodate dangerous human drivers. For example, would the owner of the speeding driverless car be fined? That would seem unfair, but then so would the opposite—that only human drivers are liable to be penalized.

During the transition period, human-driven cars may be able to game the system. Because driverless cars will brake quickly to avoid collisions, humans behind the wheel may become cavalier in their behaviour, knowing that they can safely get away with being more reckless.

There are also technical problems about identifying threats. Humans can easily tell that a brick on the road poses more of a danger than a plastic bag. The driverless car has to learn to distinguish what in its path needs to be avoided and what can be ignored.

So these are all high hurdles for the driverless car to surmount. But this future vehicle also raises ethical challenges—and these may prove even more problematic.

*

Here's an extract from a newspaper article published on November 9, 2041:

> Yesterday, there was a fatality alongside London's busy A40 road. Eyewitnesses say that a child had run onto the road, and the child's mother had sprinted after her. To avoid them, a car travelling at the legal limit of 40 mph had swerved and mounted the pavement – hitting a young man. An ambulance arrived within minutes, but it was too late to save the man's life. The mother and child are reported to be shaken but physically unharmed.

I will return to this story soon. But before I do, I want to envisage future life with the driverless car. Back in the twentieth century the invention of the car was crucial to the growth of suburbs—cars meant that people no longer needed to be so close to work or to amenities. My prediction is that the driverless car will have an equally trans- formative impact, and that it will prove the biggest change to happen to the car since its invention.

A city like London is currently clogged with traffic. Parking places are scarce and sometimes frustrating to locate. Parked cars have the effect of reducing the width of many roads. The city is cluttered with signage to assist and direct human drivers. In the suburbs, space at many houses is taken up with garages or drives.

The city of the future is going to look and feel very different. One plausible scenario is that in a few decades, car ownership will be a luxury confined to the wealthy. After all, most of us use our cars for only a fraction of the day. So in the future we are likely to dispense with our own vehicles and instead call up a driverless car only when it's needed. Perhaps most driverless cars will spend their nights in huge car parks dotted in or just outside town.

This would produce a fundamental shift in the architecture and ambiance of the city.

Of course, none of this is inevitable. Indeed, in theory we could discourage or prohibit the driverless car. But if we were to adopt a utilitarian approach—utilitarianism being the theory that we should determine whether something is right or wrong by whether it produces the greatest good or happiness for the greatest number—then we should surely embrace this car of the future. For the advantages would seem to vastly outweigh the drawbacks.

Here are just a few of the benefits.

1. Safety. This is the principal advance. At present, well over a million people die in road accidents each year. More than twice as many Americans lose their lives this way each year than in the worst year of the Vietnam War. Most of these deaths are due to human error. Driverless cars wouldn't get distracted by singing along to the radio or by an annoying spouse in the passenger seat. They wouldn't get tired and fall asleep at the wheel. They wouldn't consume five beers at a party and be confident that they were nonetheless safe to be behind the wheel.

2. Social benefits. Many people are physically and socially isolated because they cannot drive. Perhaps they're too old to drive safely or perhaps they have a disability that makes driving impossible. Perhaps they can drive but cannot afford a car. Of course, in theory such people can move around by taxi or minicab. But in practice this is only a partial solution. For most of us taxis are expensive. Regular use for mundane trips to a café, or shop, or to meet a friend, is not feasible. The biggest component in the cost of taxis is the pay of the driver. The driverless car will offer taxi journeys at a fraction of today's price.

3. Financial benefits. We have already mentioned that using a driverless car will be much cheaper than taking an Uber cab. Indeed, it seems likely that Uber and all the other car apps have always foreseen an endgame in which they control a fleet of cars without having to pay the humans who operate them. But in addition, there will also be savings to be had on insurance. Since cars will be much safer, the insurance on them will be correspondingly reduced—and all car users should benefit.

4. Environmental benefits. It seems likely that all cars, driverless or not, will become electric. The increase in demand for taxi journeys in a driverless car environment might raise overall mileage. But nonetheless the driverless car should have a positive environmental impact. There should be less congestion because the flow of traffic will be better regulated (cars will be able to drive at the same speed and closer together) and there will be many more opportunities for journey sharing. Since each car will be much more fully employed, there will be far fewer of them.

5. Racial justice. In the United States, African-Americans have long complained about being pulled over by police on some pretence but really for the crime of DWB (driving while black). In the UK too there is a history of the black community being discriminated against and being targeted by the police. In the driverless car regime, such injustices will hopefully disappear altogether.

6. Relaxation and productivity. Some people enjoy driving. But for the rest of us, it is boring and stressful. Busy roads require vigilance, not knowing the route can lead to anxiety. We could instead be sitting in the back seat, reading a novel on our electronic device or dictating emails through our voice-recognition phone. There's also car upkeep: in the future, the cleaning, parking, and maintenance of cars will be subcontracted to the operators.

These potential benefits from the driverless car are substantial. On the negative side of the ledger the list is shorter. Certainly, there will be significant upheaval in certain industries. Tens of thousands of taxi and lorry drivers will lose their jobs. Other downsides are more difficult to foresee—perhaps, for example, there will be an increase in alcoholic consumption because people won't need to drive themselves home.

More concerning are dangers from the technology underpinning the driverless car. In the future there will be a data record of all our journeys. This raises issues about privacy. An autonomous car has been described as "basically big brother on wheels".[1] And then there's hacking. Could a malicious agent hack the controls and drive a car over a cliff?

Nonetheless, on balance the negatives of the autonomous car are vastly outweighed by the positives. In any case, technological advance is not easy to frustrate: it seems very likely that sooner or later the era of the driverless car will be upon us. Time to return to that newspaper article from 2041.

The Trolley Problem

The Trolley Problem is a famous dilemma in moral philosophy. It stems from an article written by the Oxford philosopher Philippa Foot in 1967 and then a follow-up article, nearly two decades later, by the American philosopher Judith Jarvis Thomson.[2]

The original puzzle goes something like this. Imagine you are standing by the side of the track and see a train hurtling towards you. Clearly its brakes have failed. Worse, five people are tied to the track ahead and they face certain death if hit. You are by the signal lever: if you pulled the lever you would divert the train down a side-track, a spur. Unfortunately, one person is tied onto this spur track and if you redirected the train he would be killed. What should you do? Call this scenario 'Spur'.

The second puzzle is an adaptation of this. Once again there is an out-of-control train heading towards five people tied to the track. This time you are on a footbridge overlooking the track, standing next to a fat man. If you were to push this man over the footbridge to his death below, his sheer bulk would stop the train and save five lives. What should you do? Call this scenario 'Fat Man'.

In multiple studies around the world, people of all ages, classes, religions, and nationalities, tend to give the same answers. The right course of action, they say, is to alter the direction of the train in the first scenario, but not to push the Fat Man in the second.

In a way this is baffling. Why do people have such conflicting intuitions given that in both cases the choice is between taking one life and saving five? The search for an answer to this conundrum has spawned a mini philosophical industry. My own preferred solution draws on what's called the doctrine of double effect.[3] There is a distinction between 'intending' an outcome and merely 'foreseeing' it. We foresee but do not intend the death of the isolated man in Spur, and if he were somehow to extricate himself from the track and run away before being hit we would be delighted. But we do intend the death of Fat Man: we need him to block the train, otherwise the five lives would not be spared.

Intellectually absorbing though it is, until recently The Trolley Problem has not troubled the sleep of many non-philosophers. But in the era of autonomous machines and the driverless car, it now needs to be faced up to. For variations of it, like the scenario described in the 2041 newspaper article, may actually occur.

True, they will be very rare. In most situations a car will be able to stop and avoid any injuries or fatalities. But no system is failsafe.

Choices, Choices

The possibility that the driverless car will have to be programmed to choose between the life of a child and a mother on the one hand and a young man on the other, raises some thorny issues. In the real world, as opposed to that imagined by philosophers, there's a lot of uncertainty: we can't be sure what outcome will follow from our decisions. That important caveat aside, however, what criteria should we use to assess the right course of action? How should the driverless car be pre-set to act? As mentioned earlier, responses to The Trolley Problem reveal that most of us are not crude utilitarians—that is, even though turning the train in Spur and pushing the Fat Man both take a life, most people judge the latter act to be worse than the former. However, when it comes to 'choices' to be made by autonomous vehicles, people have more utilitarian instincts. Surveys suggest that they believe that the driverless car should save the maximum number of lives.

This must be—I contend—because we find it more difficult to attach the concept of 'intention' to autonomous machines than to human beings. We think that the mental content of a human when pushing the Fat Man is not the same as when turning the switch in Spur. Of course, the driverless car is programmed by humans, but human involvement in the 'choice' of how a driverless car responds in a life-and-death dilemma feels more remote.

The data suggests there is one exception to the utilitarian preference. True, if turning the car left kills one bystander and turning it right kills two, the driverless car should, people believe, turn left. But many people don't believe that this principle should be used when it comes to weighing up the lives of the passenger against those of pedestrians or passengers in other vehicles. That is to say, people don't want to take a journey in a car that would sacrifice their life to save other lives.

From an ethical point of view, that hardly seems like a defensible position. How could anybody justify the principle that someone else's life be sacrificed to save two lives, but that in any calculation or comparison between lives *their* life be privileged? It seems to clash with a golden rule—the idea that we should treat others as we want to be treated. If we demand a selfish car, others should be allowed to demand one too.

However, if the survey data is accurate, and driverless cars were run on purely impersonal utilitarian lines, then people might be reluctant to use them. That would be regrettable if, as I believe, the driverless car promises huge societal benefits. The hope is that users could be persuaded that the risk that their car sacrificed its passenger(s) would be miniscule—and that overall they would be much safer in a driverless car world than they are at present.

But in any case, whose decision will it be to determine how a driverless car responds in these very rare cases where an accident is inevitable? The government's? The manufacturer's? The owner's or passenger's? Will we be able to choose the morality of our automobile—"I'd like a maroon Kantian, Porsche convertible please"? That sounds like a recipe for confusion—a regime in which different vehicles were darting about operating under a variety of ethical algorithms would be unpredictable and generate feelings of insecurity.

Then there's the matter of liability and insurance. Currently, when there's an accident we apportion blame. If John's car collides with Mary's, a decision has to be reached as to who's at fault. If John was responsible, then, in a typical case, his insurance would pay for the damage. But it doesn't seem reasonable to blame John if the car was driving itself. In which case, should the manufacturer settle any bills? Lawyers are already pondering solutions to this issue: one option might be that there is a user insurance surcharge—paid into a giant pot. Rather than owners or users of driverless cars having individual insurance policies, any damages would come from a collective fund.

Questions of liability will be even more complex in the transition period, in which there are both driverless cars and human-driven cars on the same roads at the same time. I have already pointed out that many people enjoy driving—but given that the driverless car will pose much less of a threat than the human-driven one, it seems to me that those who persist in driving should, at the very least, be forced to pay some kind of tax premium.

*

That there are tough technical challenges to the driverless car is undeniable. And to make the driverless car as safe as possible, there will need to be investment in electronic furnishings on and near roads—signals to facilitate navigation. I don't want the driverless car to illustrate a Zeno Paradox: I want it to reach its destination— appearance on our roads—and as quickly as possible. When it does so, it will save many lives.

Most people who dismiss the viability of driverless cars point to the admittedly significant engineering and infrastructure difficulties. But it's the tricky ethical and legal issues which may prove the real roadblock to their emergence.[4]

Further Reading

Edmonds, D., *Would You Kill The Fat Man?* (Princeton, 2013).

Notes

1. P. Lin, quoted in Philosophers are building ethical algorithms to help control self-driving cars, *Quartz Magazine*, 11 February 2018.
2. For more background on The Trolley Problem, see D. Edmonds, *Would You Kill the Fat Man?* (Princeton, 2013).
3. For more on the Doctrine of Double Effect, see Edmonds (2013).
4. Thanks to Sven Nyholm for helpful comments on this chapter.

Future Communication

12

The Future of Privacy

Carissa Véliz

When we look back at how humanity has behaved throughout history, most people agree there is much to be ashamed of: centuries of human beings abusing one other, and making bad decisions that have brought about much unnecessary turmoil and suffering. Among the many reasons that can partly explain why people have failed to act better in the past are greed, selfishness, chauvinism, short-sightedness, negligence, and other faults and biases that have obstructed our moral vision. Even though the world is still ravaged by unnecessary suffering, some parts of it have improved. The Universal Declaration of Human Rights, the instantiation of universal suffrage, and the development of medical ethics are some examples of initiatives that have led human beings to treat others better. When we contemplate the past, we seem to have a better perspective than the protagonists of the stories we study to judge what was wise and unwise.

One reason why, arguably, we have more moral clarity on the past than the present is because we know how the past panned out. In the present we can only imagine the places that our current actions might take us.

A second reason why we can enjoy more moral clarity about the past is that when it comes to the past—especially the quite distant past—we are less likely to have skin in the game. We have no commercial interest in the Industrial Revolution, for instance, so it is easier to perceive just how morally unacceptable worker conditions were. When we think about Romans forcing people to be gladiators, we can more easily be outraged because we don't feel the excitement of the battle, or the allure of business. Not being a stakeholder in the past allows us to have a more unbiased moral perspective.

Imagining how ethicists in the distant future will perceive our present practices, or our practices in the more immediate future, can thus be a useful heuristic to help us assess them. It can allow us to move away from our present conditioning, even if only slightly— and that sliver of perspective can prove enlightening.

How do you think a future ethicist will regard how we currently treat privacy in the context of the data economy? As a brilliant idea that led to scientific progress, political stability, and individual well-being? Or as a terrible idea that exploited people's rights and led to unfairness, political unrest, and unnecessary suffering? Let's start by taking a look at the current state of affairs, and then assess whether privacy-eroding trends are more likely to lead us to a brighter or darker future.

Privacy Today

Today, British, European, and American citizens have much less privacy than they did in the 1990s. Back then, most corporations knew little, if anything, about individual customers. Governments held some data on citizens with a criminal record but very little on those who were law-abiding, and much of it was scattered across different agencies. If the police suddenly suspected a person might be a criminal, the data for the ensuing investigation would start at that point, and not before.

Privacy matters because it protects individuals from abuses of power. It is like a blindfold forcing the system to treat everyone equally. A prospective employer could not discriminate against someone on account of his health status because they didn't have access to that information.

That gradually changed during the first decade of the 21st century. Google and other tech companies realised that they could use the data produced by users to build profiles of these users. The aim was to allow the personalisation of ads. Google, and others, didn't ask permission to collect this data from either users or governments. They just did it. By the time it became widely known, the system was already in place. By then, governments were not motivated to regulate the data economy because they realised they could make a copy of the data being collected by private companies and use it for their own purposes. The government's thirst for data increased after the 2001 terrorist attacks on the Twin Towers—for security reasons they wanted as much data on everyone as they could get their hands on.[1]

Today, businesses and governments can learn a huge amount about almost any person in the world with a few clicks. Nearly everyone carries a spy in their pockets, better known as a smartphone. Among the personal data routinely collected about everyone who uses digital technologies is location data, contacts, communications metadata (whom you've called or messaged, when, from where, for how long, etc.), purchasing records, browsing history, and biometrics (e.g. face prints). This data is incredibly sensitive. With it, someone can infer where you live and work, whom you sleep with, whether you have had an abortion or do drugs, whether you go to church, your diseases, your purchasing power, your political beliefs, and much more. If the police become suspicious that a person might be a criminal, they can plunge into years of past personal data and fish for possible crimes. They could look for anything suspicious or antisocial you have said or done in the past, often taking it out of context. A prospective employer who's bought a file on you from a data broker—data brokers are companies that collect personal data in order to sell it to other companies—could discriminate against you for all kinds of reasons— religion, politics, health—and you will probably never know about it.

That's a sketch of privacy today. To take an imagined perspective from the future, so as to assess whether trading personal data is a good idea, we need to picture where current trends might lead us. What might the future look like if the process of trading personal data accelerates? What are the implications for privacy?

A Future without Privacy

Your smartwatch vibrates. It's time to wake up. 'Good morning', says your digital assistant, 'I've noticed that your heartrate was a bit fast last night. Maybe you need to exercise more. How about starting the day with a run?'

You really don't feel like going for a run. You're tired, you have a slight headache, and you'd rather read the newspaper. But rejecting your digital assistant's advice means losing points on your health insurance account, which will make your premium more expensive. That information is also sold to your life insurance company, your employer, your bank, and your government, among others. Any one point lost could cost you a pay raise or the chance to access a loan. You go for a run.

You feel queasy during your run. You wish you could stop for a break without it being recorded by your smartwatch. Today is one of those days when you feel like calling in sick to work. But you won't, as that would trigger an immediate appointment with your doctor that would only make your headache worse. The extra scrutiny wouldn't help the stress you're feeling; you know you just need time to relax, but you soldier on.

Back home, your digital assistant suggests porridge for breakfast. You are sick of porridge. Apparently, oats are good for lowering cholesterol. Not eating your porridge might cost health insurance points. You eat your porridge.

You open your laptop. Even though you've worked this way for years, it's still hard to keep in mind that everything you do on your computer is being recorded and sent to your boss. It's stressful not to be able to take a second off to write a personal message or read the news. Work software (in the old days software like this used to be called 'spyware') monitors your attention, and how many words you type per hour, among other things.[2] It links up to your digital assistant, and anytime you slack, it nudges you back to work. 'You seem to be distracted', says your digital assistant. Your digital masters are so strict that if you take one bathroom break too many, you will not achieve the daily goals they set for you. The irony is that you're not more productive than you used to be; you may write more words, but the quality is worse and more of it is waffle and padding.

When your workday is finally done, you lie down on your couch for a rest. Your head still hurts. You check your smartphone. The way you type, tap, and scroll is being analysed by machine-learning algorithms to infer your emotional state of mind and your cognitive abilities.[3] The thought that such a mundane detail—a swipe too slow—could reveal whether you have depression, memory problems, or an attention disorder, adds to your anxiety. For all you know the algorithm is hopelessly faulty, but your employer takes whatever the algorithm says at face value.

An email alerts you that your bank account has been hacked. Again. You wonder how many hours and how much money it will take to sort things out this time.[4] But you can't deal with it now, so you go for a walk.

You remember the days when you could explore the city anonymously. You could stroll anywhere you liked without being recorded, noticed, analysed. You could get lost in unknown neighbourhoods, full of corners and cafés waiting to be discovered. These days it's too risky. Drones and satellites watch you from above. Facial and gait recognition identify you with every CCTV camera you pass. If you end up in a bad neighbourhood, you could be deemed suspicious; you could lose points on your social credit. If you end up somewhere near a protest, you could be added to a blacklist. It's been decades since you have protested anything—and not for want of injustices. Better stay in the safe touristy areas.

You pass a bookshop. You miss browsing freely in a bookshop, buying and reading books about politics, sex, love, and health. You don't do that any more. It's too revealing. There are rumours of underground bookshops cropping up here and there; places in which there are no cameras, where no digital devices are permitted, and that use a system of barter instead of electronic payments. But just taking off your smartwatch is enough to land you in trouble. You don't want to attract the attention of intelligence agencies or other investigative authorities. Since the coronavirus pandemic, you are required by law to wear your smartwatch at all times. Among other things, your smartwatch tracks your heart rate, temperature, and skin conductance (whether you are sweating). It's meant to prevent future pandemics. If only that data were used for that alone.

You wish you could consult with a lawyer about some of the ways your data is being used. You are not sure they are legal ways, but contacting a lawyer is also too dangerous. It is common sense to assume that lawyers are bugged along with everyone else.

You return home and turn on the TV to watch the news. The Prime Minister is going on about how your country's economy is world-beating; how his administration is making the nation great again. You try to keep a straight face. Emotional surveillance companies record and analyse your emotions through the camera on your smart TV, and they share that data with the authorities. Governments and corporations insist that emotional surveillance serves democracy.

The government claims that your political opinions can be inferred from your data, thereby making voting superfluous. They say citizens have been liberated from the burden of voting. You miss voting though. You don't trust algorithmic inferences, particularly given that the media you consume is personalised. Isn't there some kind of vicious cycle in content being tailored to you and then used to infer your opinions on matters of public interest?

You feel bad for all the young people who never got the chance to vote. Democracy is partly a tradition, a know-how, something that your elders taught you how to engage with, and you fear this tradition is being lost. When you went to university, you were still taught that good governments derived their power and legitimacy from the consent of their citizens—not from their data. How things have changed . . .

Privacy, Freedom, and Democracy

A critic might argue that I have painted too bleak a picture: surely the use of personal data doesn't have to lead to the erosion of freedom and democracy. Can't we use personal data to avoid pandemics, to develop personalised medicine, and to better fulfil our worldly desires without it affecting our freedom? Perhaps. But only if we regulate the data economy properly.

What kinds of safeguards should we put in place to avoid the future I depict? Well, for starters we should ban personalised content. As long as politicians and rogue actors can segment the population, information ghettos will erode democracy. To have a well-informed citizenry, we all need to have access to the same content, so that journalists, academics, and citizens in general can fact-check and criticise it and push politicians to be consistent in what they stand for, as opposed to tailoring different messages to different sectors of the population.

To avoid discrimination and unfair uses of data, we need those who collect and analyse personal data to have fiduciary responsibilities—

requiring them to put the interests of data subjects above all else. Our data should not be used against us. Just as your doctor can only use her position of power to help you, people who manage your data should use it only in ways that benefit you. If your smartwatch tracks your heartbeat, the data should not be sold to your employer or to data brokers who do not have your best interest as their main objective.

To further incentivise correct uses of data, we need to ban the trade of personal data. Information about who you are, what you do, and what your weak points are, should not be the kind of thing that can be bought and sold. That we allow data brokers to line their pockets by selling, for example, databases of rape victims and HIV patients, is inexcusable.[5] Those who buy that data are people who take advantage of people's vulnerabilities. If personal data is profitable, there will always be an incentive to collect more of it than is absolutely necessary, and to sell it to whoever wants to buy it. Data brokers have even sold personal data to fraudsters.[6] If we ban the trade in personal data, we disincentivise bad data practices.

With a few more adjustments in place, such as banning sensitive inferences (e.g. inferring sexual orientation from musical preferences), we can start to imagine a world in which freedom and democracy can thrive, and personal data is used to further science and technology.

The limits that I propose to protect freedom and democracy are those that protect privacy too, because we can't get the former without the latter.

We need privacy to avoid interference with our autonomy. When others know too much about us, there is a temptation to interfere with our beliefs and behaviour. For example, a casino might use adverts to target, very accurately, those tempted to gamble—good for the casino, but possibly harmful for the gambler. We need privacy to be able to protest anonymously, vote in secret, contact doctors, lawyers, and journalists in confidence, read whatever we are curious about; all these things and more make up the foundations of freedom and democracy. It is not a coincidence that totalitarian regimes like the German Democratic Republic and the Soviet Union were experts at surveillance, using the Stasi and the KGB to spy on and terrorise their citizens.

Modern totalitarian tendencies tend to involve the corporate world. Contemporary surveillance stems from a collaboration between governments and the private sector. The Chinese social credit system is a good example of a model to avoid, but one which we are dangerously approaching. Chinese citizens are rated for trustworthiness. According to the system's founding document, the objective is to 'allow the trustworthy to roam everywhere under heaven while making it hard for the discredited to take a single step'.[7] Playing too many video games, jaywalking, buying alcohol, playing loud music, or spreading 'fake news' are examples of the kinds of actions that harm people's scores. Data is collected and shared between businesses and public agencies. An infraction like smoking on a high-speed train can be enough to get you publicly shamed, and on a blacklist that excludes you from accessing hotels, loans, and even from travelling.[8] By the end of June 2019, China had banned almost 27 million people from buying air tickets, and almost 6 million people from using the high-speed rail network.[9] Having a low score can mean not being able to find a job or buy a property. It might even affect your dating—for example, how prominently your profile is displayed on a dating app.[10]

Choose Your Own Adventure

Privacy is currently at the centre of a fierce battle. On one side, powerful data companies like Google, Facebook, and major data brokers are collecting and analysing as much personal data as they can. They are lobbying governments around the world, and trying to get governments to depend on them. During the coronavirus lockdown, for instance, governments depended on platforms to conduct their meetings online. The analysis of data is increasingly outsourced to companies like Palantir, which has contracts with American and British public institutions. Intelligence agencies and public health authorities argue that they need as much data as possible to keep us as safe as possible. On the other side of the privacy battles, a techlash from consumers, human rights organisations, privacy experts, a few businesses, and new regulation such as Europe's General Data Protection Regulation (GDPR) and California's Consumer Privacy Act, represent forces that are pushing corporations and governments to respect our privacy. It is up to citizens to decide what kind of future we want. We can use and analyse personal data. But to prevent abuses of this data we have to protect privacy, which in turn will help us protect autonomy, freedom, and democracy.

Further Reading

Véliz, C., *Privacy Is Power* (Bantam Press, 2020).

Notes

1. For a more extensive narrative of the development of the data economy, see B. Schneier, *Data and Goliath* (W.W. Norton & Company, 2015); S. Zuboff, *The Age of Surveillance Capitalism* (Profile Books, 2019); and C. Véliz, *Privacy Is Power* (Transworld, 2020).
2. A. Satariano, How my boss monitors me while I work from home, *New York Times*, 6 May 2020; B. Allyn, Your boss is watching you: Work-from-home boom leads to more surveillance, *NPR*, 13 May 2020; W. D. Heaven, This startup is using AI to give workers a 'productivity score', *MIT Technology Review*, 4 June 2020.
3. R. Metz, The smartphone app that can tell you're depressed before you know it yourself, *MIT Technology Review*, 2018.
4. The features of the internet that make it easy for corporations and governments to collect personal data, also make it easier for hackers to access data.
5. M. Hicken, Data brokers selling lists of rape victims, AIDS patients, *CNN*, 2013.
6. N. Singer, Data broker is charged with selling consumers' financial details to 'fraudsters', *New York Times*, 2014.
7. S. Mistreanu, Life inside China's social credit laboratory, *Foreign Policy*, 3 April 2018.
8. F. Tang, China names 169 people banned from taking flights or trains under social credit system, *South China Morning Post*, 2 June 2018.
9. O. Wang, China's social credit system will not lead to citizens losing access to public services, Beijing says, *South China Morning Post*, 19 July 2019.
10. A. Ma, China has started ranking citizens with a creepy 'social credit' system, *Business Insider*, 29 October 2018.

13

Persuasive Technology

James Williams

Let's imagine that it's the middle of the twenty-first century, and the most immersive, persuasive technology ever conceived has just transformed the human experience.

*

It all started when a quixotic neuroscientist-turned-inventor released to the world the alpha version of a device he called the Spectacles, a non-invasive neurological interface that syncs to, and simulates content in, users' visual and auditory streams. You wear it like a pair of glasses, but there's no frame or lenses—yet it overlays the most realistic augmented-reality sounds and visions imaginable. The device's core technological innovation was quickly recognized as world-changing, especially in light of its simplicity and trivial development cost. Within a year, the academic paper describing the technology, titled 'A Novel Method for Manipulating Human Perception', became the most cited publication in history.

It's difficult to adequately describe the experience of using the Spectacles to someone unfamiliar with them. If you're old enough to remember movie theatres, you may remember walking out of the theatre after a movie and having the feeling that the movie was still playing in your mind: you carried the attitude of the action hero or detective or whatever out into the real world with you for a few minutes, until it faded away like a siren dopplering off behind you. Imagine that same feeling—of your mind overlaying narrative meaning on the world—but rather than fading, it swims up into your eyes and ears and becomes real until you turn it off, which you never want to do.

The effect of the Spectacles on human life and society has been profound. During the device's limited public beta, the lucky bespectacled few were mobbed and envied. Many people pretended to have one on when they didn't, for instance by acting like they were doing battle against nonexistent entities on their way to work. Distraction suddenly became cool. Daydreaming became a status symbol overnight.

After the official launch of v.1, adoption of the Spectacles was similarly swift. Now, just two years later, 83% of adult humans are spending the majority of their waking lives (and, after Spectacles v.3, most of their dreaming as well) partaking in its controlled hallucinations at scale. People's wildest dreams have become routine as their imaginations become immanent. It is difficult to know, or care, where the Spectacles end and the baseline world begins. The primary function of the physical environment is now like that of a projector screen: blank, flat surfaces are preferred so that there is minimal perceptual conflict with the experiences the Spectacles are producing. The Spectacles have spawned a whole new ecosystem of content creators with job titles like Behavioural Experience Architect, Lead Life Journey Analyst (Quantitative), and Director of Narrative Neuroexperience.

Places generally have become less important. When anyone or anything can appear before you instantly, terms like 'work' and 'home' are losing their meaning. If these places involve being around certain people in a certain type of environment, and you can call forth both the people and the environment anywhere you are, then that place is potentially everywhere (and nowhere).

Some people are even using the Spectacles to speak with the dead—not literally, of course, but algorithmically. As they walk through life, they consult artificial approximations of deceased friends or family members that have been trained on the corpus of all the digital audio, video, image, text, and behavioural records those people left behind. It is like the Roman tradition where families hung their ancestors' death masks on the walls of their home and traced out the relations with thread—except instead of telling stories about them, they are having coffee with them and asking them for advice.

The boundaries between people have simultaneously hardened and softened. People have become more theatrical as it is harder and harder to get anyone else's attention, at least without paying to put 'suggested experiences' in their streams. Yet this increased social need to expand one's self to others has come into awkward conflict with the new paucity of opportunities for calm, quiet, and reflection that the Spectacles' constant parade of stimuli has left us with.

Pushback against the Spectacles has been minor. There was brief resistance by some religious groups who denounced it as 'the mark of the beast', as well as by an organised cadre of self-termed 'cognitive libertarians' who objected to the political economy behind its design, demanding 'no manipulation without representation'. While most neo-democratic countries have already adopted the Spectacles as next-generation voting machines, the code and decision-making processes employed by the company's Democracy Protection team have remained secret, largely due to intellectual property concerns. In any event, the company maintains that it would be impossible to subject the Spectacles' workings to outside control due to the high degree of automation involved—most of its algorithms are emergent and never even seen by a human—as well as undesirable, since injecting human bias into the machines would undermine the platform's neutrality. Rejecting this logic, a sizable portion of cognitive libertarians who espoused more extreme methods of resistance soon branched off into the Attention Rebellion movement, which no longer officially exists but has survived informally as a ragtag underground network. Yet these and other critical reactions against the Spectacles have failed, in large part because they were quickly muted by the 'safety filters' of the Spectacles themselves.

A key component of the Spectacles' success was its v.1 launch strategy; its rhetorical framing served to preempt many potential ethical objections. The approach, conceived by the inventor and his team at Bloom, Inc., was informed by a close study of the dynamics of the so-called 'tech-lash' against digital technology companies in the early twenty-first century. As a result, by the time of its launch the Spectacles had already been full-throatedly endorsed by well-known thought influencers and public philosophers, all of whom hailed it as the most intentional computational expression of 'know thyself' the world had ever seen.

Essential to this strategy was the way in which Bloom seized the language of wellbeing in its initial selling of the Spectacles. At the public v.1 launch event, the company's Chief Product Philosopher walked on stage and began his presentation with that now-famous phrase: 'We keep ourselves whole by keeping our environments whole.' He concluded the talk with a masterful display of enigmatic distraction, by reciting a rhyming quatrain whose meaning has, presumably as intended, been the subject of multiple self-help podcast episodes, discourse journal articles, and business school case-studies.

The core, unstated design assumption of the Spectacles is that we give attention to what is worth giving attention to. The error of this assumption is rarely questioned or remarked upon. Even more importantly, its direct conflict with Bloom's business model—persuasion—is barely apparent even to those who are inclined to take a critical stance toward the system. Evidence of successful persuasion is simply taken as evidence of user intention. Why else would a man walking to work stop and fist fight for thirty minutes with an Old Spice-sponsored bio-approximation of Ernest Hemingway if he didn't want to in the first place?

The way the Spectacles have been quickly monetized—and how Bloom has become the most valuable company on the planet—is by allowing anyone to put a 'suggested experience' in anyone else's perceptual stream. In an earlier era these would have been called 'advertisements', though here there is virtually no limit on what they can consist of, what persuasive mechanisms they can employ, or the particular end goals of the sponsors who pay to deploy them for persuasive ends. The entire environment is persuasive, and this is just one more mode of persuasion. Of course, transparency of a sort has been required: anytime a suggested experience appears in your stream, you see a little black-and-white smiley-face icon to indicate that it's sponsored. And of course you're not forced to allow them in your stream: you have to consent at least semi-cognitively in order for them to start playing (unless you have auto-play enabled). But in reality, no one stops and affirms every single little smiley face—who has time for that? Most people just mentally smile across all of them at once and allow them to do their thing so that the prompts will go away. Besides, if you were to think individually about each prompt, all the sponsor has to do is target you in your most receptive moments, which the system makes really easy via the 'Perfect Time' targeting feature.

This is how the Spectacles are monopolizing human attention, becoming the primary platform for human life and culture in our century, and giving us the most powerful tool of influence the world has ever seen. We can't go back and undo their creation—I mean, we're not Luddites!—but maybe we can learn the right lessons so that we'll be ready when the next big technological change comes along.

*

This scenario is largely an extrapolation of trends in technology and culture that are already visible in our world today. I've leaned into the fictive details in order to go beyond a focus on the design features of the technology, and to paint a wider view of the *phenomenon* of the technology in society. The Spectacles represent a number of trends familiar to us: the conquest to own our experiences and reach us in our innermost selves; the deflections of clever marketing; the incursion of the device paradigm upon the body; the ways in which technology adoption often occurs on the basis of social-signalling, rather than instrumentalist, reasons; the appeals to status and other egoistic motives; and attention-economic business models that sell to others the opportunity to make us think and act in ways we otherwise would not. It's largely a more advanced composite version of our current media environment, which, as the essayist and novelist Marilynne Robinson has put it, 'is addressed to our nervous systems, never to our minds'.[1]

As such, the Spectacles example suggests new ethical considerations that are likely to emerge and also casts a helpful light on ethical issues we're already dealing with today. A technology of its nature—one that commands such a totalizing influence over the human experience— would naturally touch on virtually every ethical issue imaginable. Perhaps the closest analogue in our time would be the internet. However, we can make a useful high-level distinction between two types of ethical issues: those pertaining to content within the system, and those pertaining to the form of the system.

For example, upon the Spectacles' wide public adoption, there would no doubt be vigorous discussion about what kinds of experiences ought to be permitted, what kinds of fantasies ought to be entertained, how children ought to be protected from various dangers, which elements of one's own spectacular experience ought to be visible to others by default, whether a person ought to be algorith-mically simulated without their consent, and so on. These all relate to issues of *content* within the system. Issues of *form*, however, would include questions about what the system is fundamentally designed to do, whether its ultimate design goals align with those of users, how its stated design goals may be validated, whether the systemic incen-tives (e.g. business models) that inform its design enhance or under-mine desirable design goals, whether it enhances or detracts from users' autonomy, and so on.

Many of the most pressing ethical questions that have to do with the form, rather than the content, of such a technology relate to the dynamics of influence—persuasion, coercion, manipulation, and the like—and particularly their implications for users' freedom or auton-omy. It's worth giving attention to a few of those dimensions here.

Freedom of thought—Freedom of thought is central to questions of autonomy. It's articulated as a fundamental freedom in Article 18 of the *Universal Declaration of Human Rights*. In *On Liberty*, John Stuart Mill writes that the 'appropriate region of human liberty . . . comprises, first, the inward domain of consciousness', which includes 'liberty of thought and feeling; absolute freedom of opinion and sentiment on all subjects, practical or speculative'.[2] In the context of increasingly compelling and powerful persuasive technologies, there's a major opportunity to better theorize freedom of thought so that it may be better protected. A similar task of development is needed for the concept of attention, in particular to enable the development of better ways of valuing it. For example, imagine that the Spectacles show you three options for a product you want to purchase, but it puts them in a certain order, describes them with a certain voice, and plays a certain song in the background such that there is a 95% chance you'll choose the option it wants you to. If this infringes on your freedom to choose for yourself, how and where does it do so? At what point does the persuasion spill over into unacceptable manipulation?

The reasons for technology adoption—The first act of per-suasion that any persuasive technology must succeed at is getting a user to start using it. The moment of adoption is a crucial point at which it can be easier to ask certain questions about a technology's purpose and design. Often, technologies are adopted on the basis of their novelty, their social value, or some other reason that differs from their stated design purposes. In the case of the Spectacles, it was initially their value as a status symbol. These kinds of reasons for adopting a technology are not necessarily morally objectionable, but they can make it less likely that a person will reflect as critically in the decision process about what they want the technology to do for them. Yet it's often much easier to ask these questions at the outset rather than revisiting them post-adoption, when network effects or sunk-cost reasoning may dramatically increase the perceived costs of discontinuing its use. In the case of the Spectacles, this would have meant critically assessing its reasons for existence and its wider set of possible implications upon its unveiling, rather than waiting to do so until it was embedded in users' day-to-day habits.

Awareness and validation of persuasive design goals—A person's autonomy is undermined when a persuasive system obscures or misrepresents the goals it has for his or her thinking or behaviour. The same is true when the stated design goals of a system can't be reasonably validated by the user, for instance by the absence of a sufficient view of the metrics or signals toward which the design is being optimized. In the example of the Spectacles, the stated design goal was 'wellbeing', but there was no explanation about what the designers understood that to mean, how specifically it was being measured or calculated, and so on. When a persuasive technology claims it's doing something for your life, you ought to be able to reply, 'Prove it', and get a clear and meaningful—and true—answer. If the Spectacles had provided users with a line of sight from any given design element to the system's high-level persuasive goals, then there would have been greater accountability and users would have had greater justification for trusting the system to guide the turn-by-turn decisions of their lives.

Alignment of system goals and user goals—When the design goals of a persuasive technology differ from the user's goals, it's adversarial in nature and unworthy of the user's trust. In order to ensure that the goals of the system and the goals of the user are aligned, it's necessary for the system to, in some way, know the user's goals. Depending on the technology, this can be done by, e.g., asking the user their reasons for using the technology at the outset, engaging in ongoing conversation with them about their preferences, or capturing signals of intention to infer the user's goals which can be later validated with them explicitly. For example, the high-level design goals of the Spectacles might be to maximize the user's 'donned time' (the percentage of their day spent wearing the device) or their engagement with sponsored rather than non-sponsored experiences, whereas the user's goals for the week may be to finish that philosophy book or start learning how to programme in Python.

A grammar of influence—When it comes to understanding and ethically assessing the varieties of influence, our linguistic and conceptual toolkit is woefully inadequate. We currently have a field of scattered terms—including persuasion, manipulation, coercion, 'nudging', brainwashing, and countless others—whose boundaries are insufficiently clear. What's urgently needed is a project to defragment and map out our language for the varieties of influence. In particular, these distinctions will prove especially important for the task of equipping ourselves to speak more clearly about the ethical dimensions of non-rational influence. We already trust therapists, coaches, artists, and people in many other roles to non-rationally influence our lives toward better ends. How can we develop a similar language and understanding in the context of technology?

The ethics of non-rational influence/persuasion—Over the past half-century, psychologists have identified an enormous number of non-rational biases present in human decision-making. Digital technologies routinely exploit these cognitive biases for persuasive ends. Yet there is very little clarity about the ethics of such non-rational influence. When does non-rational persuasion inhibit a person's ability to choose for themselves? Are there certain biases whose exploitation presents greater ethical problems than others? To what degree should we desire that a user be aware of it when a technology attempts to persuade him or her via non-rational avenues? In a similar way that we strive to protect vulnerable members of society from undue exploitation, are there vulnerable parts of our cognition that deserve special protection?

Enhancement or hindrance of user reflection—Reflection is an important component of autonomy, for instance in the development of preferences, values, and volitions. If a persuasive technology is optimized for user engagement, and so presents the user with an endless parade of stimuli it thinks they will find most interesting, it may crowd out opportunities for reflection and thereby undermine a person's autonomy. Conversely, a persuasive technology could conceivably enhance a person's reflection, for instance by asking a useful question at the right time which prompts the user to be more critically reflective about their thinking or behaviour. A system that enabled such reflection would be—to reverse Marilynne Robinson's quote from above—one that addresses our minds, not our nervous systems.

*

The Spectacles do not yet exist, but their persuasive design elements are already with us. And the extent of their ethical challenges is already becoming clear. We would do well to wrap our heads around them—before we put them on our heads.

Further Reading

Williams, J., *Stand Out of Our Light: Freedom and Resistance in the Attention Economy* (Cambridge University Press, 2018).

Notes

1. M. Robinson, *Absence of Mind* (Yale University Press, 2010).
2. J. S. Mill, *On Liberty* (1859).

14

Conspiracy Theories?

Steve Clarke

Introduction

The popularity of apparently unwarranted conspiracy theories is at disturbing levels. In a 2006 poll, 36% of respondents endorsed the assertion that 'federal officials either participated in the attacks on the World Trade Center or took no action to stop them'.[1] A 2013 poll suggested that 20% of respondents endorsed conspiracy theories regarding a link between childhood vaccination and autism.[2] Popular conspiracy theories alleging that the 2019/2020 coronavirus (Covid-19) pandemic did not have a natural origin sufficiently worried public health scientists that 27 of them wrote a letter, published in the prestigious medical journal *The Lancet*, condemning such theories.[3] We should be concerned by the popularity of apparently unwarranted conspiracy theories and by the rapid rate at which they can spread in the age of social media.[4]

Here, I will try to answer a practical question: what, if anything, should governments in Western liberal democratic societies do to reduce rates of acceptance of unwarranted conspiracy theories? What short- and long-term strategies might they adopt? Before I go on, though, I need to address a few concerns about the project I am undertaking. One is that it is unclear what counts as a conspiracy theory. A second is that it might be supposed that the acceptance of unwarranted conspiracy theories is not harmful. And if the acceptance of unwarranted conspiracy theories is not harmful then it is unclear why governments should be trying to reduce their rates of acceptance. A third concern is that it's unclear that we should be encouraging governments to undertake the project of reducing the popularity of unwarranted conspiracy theories, given that sometimes governments themselves have been known to mislead us about conspiracy theories.

Three Concerns

What is a conspiracy theory?

I will work with Brian Keeley's definition of conspiracy theories: 'a proposed explanation of some historical event (or events) in terms of the significant causal agency of a relatively small group of persons – the conspirators – acting in secret'.[5] This captures key aspects of what we ordinarily mean when we refer to a 'conspiracy theory'. The qualification that a conspiracy theory postulates the agency of a 'relatively small group of persons' appears necessary, because large numbers of people acting in concert are not usually thought of as conspirers. The qualification that conspirators act in secret seems necessary because if the small group of persons in question is openly aiming to achieve a particular goal, then they are not usually thought of as conspiring.

One problem with Keeley's definition is that it departs from ordinary usage in a striking way. In ordinary usage, a conspiracy theory ceases to be considered a conspiracy theory when it attains 'official status', whereas, by Keeley's definition, it remains a conspiracy theory. It is generally accepted, nowadays, that a small group of members of Al Qaeda conspired to hijack passenger aircraft and fly these into the World Trade Center and the Pentagon, on 11 September 2001. However, we would not typically refer to someone who endorsed this 'received view' as a conspiracy theorist, even though this theory fits Keeley's definition. Ordinary usage contrasts conspiracy theories with 'official stories'.[6] Nevertheless, I will stick with Keeley's definition because I want to focus on what governments might do to reduce the acceptance of unwarranted conspiracy theories, and not on the separate issue of whether or not particular theories happen to have obtained any kind of official status.

Unfortunately, governments sometimes grant theories involving conspiracies official status even though they lack warrant. A clear example of this happening is the Bush administration's promulgation of the allegation that the Iraqi leader Saddam Hussein conspired with

Al Qaeda to facilitate the events of 11 September 2001. It is unlikely that key members of the Bush administration, including Dick Cheney and Karl Rove, ever managed to make themselves believe this allegation, but even if they did, they would have been well aware that there was a striking lack of evidence in its favour.[7] The theory was promulgated by them not because it seemed warranted but because they were aware that having it widely accepted in the US would help the US Government win public support for the 2003 US invasion of Iraq.

So are conspiracy theories harmful? On the face of it many 'non-official' conspiracy theories seem harmless. Why should governments care if some of their citizens happen to believe that Elvis Presley faked his own death or that Paul McCartney died in a car accident and was secretly replaced in the Beatles by a look-alike? These idiosyncratic conspiracy theories seem more entertaining than harmful.

But there are more worrying conspiracy theories. In retrospect, that widespread acceptance, in the US, of the unwarranted theory that Saddam Hussein conspired with Al Qaeda in the events of 11 September 2001 was clearly harmful, both to Americans and to Iraqis, because the war it facilitated was harmful to both Americans and Iraqis.

What's more, the popularity of political conspiracy theories, such as the theory that the US Federal officials were involved in the 2001 attacks on the World Trade Center, or had advance warning of the attacks and nevertheless allowed them to go ahead, are harmful because they undermine public trust in government. However, this harm must be weighed against the benefits to society that are accrued when conspiracy theorists succeed in uncovering actual conspiracies involving the complicity of government officials—such as the plot by Nixon administration staff members to bug the Watergate Hotel rooms used by the Democratic National Committee. By helping to uncover actual political conspiracies, conspiracy theorists contribute to the transparency and accountability of governments.[8] Arguably, we are better off if we do not encourage our governments to undermine the credibility of political conspiracy theories, because this would give them an additional excuse to cover up conspiracies that they are involved in.

However, it doesn't follow that governments should refrain from undermining *every* conspiracy theory. If we can identify them, we should encourage government to undermine classes of unwarranted conspiracy theories, that are clearly harmful, and which governments have little motivation to deceive us about. One such class is theories about the efficacy and purpose of government health programmes. Conspiracy theories about HIV/AIDs being a plot against African-Americans have led to poorer knowledge about HIV/AIDs and have made it more difficult for healthcare workers to promote HIV/AIDS prevention amongst African-Americans.[9] Acceptance of conspiracy theories about vaccination predicts people's intentions to vaccinate and so leads people to expose themselves and their children to preventable diseases.[10] Also, conspiracy theories about the Zika virus—such as the theory that the virus was created by pharmaceutical companies to create a need for a vaccine or drug they could sell—made it difficult for public health officials to implement mosquito abatement programmes in affected places in the US, such as Miami.[11] Unwarranted conspiracy theories about public health programmes have led to a slew of harms—it seems clear that governments should do what they can to reduce the public acceptance of these theories.

Our third concern was whether we should be encouraging governments to try to reduce the acceptance of unwarranted and harmful conspiracy theories given that governments have misled us about conspiracy theories in the past. Unfortunately, as we've seen, governments sometimes promote conspiracy theories because it is in their interest to do so, even when this harms the population they represent. Unfortunately, also, government officials sometimes fail to speak out against unwarranted conspiracy theories. One such case occurred in 2015, when the Texan talk show host Alex Jones promoted the theory that the US army was planning to take over the State of Texas, disarm the population, and incarcerate its leaders. Perceiving an electoral advantage in having this theory popularized, the Texan governor, Greg Abbott, conspicuously failed to criticize the theory and, indeed, sought to enhance its credibility by tasking the Texas State Guard with monitoring a US army training operation taking place in Texas.[12]

So governments cannot always be relied on to reduce the popularity of unwarranted conspiracy theories and to refrain from disseminating unwarranted conspiracy theories. The interests of governments and citizens are not always aligned. But the fact that governments sometimes do the wrong thing is not a good reason to cease pressing them to do the right thing. Also, when public health is at stake it is very rarely in the long-term interests of Western liberal democratic governments to deceive people about the efficacy and purpose of government health programmes. Attempts at such deception can endanger large numbers of lives and by so doing threaten to dramatically reduce the popularity of government administrations that, of course, want to be re-elected.

Short-Term Strategies

One strategy that governments could employ to combat the popularity of unwarranted conspiracy theories about public health, is to provide official rebuttals of those theories. A problem with this approach is that there may be members of the public who were hitherto oblivious of a conspiracy theory and who only hear of it (and are perhaps inclined to accept it) via the attempted rebuttal. A second problem is that even among those who've already heard about the theory, the official rebuttal may lend it credibility. An impartial member of the public may reason that there must be something to the theory if it is worth trying to rebut. A third problem is that once people have accepted a conspiracy theory and begun to identify with a group that accepts that theory, along with a set of beliefs that are commonly associated with it, they tend simply to ignore rebuttals.[13] True, some conspiracy theorists may be persuaded by official attempts at rebuttal, but overall this looks to be a strategy of limited value.

A second short-term strategy is one that has been controversially proposed by Sunstein and Vermeule:[14] 'cognitive infiltration'. The idea is that governments employ people to covertly join networks and groups that promulgate conspiracy theories, while pretending to be legitimate members, with the aim of introducing 'cognitive diversity' into those groups and networks. This could involve raising doubts about the beliefs on which particular conspiracy theories are premised, about the logical structure of those theories, and about what implications they might have for political action. One worry about this strategy is that it is likely to be ineffective. As we have seen, people who are committed to a particular view and identify as members of a network or group tend to ignore rebuttal attempts—regardless of whether or not a rebutter identifies as a member of the network or group. A second concern is that cognitive infiltration is liable to backfire. If groups and networks that are cognitively infiltrated discover what's going on, and the conspiracy theory that they adhere to involves the postulation of government involvement in the conspiracy, as many such theories do, then their members may well take cognitive infiltration to be further evidence of government involvement in the conspiracy in question.[15]

A third short-term strategy is to try to anticipate the spread of conspiracy theories and to prime resistance to their acceptance. One way to do this is to provide reliable factual information about a topic that is likely to become the subject of future conspiracy theories.[16] It can also be helpful to provide people with effective counterarguments before they become committed to particular conspiracy theories.[17] It is easier to prevent people from accepting particular beliefs than to persuade them to change their minds about something that they believe.[18]

There are two limitations to this strategy, however. The first is that nowadays, with the internet and social media, conspiracy theories can be disseminated extremely fast, and conspiracy theories about the causes of an event often tend to be postulated and disseminated soon after that event has occurred.[19] It may simply be impractical to anticipate and respond to conspiracy theories before they obtain widespread acceptance.

The second limitation is that it can be difficult to anticipate the content of conspiracy theories. Consider, for example, the unwitnessed death of the Australian Prime Minister Harold Holt in 1966, while swimming alone in rough surf. While it was realistic to expect that conspiracy theories would emerge about his death, it would have been hard to anticipate which theories would go on to become influential. There would have been many contenders. Holt could have been assassinated, by representatives of some or other criminal group, ethnic group, religious group, or government agency. There are also possible theories that would involve him faking his own death for this or that reason. But who could have predicted the theory that actually became influential—that Holt was picked up by a Chinese submarine and secretly relocated to China?[20]

Long-Term Strategies

I've considered three short-term strategies—the ones most discussed in the academic literature—for governments to reduce the popular acceptance of unwarranted conspiracy theories, and shown that all of them have limited value. So, it seems best to concentrate on long-term approaches. The first of these is to promote critical reasoning skills through schooling and other forms of public education. The study of critical reasoning promotes analytic thinking. Some, but of course not all, conspiracy theories are built on fallacious but intuitively appealing reasoning patterns. When people think more analytically there's evidence that they are less liable to accept intuitively appealing conspiracy theories which tap into existing anxieties, but which defy logic, or lack an evidential basis.[21] An example is the theory that HIV/AIDS was created by the US Government for the purpose of restricting the growth of the black population, a theory that has been accepted by over 20% of African-Americans.[22] There is no credible evidence for this theory and it disregards the massive harms that HIV/AIDS has caused amongst non-black populations.

A second long-term strategy is to promote knowledge of the media and how it works. Many unwarranted conspiracy theories involve accusations that sections of the media have knowingly colluded in the suppression of the truth about conspiracies. An example is the theory that, contrary to the official story, the 1995 Oklahoma City bombing was carried out by US Government Agencies, to create a pretext to expand their law-enforcement powers.[23] There is evidence that when people become increasingly familiar with the processes by which media outputs are produced, they become less inclined to accept such conspiracy theories. This is because greater knowledge of the workings of the media leads people to become better at assessing the relative reliability of different media sources. This, in turn, usually leads people to reduce their exposure to unreliable non-mainstream news sources—which are often hotbeds for conspiracy theories.[24]

A third long-term strategy is to make government operations more transparent and accountable.[25] Some conspiracy theories about nefarious government activities, hidden from the public, are justified. However, it's difficult for government officials to participate in conspiracies if they are also required to behave in a transparent and accountable manner. The more transparent and accountable a government has to be, the less scope there is for government officials to participate in conspiracies. So, the less reason there is to suppose that officials in that government have participated in conspiracies.

Concluding Remarks

I've looked at a range of short-term and long-term strategies that have been proposed to reduce the popularity of unwarranted conspiracy theories. I've argued that governments ought to try to reduce the popularity of some classes of harmful unwarranted conspiracy theories and I've identified public heath conspiracy theories as a good example of a class of such harmful theories. I have also argued that the short-term strategies most discussed in the academic literature are of limited value. Much more effective are the three long-term strategies that I've considered. Unfortunately, we live in a world which is awash with unwarranted conspiracy theories, many of which are widely accepted. If governments want to significantly reduce the rates of acceptance of such theories, they should take steps to improve people's critical reasoning abilities and knowledge of the media. They should also introduce increased transparency and accountability into their own operations. This last step may be the most effective of all.[26]

Further Reading

Dentith, M. R. X., *The Philosophy of Conspiracy Theories* (Palgrave Macmillan, 2014).

Notes

1. Cited in C. R. Sunstein and A. Vermeule, Conspiracy theories: Causes and cures, *Journal of Political Philosophy*, 17/2 (2009), 202.
2. D. Jolley and K. Douglas, Prevention is better than cure: Addressing anti-vaccine conspiracy theories, *Journal of Applied Social Psychology*, 47/8 (2017), 459–60.
3. C. Calisher and 26 other authors, Statement in support of the scientists, public health professionals and medical professionals of China combatting COVID-19, *The Lancet*, 2020, DOI: https://doi.org/10.1016/S0140-6736 (20)30418–9.
4. S. Craft, S. Ashley, and A. Maksl, News media literacy and conspiracy theory endorsement, *Communication and the Public*, 2/4 (2017), 388–401;

J. M. Connolly, J. E. Uscinski, C. A. Klofstad, and J. P. West, *Communicating to the Public in the Era of Conspiracy Theory (Public Integrity)*, 21 (2019), 469–76.

5. B. Keeley, Of conspiracy theories, *The Journal of Philosophy*, 96 (1999), 116.

6. D. Coady, Conspiracy theories and official stories, *International Journal of Applied Philosophy*, 17 (2003), 198–9.

7. F. Rich, Editorial: Dishonest, reprehensible, corrupt . . . , *New York Times*, 27 November 2005.

8. S. Clarke, Conspiracy theories and conspiracy theorizing, *Philosophy of the Social Sciences*, 32 (2002), 148.

9. L. M. Bogart and S. Thorburn, Are HIV/AIDS conspiracy beliefs a barrier to HIV prevention among African Americans?, *Journal of Acquired Immune Deficiency Syndromes*, 38 (2005), 213–18.

10. Jolley and Douglas (2017).

11. J. M. Connolly, J. E. Uscinski, C. A. Klofstad, and J. P. West, Communicating to the public in the era of conspiracy theory, *Public Integrity*, 21 (2019), 471.

12. R. Muirhead and N. L. Rosenbaum, Speaking truth to conspiracy: Partisanship and trust, *Critical Review*, 28/1 (2016), 64–6.

13. F. Zollo, A. Bessi, M. Del Vicario, A. Scala, G. Caldarelli, L. Shekhtman, S. Havlin, and W. Quattrociocchi, Debunking in a world of tribes, *PLOS ONE*, 12/7 (2017), Doi: e0181821.

14. C. R. Sunstein and A. Vermeule, Conspiracy theories: Causes and cures, *Journal of Political Philosophy*, 17/2 (2009), 224–6.

15. D. Coady, Cass Sunstein, and Adrian Vermeule on conspiracy theories, *Argumenta*, 6 (2017), Doi:10.23811/56.arg2017.coa.

16. E. J. Avery, Public information officers' social media monitoring during the Zika virus crisis, a global health threat surrounded by public uncertainty, *Public Relations Review*, 43 (2017), 468–76.

17. E. Bonetto, J. Troian, F. Varet., G. Lo Monaco, and F. Girandola, Priming resistance to persuasion decreases adherence to conspiracy theories, *Social Influence* (in press).

18. Jolley and Douglas (2017).

19. Jolley and Douglas (2017).

20. A. Grey, *The Prime Minister was a Spy* (Hodder & Stoughton, 1983).

21. V. Swami, M. Voracek, S. Stieger, U. S. Tran, and A. Furnham, Analytic thinking reduces belief in conspiracy theories, *Cognition*, 133 (2014), 572–85.

22. See P. R. Leman, The born conspiracy, *New Scientist*, 195/2612 (2007), 35–7.

23. Keeley (1999), p. 122.

24. Craft et al. (2017).

25. V. Swami and A. Furnham, Political paranoia and conspiracy theories. In J. W. van Prooijen and P. A. M. van Lange (eds.), *Power Politics, and Paranoia: Why People Are Suspicious about Their Leaders* (Cambridge University Press, 2014), p. 231.

26. Thanks to Suzie Gibson and Dave Edmonds for helpful comments on an earlier draft of this chapter.

Future Bodies

15

Mind-Reading and Morality

Stephen Rainey

What are the prospects, promises, and perils of neurotechnology that aims to reveal our thoughts by recording our brain activity?

*

Ada is walking to work. Unfortunately, the fallout from last night's visit to the pub is coming with her. Her head is sore, and she's been worrying about whether she should have said all of *those things* to people she barely knows. She opens an app on her phone and adjusts a few sliders. The interface reads: *entering headache mode, anxiety reduction enabled*. Soothing music begins to play. Soft blue lights indicate the electrodes embedded in the fabric of her collar are activating. She rounds a corner and a digital billboard advertises *Fast, effective hangover relief* just as she looks up. Her phone displays a map to the pharmacist. This bad morning might yet turn into a good day. And all thanks to the HeadSpace system!

HeadSpace is a brain monitoring system invented 10 years from now. It analyses levels of activity across a user's brain, through a set of electrodes worn on the head. Ada has the latest model, which includes magnetic field generators which can detect and intervene in brain activity automatically, or be controlled from her phone. Via her phone, the system also has an 8G connection to the Internet of Things. Even before she awoke, HeadSpace was reading her sleeping brain, and modulating the activity in order to maximise restful sleep. From the morning's readings, the system had detected the sorts of activity that indicate discomfort for Ada. Some unobtrusive music, played wirelessly to Ada's earbuds, was chosen automatically from her phone's music library.

At the same time, the system had begun to inhibit hyperactivity of some of the stress-response regions of her brain, through targeted generation of magnetic fields. Having performed a search for nearby pharmacies, and efficient painkillers, HeadSpace had connected with mobile phone masts, beaming Ada's hangover requirements to nearby, web-connected billboards and downloading the locations of pharmacies along the route to work. The system magnetically stimulated her visual system as Ada approached the nearest billboard, stimulating her visual field to recognise it, and sent directions to her phone. The HeadSpace system made sure Ada's night was as recuperative as could be, and over the morning it would help her feel better. Everything was set up for a great day ahead!

More 'Science' than 'Fiction'?

The idea of technologies converging to make life easier is an enduring one. Technology-based utopias have been the stuff of science fiction for as long as the genre has existed. Many of us want technology to take on some of life's burdens, or even just the boring bits. That leaves us with more time to do our own thing, at our own pace. The idea of HeadSpace—dealing with our hangover—holds some of that appeal. Ada's is certainly a futuristic story. But the kinds of technologies that would make it a reality are already being researched, used in clinics, or marketed to the public.

Everything we think or plan to do, every bodily movement we make, and sensation we undergo, has a neural correlate—some sort of electrical trace in the activity of neurons in the brain. By recording the activity and analysing it with algorithms, it can be decoded, providing clues about those thoughts, plans, movements, and sensations. For example, present-day neurotechnology companies market a variety of devices, including some which record a user's brain activity so that the user can see measures of distraction and stress levels. By monitoring these levels, users can take steps to respond to how their brain is registering events around them, maybe by trying relaxation techniques to calm down. Ada's futuristic device works like this, but has an automatic response built in, via those magnetic field generators.

Transcranial Magnetic Stimulation (TMS) is a non-invasive technique whereby magnetic fields are used to affect the ways in which neurons operate. Experiments in the 1980s showed the potential for TMS to create limb movements by stimulating the brain. More recently, it has been used as a therapy for mood disorders. Whereas drugs can be used to treat anxiety or depression chemically, TMS promises similar effects by altering the electrical activity of the brain through magnetic fields generated by a magnetic coil placed on the scalp. TMS has also been used in treating addictions by the same mechanism, without the side-effects of drug therapies.

The Internet of Things, meanwhile, promises new levels of integration between software and hardware and the very environment itself, pre-empting or reacting to inputs provided via the data we produce in day-to-day living. Neuroscience is also developing an increasingly sophisticated understanding of how our attentiveness to the environment works—not just how our brain processes signals from our eyes, ears, and touch on our skin, but also which stimuli we are paying attention to. A not-too-distant device could use this understanding to make sure we never miss a thing, by, very literally, grabbing our attention, maybe through the same sort of TMS that might help mood regulation. A device could ensure Ada noticed the billboard showing what drugs she needed to ease her headache.

A seamless chain from our inner lives, via the activity of our brains, out into the world, bypassing the need to make decisions, is technically possible—the world responding to our needs before we have to think about them. As we go about our day-to-day lives with something like HeadSpace, as our desires are met and suggestions made to improve our experience, we might be tempted to think: *Wow, the system really read my mind!*

Behind the System

Ten years from now, SkullScope begins selling the HeadSpace system. Jeff has been working as a data analyst for SkullScope for the past five years. This morning, he has been monitoring data streams from hundreds of users, including Ada. He notices *headache mode* and *anxiety reduction* have been enabled. He makes an educated guess—*hangover*.

Jeff scrolls back through Ada's records to the night before, to see if there is interesting information about her evening in the pub. Another HeadSpace user, Walter, was in the pub too, and so Jeff can correlate their data. He watches as their inhibitory brain functions slacken, and identifies the point that each had had too much to drink. He can't, at a glance, determine if they know each other, so he sends off their combined data for computer analysis. Data recorded from interacting HeadSpace users can provide clues about relationships between people, and about their ideas and behaviour. The computer determines that the kind of brain activity each user exhibits shows that they are (were?) attracted to one another. In fact, the computer has made an error here—what the brain activity really indicated was a mix of apprehension, embarrassment, and mild anxiety of a socially awkward interaction. Jeff can't know the computer has erred. He tags their HeadSpace user data with the status 'in a relationship', as the computer analysis has suggested.

Jeff scrolls forward again to the morning. Ada's HeadSpace system is recording activity that shows she is walking to work. Jeff is relieved that he doesn't have to alert the authorities that she may be driving while still inebriated. SkullScope has partnerships with a variety of collaborators, including law enforcement and Ada's bank. Cross-referencing her account activity with the frequency of hangovers, SkullScope's automatic analysis recommends lowering Ada's credit score. Too many hangovers suggest she's irresponsibly spending too much money—and time—in bars, and should be considered a repayment risk.

Jeff notices the calming music HeadSpace is playing for Ada. Another SkullScope partner, NeurAdvertising, receives the instruction to include this genre of music in ads targeted to her. The marketing company also takes delivery of the data relevant to Ada's anxiety: what it looked like when she was anxious, and at what level she felt calm. NeurAdvertising can now recognise how Ada responds to differently constructed adverts, sending only the most effective to the billboards around her. This data was also sold on to the police and security services.

By examining the recorded stress dynamics from the users of HeadSpace systems, the police hope to develop systems for detecting criminal intent, based on anxiety patterns in brain activity. The security services are also in negotiation with SkullScope to gain access rights to the magnetic generators of users' HeadSpace systems. They would like to stimulate brain activity to help in emergency response scenarios. If they could quell stress responses in emergencies from *inside the head* it would go a long way to ensuring crowd safety. Jeff is on the team developing this neuro-security project, and is excited to tell the police about visual field stimulation as well. The police would like to use the technology to ensure victims in emergency scenarios don't miss safety notices and other instructions. Ada's brain data, when she was prompted to spot the painkiller advert, was useful in demonstrating this principle.

Ethical Problems

It seems clear from looking at Jeff's side of the story how ethically problematic HeadSpace and SkullScope could be. But it's worth highlighting a few issues, to demonstrate how seemingly innocuous, useful, or fun neurotechnologies can harbour searching ethical questions.

Should we think about ourselves, our bodies, our brains, as instruments to be used towards some ends? The neurofeedback parts of HeadSpace's design might prompt such a thought. Doubtless there are times when it would be helpful to fine-tune our responses to circumstances. To engineer a good night's sleep, or to adjust a stress reaction before a job interview or an exam, could be the difference between success and failure. But maybe a stress reaction in advance of a test is appropriate. By tuning it out, we may be depriving ourselves of experiencing what it is like to overcome this kind of adversity. Using a machine to feel better might inhibit our learning about our own resilience. And what we learn in facing adversity might prompt us to reflect on our character, perhaps encouraging edifying changes in how we engage with the world.

Distress might be another example. While it is often unpleasant to *feel* distressed by something, it may nevertheless be appropriate to *be* distressed. Tuning it out would allow the distressing circumstances to remain, altering merely how they are encountered. Better, surely, would be to change the circumstances. Faced with widespread social injustice against marginalised groups, for instance, should one find a means of intervening in the brain to feel less distressed by that injustice? Surely it would be preferable to engage with ways of removing the causes of the injustice, say, by political campaigning.

Control over our otherwise autonomous bodily and mental reactions seems positive in a few easily imaginable contexts. A hangover is one such case. But it does raise the question of how we know what level of reaction is preferable to another. In the HeadSpace system, this is handled automatically: the system detects hyperactivity and brings that activity down to 'acceptable' levels. How this acceptability is quantified and programmed into the system is problematic from an ethical point of view. The automatic operation of the machine might work against what could be appropriate reactions. On the face of it, a real but relatively rare occurrence like a bereavement is a bad time to keep reactions within parameters specified for day-to-day life.

For all the automaticity promised by hi-tech applications, there are frequently human beings in the mix. Where there is no seamlessly automatic system there may be unusual interpersonal relations—as with Jeff and Ada. Ada's privacy and dignity are impacted through Jeff's work, even if Ada never realises this. To her it might seem almost magically technological and have a satisfying scientific objectivity surrounding it. Nevertheless, a human is behind the scenes, picking data for processing and selling bits and pieces of her neural life for the commercial purposes of a company. Were Ada to discover that Jeff had raided her diary and marketed his judgements about what kind of a person she was, based on its entries, she would probably be appalled. Yet dressed in scientific garb, this intrusive dimension of the technology is obscured. Should we be happier about neuro-surveillance than we are about the plunder of a diary?

What's more, there are secondary uses of that data that go beyond any purposes the user might have imagined their actions could serve. Users would be unlikely to think that buying painkillers would somehow contribute to security research—yet this is what happens when SkullScope shows Ada's painkiller purchase data to the security services. Every HeadSpace system simply aggregates data into a general-purpose pool for analysis for whatever means can be successfully marketed to whatever buyer. The user could not anticipate, let alone consent to every particular use, as each instance of data collection, processing, analysis, and marketisation happens as part of an overall system-company data ecosystem.

In the hands of private companies, with economic interests of their own, there would always be incentives to treat consumers' brain data as an asset to be exploited like any other. Can we really afford to have sensitive brain recordings, processed by algorithms, regulated only by market interests? A future in which corporations might market products based on brain-based profiles of consumers, or in which political parties might develop policy based on brain-based predictions about hidden desires, is not inconceivable. Police and security services could seek to prevent criminality and terrorism by identifying ill-intent through brain types, not manifest behaviour. Not only would the prospects for errors make this concerning, but underlying it all is a change in the focus of how we deal with people, reducing them to brain activity via algorithms. Whether we ought to accept such a reduction is ultimately a moral question.

The judgements made of Ada, regarding her relationship status and her credit rating, resulted from computer-based data processing. This is part of the reason we ought to consider neurotechnological advances now, despite there being no HeadSpace system yet. Because of the ways many computer algorithms learn, the more data they have to operate on the more versatile they become. If there are very large datasets, algorithms can detect patterns at a scale impossible for human beings, and at speeds beyond human capacity. This is why we already see artificial intelligence being used to screen for cancers more reliably than some doctors, and to predict novel effective drugs. But they can also be difficult to control, as much of their processing is done via practically impenetrable mathematical operations. This is what people mean when they describe algorithms as 'black boxes'— their internal operations are not open to steering. They simply crunch data.

In neurotechnological applications, recordings can be processed by algorithms aimed at predicting brain-related activity, including its relation to mental states. In processing brain recordings in these sophisticated ways, a means is provided of predicting fundamental relations between the brain and the mind, or making judgements about the person more broadly. A future of vast brain recording databases, processed algorithmically, could lead to far-reaching predictions about our minds. We may be entering a world of neuroprofiling—judgements being made about persons, on the basis of data, beyond relationships and credit ratings. Job interviews might be replaced by brain-based predictions of suitability for an occupation, suggesting that a person applying for a job as a used car-salesman would be more suited as a prison officer. Such neuro-predictions might also find their way into education: why take those exams, or study for that course, when your brain data can exhibit your intellectual aptitudes?

Neuroprofiling would have people assessed as a profile not an individual. All profiling has this potentially demeaning characteristic of judging a person by means of categories, rather than character. But neuroprofiling has an extra dimension; whereas most behaviours can be voluntarily altered to adjust for circumstance, brain activity occurs without volition. What's more, a particularly undermining dimension of neuroprofiling is that some will claim that brain activity is a better marker of a person's dispositions and emotional states than their own testimony. Yet neuroprofiling won't be fail-proof. From parameters gleaned from brain data, a person might be categorised one way or another, or related to others in ways that may or may not reflect reality (remember the incorrect inference about Ada's 'relationship').

Putting aside concerns about profiling and errors, there's an even more fundamental concern. On the one hand, if brain activity was likely to be recorded, a person might begin to worry about which thoughts they think. On the other, they might fear misinterpretation of a thought. Ordinarily, it seems reasonable that anyone should be free to think anything, whenever they choose. This is a matter of cognitive freedom. There may be perfectly good or innocent reasons even for consideration of reprehensible things—for instance, in considering an ethical dilemma, writing a play, or empathising with a bad character. If we feel inhibited about what we can think, how free can we possibly be more generally, in formulating opinions and actions?

Conclusion

Our understanding of the brain, and its connections with the mind, is becoming more and more sophisticated. The research seems capable of providing tantalising insights into hitherto rather arcane-seeming brain and mind processes. There is no genuine near-term prospect of mind-reading of the sort often seen in science fiction. But there remain mind-reading risks from the advance of neurotechnologies. This is especially centred upon how data processing works in technologies developed outside of clinical and scientific research. Neurotechnologies will begin amassing ever-growing databases of brain recordings. Technology companies will continue developing algorithms capable of discerning patterns that no human data analyst could spot. In combination, these will amount to a great many *opportunities* for predicting things about brains, and *inferring things* about minds. We need to think now about whether this is something we want to undergo, or something over which we should demand control.

What would Ada think of Jeff and the SkullSpace data ecosystem mining her hangover response? Would she be happy about the ways NeurAdvertising monetised her dispositions? If she learned that the police took an interest in her brain activity, she might think twice about using her device again. Having her attention grabbed by that billboard was helpful, but thinking it over some more, Ada could start to feel a little like a puppet, with SkullScope pulling the strings. Now put yourself in her shoes: having read this chapter, standing before the heaving shelves of the neurotechnology superstore, will you be buying yourself a HeadSpace system?

Further Reading

Gibson, W., *Neuromancer*. Ace Science Fiction (Ace Books, 1984).
Levy, N., *Neuroethics: Challenges for the 21st Century* (Cambridge University Press, 2007).

16

Love Drugs

Julian Savulescu

Kara gets up. She has a job interview for a position as a staff writer for a major news website. She picks out a suit and puts on make-up. The job itself will be largely home-based and does not require either. Most of the time, Kara is a casual dresser, preferring to work in tracksuits. But Kara knows that when she is meeting people, a suit and make-up will make her feel more confident and perform better; she also believes that if she dresses up, the interview panel will respond to her more positively. She brings along her iPad, where she has used a MindMap programme to help her organise her thoughts around topics that might come up. She takes a beta blocker to help her keep calm.

In the afternoon, Kara is planning to go for a CrossFit class. Alongside her gym clothes, she packs a concentrated beetroot shot because she read a study that says it increases time to exhaustion. It will help her perform at the class despite her mental tiredness from the stressful morning.

After the class, Kara gets a call about her interview. She's got the job! Kara is invited to join her new team for their regular after-work drinks. She accepts, and purchases a glass of white wine when she arrives. She doesn't like the taste, but knows that the alcohol will help her relax and bond with her new team with less inhibition.

Human Enhancement

Human enhancement at its most basic is anything that has the goal of improving our capacities.[1]

Kara uses various tools and substances to enhance her performance at the interview, at the gym, and at the social event. Nearly everyone regularly uses some or all of these tools. Arguably, these are all forms of enhancement.

There are a few common distinctions amongst different forms of enhancement that are considered important when it comes to deciding about whether using a form of enhancement is ethical.

Biomedical Enhancement

Kara's clothing, make-up and iPad help her performance, but are not biomedical. They are simply external tools that support her practically, socially, and psychologically. Few people find anything unethical about this. On the other hand, Kara's pre-workout shot, beetroot juice, is a biomedical enhancer. The chemicals in it interact with her body chemicals to produce the desired results.

The focus of ethical debate about human enhancement has been mainly on this group of enhancers. Biomedical human enhancement involves "biomedical interventions that are used to improve human form or functioning beyond what is necessary to restore or sustain health".[2]

Natural v Unnatural

Few people worry about the ethics of beetroot juice or a moderate amount of alcohol.

To identify the kinds of human enhancement that might concern us, a further distinction is often made between natural and unnatural biomedical enhancement. Kara's consumption of beetroot juice might be considered 'natural', whereas her beta blockers are not. This distinction can be blurred and difficult to define. For example, Kara's wine is produced from natural products, such as grapes and sugar. But a great deal of processing is required to make alcohol.

Everything we have must of course originate from something found on earth. Natural might therefore imply minimal processing, few ingredients, or ease of home production. Unnatural might imply extremely concentrated levels, a laboratory-level process for creation, or a substance that is only created by a chemical reaction between two or more other substances. This is a rough and ready category, and we need to be careful not to conflate 'safe' or 'commonly used' with 'natural'.

Safety can be a concern for both natural and unnatural products. Foxgloves are poisonous in their natural state, but the active ingredient, digitalis, is used to make life-saving medicine for heart disease. Clearly, risk of harm is a good and usually overriding reason not to use a potential enhancer. This chapter involves a thought experiment. For these purposes, we will assume that any intervention discussed has been proven to be safe in the imaginary scenarios presented, although in fact most are either untested, or carry risks. I want to use them to discuss ethical issues around the purpose of enhancement, not make a policy proposal for any particular substance.

Safety aside, many have an intuition that natural enhancers are acceptable where unnatural ones are not. I will argue that this is invalid. What matters is not how we produce a possible enhancer, or how frequently other people use it, but how it affects our overall welfare.

Controversial Forms of Biomedical Enhancement

Most of Kara's enhancers listed above are uncontroversial, even the biomedical interventions: Kara would not be banned in most countries from any of these enhancements, and nor would she be embarrassed to admit to her friends—or even on social media—to using them. But other forms of biomedical human enhancement are controversial. When that happens, it is usually (1) because of the purpose of the enhancement, (2) because of features about the substance itself (for example, if it involves a high level of risk of harm to the user), or (3) because they are used in a situation where specific rules have been made (such as professional sport).

For reason (2), many people believe that using a drug like caffeine to help focus on an important piece of work is acceptable, but using off-label prescription drugs, such as modafinil (a drug for narcolepsy, which some people believe helps concentration in healthy people), is not. We have never tested this kind of use, and it may be dangerous (physically or psychologically) to take this drug for that purpose, either acutely, or with chronic use. This is an example of a substance-based controversy around safety.

Tennis player Maria Sharapova was famously banned from competing in tennis in 2016 because she tested positive for the drug Meldonium. She had taken the drug for 10 years prior to 2016. But in the new year, a ban on that drug came into force, and so she was now breaking the rules by taking it. (There is no good evidence that the drug is either unsafe or performance enhancing.) Once the rule came into force, Maria Sharapova was treated as a cheat. This is an example of a rule-based controversy.

There is much to discuss about what level of safety is safe enough (after all, alcohol kills around 7500 people per year in the UK and is a contributory factor to many more deaths).[3] There is much to discuss about what the rules *should* be in sporting or other competitions. And there's much to discuss about other concerns regarding enhancements, such as equality of access, implicit coercion on others to take them to keep up, and deservingness of achievements following enhancement. But these are debates for another day.

This chapter will instead focus on one of the 'purpose'-driven areas of controversy around bioenhancement: substances taken with the purpose of enhancing romantic relationships, or 'love drugs'.

Love Drugs

Earlier in the chapter, we followed Kara through a number of successes, including her job offer.

Unfortunately, not everything is going so well in her life. Kara has been in a civil partnership with Sadie for 10 years and they have two young children. However, over the past year, things have become difficult. Although Kara knows that Sadie is a good person, and still respects her, she feels they have grown apart through the daily grind of childcare and work. Often, it feels like they are more flatmates than lovers. Kara has found herself attracted to other people; she has made an effort to remain faithful, but she misses the connection that seemed so effortless in the early stage of their relationship. Then, she never even thought about anyone else.

On bad days, everything about Sadie annoys Kara. She thinks about but doesn't want divorce. If she got divorced she wouldn't live with her children for at least half of the time, she would lose half of her assets, and probably half of her friends. So although she hopes to stay married, living in constant irritability and bickering is proving psychologically wearing for the whole family.

*

Studies have shown that growing apart, boredom, and loss of closeness are key factors in many divorces.[4]

It is a common TV and film trope that the main character leaves a relationship which *seems* perfect, to end up with the love of their life, who, despite perhaps having more apparent flaws, is in fact 'The One'. For example, Carrie, the lead character and narrator in *Sex and the City*, forms a serious and apparently happy relationship with Aiden, a handsome and kind furniture designer, only to leave him for Mr Big, a surly and commitment-phobic banker, at times married to someone else, who leaves her at the altar before they finally reconcile for a happy ending.

One of the beliefs that lies under this trope is that if only you can find 'The One'—unexpected and unsuitable as he or she may be—you will live happily ever after.

Yet 'ever after' is a finishing line that has receded further into the distance as our lifespans have extended. Evolutionary theory suggests that pair bonding developed to last to support bearing and bringing up children, a resource-intensive process for humans, and with much greater chances of survival with the support of two adults. But there would be little evolutionary benefit in bonding beyond the period after children have matured into adulthood. Evolution is geared to survival of the species, not individual happiness.

If an otherwise good relationship loses its spark it is not necessarily a sign that it was the wrong relationship in the first place. Nor is a spark alone enough. Carrie might be susceptible to Mr Big's advances: but that doesn't mean she will be happier with him.

Divorce has become more easily available, but it is still highly costly on a range of measures. It is associated with poor health outcomes in adults, including increased risk of early death.[5] In children, a review of recent research found that, despite researchers developing better methods for controlling for other factors, "the case that divorce and family instability reduce children's well-being remains strong".[6]

There may be many reasons for these outcomes: our social and financial structures are built around lifelong unions, often for historical, religious, political, or practical reasons, and these are likely to exacerbate the harms following divorce. Moreover, divorce may be a *result* of financial problems, alcohol abuse, and other issues that may in themselves be harmful. But ultimately, the loss of the major relationship, the inevitable additional costs of maintaining two residences, and in the case of children, a sudden drop in access to one or both parents is likely to be in itself a significant cause of stress and unhappiness.

It's no surprise then that we invest significantly in keeping our marriages alive: in the US, marriage counselling is a multi-billion dollar industry. Yet American divorce rates remain high, at 40–50% of all marriages. This is not to say that all relationships should continue. Rather, sometimes a relationship is worth trying to maintain and improve.

Biomedical Enhancement of Love

Kara seeks help, looking online for relationship advice. One tip comes up repeatedly: massage. Massage, one article explains, releases oxytocin, the so-called bonding hormone. Kara and Sadie try this, but with two young children, and two demanding jobs between them, not to mention ageing parents needing more care, there never seems to be time or energy. Another tip Kara reads is to share new experiences. But again, after one or two attempts, life gets in the way. Kara and Sadie can't afford the childcare and anyway, they want to spend the little time they have off work with their children.

There are probably as many problems that can arise in a relationship as there are people. Some problems—such as an abusive partner, or a difference in attitudes on fundamental issues—will not be resolved through biomedical enhancement.

However, there is increasing evidence that there are biological underpinnings of love and bonding that naturally fluctuate over time, and can even be genetically determined.

A range of biological processes have been identified that mediate the experience of love in humans: oxytocin, vasopressin, and testosterone are associated with various aspects of love and attraction, along with pheromones and others.

Some traditional remedies for marital discord—including massage and new, shared experiences—may owe their success to their indirect manipulation of these pathways. In our culture, we tend to praise those who 'work at' their relationship in these ways. While currently these are the best options we have, it is quite likely that over time we will discover safe and effective biomedical enhancements for love. For example, oxytocin is available as a nasal spray. Intuitively for many, taking a spray to achieve the same effect would be wrong or inauthentic. Is this fair?

Treatment–Enhancement Distinction

Some argue that while it is acceptable to use biomedical products as a treatment to cure a specific disease, it is not acceptable to use them as an enhancement to improve on a natural state.

The problem with this view is that it is a weak distinction. To give an example, one of the closest things we do have to an effective available love drug is Viagra, a drug to treat sexual dysfunction in men. Evidence suggests that both low sexual frequency and high sexual frequency relationships can be successful: problems tend to arise when one partner has a high libido, and the other a low one.

Is Viagra a treatment or an enhancement? Erectile dysfunction is arguably a natural part of ageing. Is its use to counteract this a treatment or an enhancement? Moreover, as its fame spread, many began to use Viagra despite healthy sexual function, for recreational or enhancement purposes.

If we believe in a treatment–enhancement distinction, then we should deny access to this drug for older men if their function is in the normal range for their age. But there is no reason why erectile dysfunction due to a healthy ageing is less distressing or less important to address than dysfunction due to stress or obesity.

I have argued instead for a *welfarist* approach.[7] That is, if an intervention enhances welfare, it is irrelevant whether the lower welfare was the result of a disease or part of a healthy state.

This can apply to a social situation. If a couple were in a mismatched sexual relationship where a man had a lower libido, taking Viagra could enhance his welfare by equalising their libidos, even if, had his partner happened to also have a lower libido, he would not have particularly wanted a higher one himself. If his relationship is otherwise happy, ending that relationship would reduce his welfare.

Authenticity

A second major argument against enhancement, especially in the arena of love enhancement, is 'authenticity'.

In the science-fiction film, *The Matrix*, the hero, Neo, is offered the choice of the red pill or the blue pill: the red pill is knowledge of the painful dystopian reality, and the blue the comfortable fiction he has been born into. Of course, he chooses reality.

We do not want to live in a fool's paradise. We want to experience true love. Perhaps if Kara stays, she will miss out on meeting someone who is better for her. Or perhaps she will never be able to express parts of herself that she could if she were alone. Or maybe the drug will make her happy in the relationship, until the end of her life when she looks back and feels she's wasted her time living in a make-believe. The more effective the enhancer, the greater the risk of this. The more the enhancer creates feelings, the harder it will be to distinguish the effect of the bioenhancer from reality.

For some people, this will be decisive. Yet there are reasons to be less concerned.

Earlier in Kara's story, she considered massage as a way to release oxytocin and enhance her bond with Sadie. Why is releasing oxytocin this way more authentic than taking it from an external source? In both, she has decided to take action to save her relationship, and has mediated this with a biochemical influence.

A second way in which people may use love drugs is to enhance traditional therapies. The use of drugs (such as MDMA) is currently being trialled in certain other therapeutic contexts,[8] so why not in the context of relationship therapy? In this case, the drug is a catalyst or an amplifier of the communication work. It does not work alone. Early in relationships a great many people use alcohol as an accompaniment to dating in exactly this way. The alcohol helps reduce inhibitions to ease the communication and sharing of experiences in the dating process. Whilst over-consumption of alcohol can lead to meaningless experiences or false experience of attraction, a moderate consumption combined with the 'work' of dating is generally considered to be non-problematic. Why is this different later in the relationship or with different substances? Of course, such drugs should only be used in the context of a professional relationship, prescribed and monitored by a doctor.

Finally, authenticity is not synonymous with our best interests. Deep brain stimulation has been trialled as a treatment for patients suffering from severe anorexia. It stimulates reward processing in the brain, the so-called 'hedonic hotspot'.[9] As a result, the experiences the patient goes on to have may not be 'authentic': they do not arise solely from the patient and their interaction with the world. But without it, the patient is at high risk of death. Moreover, the choice to undergo deep brain stimulation arguably *is* the authentic self making the decision. The deep brain stimulation then supports this authentic decision to create the conditions where the patient is able to act on his or her higher order decision making.

This is not a direct analogy. For one thing, anorexia is a serious mental health condition and falling out of love is not. I have included it because it highlights the problem of authenticity. Healthy people also experience conflict between our goals and our actions. We have all experienced conflicts between our higher order and lower order desires. We have started healthy regimes only to be tempted by an off-plan chocolate treat, or formed ambitions or goals only to end up scrolling through social media. Is the plan or the impulse more authentic?

If Kara looks at her life and finds it better with Sadie in it, then is using a love drug to promote this goal really less authentic than letting the relationship slip away each time they are too tired to go on a date night, too cash poor to have a romantic getaway, or too lacking in confidence to make the first move in bed?

Risk of Abuse

Another objection is the risk of abuse, or the risk of enabling someone to put up with abuse. Imagine another version of Sadie and Kara's relationship, where Sadie is emotionally or physically abusive. This is sadly not uncommon; it's believed that 10 million people in the US are affected by family violence each year.[10]

There are many reasons why people stay in these relationships. They might be practical, or financial: a lack of other options. They might also be emotional: love can be irrational, or involve a belief that the person will change.

Let's imagine that in this version of Kara's case, she cannot afford to leave. Sadie is the main breadwinner, and leaving and taking the children would likely involve a protracted court case that Kara cannot afford. There is a risk that if she cannot persuade the court of the abuse the family suffer at Sadie's hands, she will be forced to leave her children in Sadie's care. Moreover, even if she did get custody of the children Kara is advised that Sadie—who's self-employed—may hide her income in order to lower child support payments. Kara does not know whether she would be able to support her children in that case. A love enhancement might then seem tempting so as to make her feel better about Sadie, and make it more tolerable to stay with her.

It is certainly true that an effective love enhancement in this case could be extremely harmful, to both Kara and to her children. But in other cases, it might be valuable. When we are considering whether enhancement of love is a worthy goal, it is not necessary that they are valuable in every circumstance, or even that in *every* case they are non-harmful. Instead, we should consider different contexts and whether we can predict and manage any risks.

We already do this for other enhancements. For example, we saw Kara use alcohol as a social enhancement. Having a drink with colleagues can enhance social relationships and improve bonding by lowering inhibitions. Yet drinking before her job interview would likely be the opposite of an enhancement: the inhibitions are useful in that scenario.

A solution is only valid if it addresses the problem. A doctor who prescribed physiotherapy for a broken leg would be guilty of serious medical misconduct. But there is nothing wrong with physiotherapy in itself: it is a useful tool in other situations, or in conjunction with other treatments.

There may be a risk that love drugs would be misused. However, this risk can be ameliorated through education, or through providing access to such enhancements only through a trained professional. And of course, regardless of the availability of enhancements, we need to do more to provide a range of social and financial support to protect the victims of domestic violence and abuse.

A Welfarist Account

When is it wrong to use an enhancement?

This chapter has presented a welfarist account of enhancement. The welfarist account defines enhancement as "any change in the biology or psychology of a person which increases the chances of that person leading a good life in the relevant set of circumstances".[11]

This helps us to distinguish between using love drugs to support a good relationship through difficult child-rearing years against using them to endure abuse. It doesn't represent a free-for-all. It doesn't enable people to avoid addressing the difficult questions in life: e.g. is this person right for me? Is this relationship enough? It doesn't mean society can avoid addressing the kinds of financial inequalities that leave people stuck in abusive relationships, or mean that those who choose to seek happiness away from their relationship have made the wrong choice. But, just as the beetroot shot helps us make the most of our workout, or the glass of wine helps us connect with a colleague, a puff of oxytocin could help us to see past the dishes left in the sink again and get a better view of the person we love and chose to spend the rest of our lives with.

Further Reading

Earp, B. D. and Savulescu, J., *Love Drugs: The Chemical Future of Relationships* (Stanford University Press, 2020).

Notes

1. E. Juengst and D. Moseley, Human enhancement. In E. N. Zalta (ed.), *The Stanford Encyclopedia of Philosophy* (The Metaphysics Research Lab, Stanford University, 2019), available at: https://plato.stanford.edu/archives/sum2019/entries/enhancement/
2. Juengst and Moseley (2019).
3. Office for National Statistics, Alcohol-specific deaths in the UK: registered in 2018. ons.gov.uk (2019), available at: https://www.ons.gov.uk/peoplepopulationandcommunity/healthandsocialcare/causesofdeath/bulletins/alcoholrelateddeathsintheunitedkingdom/2018#:~:text=Rates%20of%20alcohol%2Dspecific%20deaths%20have%20remained%20stable%20in%20recent,of%207%2C697%20deaths%20in%202017.
4. L. Gigy and J. B. Kelly, Reasons for divorce, *Journal of Divorce and Remarriage*, 18/1–2 (1993), 169–88.

5. D. A. Sbarra and J. A. Coan, Divorce and health: Good data in need of better theory, *Current Opinion in Psychology*, 13 (2017), 91–5.

6. R. K. Raley and M. M. Sweeney, Divorce, repartnering, and step-families: A decade in review, *Journal of Marriage and Families*, 82 (2020), 81–99.

7. J. Savulescu, A. Sandberg, and G. Kahane, Wellbeing and enhancement. In J. Savulescu, R. Ter Meulen, and G. Kahane (eds.), *Enhancing Human Capacities* (Blackwell, 2011).

8. National Health Service UK, Ecstasy tested for trauma therapy, nhs.uk (2010), available at: https://www.nhs.uk/news/mental-health/ecstasy-tested-for-trauma-therapy/.

9. R. H. Park, J. C. Scaife, and T. Z. Aziz, Study protocol: Using deep-brain stimulation, multimodal neuroimaging and neuroethics to understand and treat severe enduring anorexia nervosa, *Frontiers in Psychiatry*, 9 (2018), 24.

10. M. R. Huecker and W. Smock, Domestic violence. In *StatPearls* [Internet] (StatPearls Publishing, 2020), available at: https://www.ncbi.nlm.nih.gov/books/NBK499891/.

11. Savulescu et al. (2011).

17

Technology to Prevent Criminal Behaviour

Gabriel De Marco and Thomas Douglas

The Case of Jim

Jim was arrested arriving at the house of an unattended minor, having brought with him some alcoholic drinks, condoms, and an overnight bag. Records of online conversations Jim was having with the minor give the court strong evidence that the purpose of this meet-up was to engage in sexual relations with the minor. In the course of searching his home computer, investigators also found child pornography. Jim was charged with intent to sexually abuse a child and possession of child pornography. He was given due process, and convicted, by a jury of his peers, on both counts. This is not the first time that Jim has been convicted of a sexual offence. He had been found guilty of possession of child pornography in the past, and served time for it.

What should we do with Jim? The obvious answer is that we should send him to prison. In such cases, most people think that some form of imprisonment is justified, though there would be disagreement on why it is justified: to deprive him of access to potential victims, to deter others from committing similar crimes, or just to ensure that he experiences the suffering that he deserves.

But at some point, Jim will need to be released. Most accept that there is an upper limit on how long a person can be imprisoned. At some point, the punishment will become disproportionate—too severe for the crime committed. Yet we may be concerned with the possibility of Jim's reoffending once he is released. A stint in prison can do much to change a person, but it will not always be successful at preventing reoffending—indeed, it may even have the opposite effect;[1] and remember that Jim has been here before. We might, then, think that the criminal justice system should also do something to reform or rehabilitate him.[2]

Suppose that Jim feels remorseful, and he felt remorse after the first time as well. Getting caught the second time has made it very clear to him that, for him, remorse isn't enough. If he is going to change, he needs more than remorse; he needs help. Should we offer him help? It is very plausible that the answer is yes. Jim did something bad, and he wants to change, but doesn't know how. If we have means available to us to help him with this, it would seem difficult to justify withholding them from him. Even if one is not concerned with helping Jim to be the person he wants to be, one is likely still going to be concerned with whether he commits further crimes, if and when he is released.

So how do we go about helping Jim change? There are a variety of things we might try to do. Suppose we were to offer Jim a device that could detect when he is about to get some of his problematic urges and release a drug meant to neutralize them. Some would find these sorts of methods strange, and perhaps intuitively problematic. Using technology to solve social problems, like crime, tends to give us pause. But in the following, we will argue that using technology to prevent crime isn't necessarily problematic; insofar as we are comfortable using more conventional means for rehabilitating Jim, we should be comfortable with using some technological methods as well.

What We Might Do with Jim

So what might we do with Jim? Perhaps we could offer him an educational programme, involving a series of courses that Jim can participate in while incarcerated. Suppose that these courses are designed to help him think through the consequences of his actions, to reflect on the type of person he wants to be, and to improve his thinking skills more generally. Suppose that during his first term in prison, Jim took these courses. They did help him a bit, but obviously not enough to prevent him from reoffending once released. When asked why the educational programmes didn't help much, Jim says he doesn't know, but he has some ideas. He often found it difficult to focus during the courses, and because of this, he may not have taken the information on board, or retained it, as much as he may have liked.

Now suppose that we have an inexpensive pharmaceutical, say Adderall, which helps to solve this problem by helping him to concentrate on the courses. Were we to offer the drug to Jim to take in conjunction with the educational programme, he might do better this time around. Should we offer it to him? Some might think that he shouldn't get it without a prescription from a doctor, a doctor who has assessed him as having a clinical condition for which Adderall is an approved treatment—say, Attention Deficit Hyperactivity Disorder (ADHD). Suppose he doesn't have one of these conditions, but we still think that the Adderall could help. Why not offer it to him, if it could help him get more from the courses?

When people object to the use of Adderall by those who do not have a prescription or a diagnosed condition for which it is a licensed treatment, they are normally thinking about cases very different from that of Jim. For instance, one concern is that the use of Adderall without a prescription is illegal. But this would clearly not be a problem here, since we are discussing what the state should do, and the state could simply make it legal for Jim to take Adderall. Some argue that the use of drugs like Adderall to improve, say, a college student's performance, is problematic because one of the goals of the educational system is to evaluate students on their merits, and the use of so-called 'smart drugs' interferes with this. This might make it difficult for future potential employers to make reliable assessments of job candidates. Also, it may simply be unfair that some students get an advantage over others not through hard work or ability, but through using a drug. And we might worry that the achievements students make while using Adderall are not as worthy as those of others who achieved the same without the use of enhancers.[3]

We don't wish to get into that debate here; however, it is important to note that, in the context of rehabilitating individuals, merit does not have the significance that it does in the general education system. Here, we're not primarily concerned with Jim getting the evaluation that he merits, with whether he is getting an unfair advantage over others in the education programme, with whether his achievement, if he manages to refrain from further offending, is worthy, nor with whether his performance on the programme will be a good marker for future employers. Our main goals are to prevent Jim from reoffending and, perhaps, to help him become a better person. If giving him Adderall can help with this, then it's not clear why we shouldn't offer it; the typical arguments against the use of Adderall without a medical need won't apply here.

Would this be enough—an educational programme and a smart drug like Adderall? Sure, Jim might get better at recognizing the consequences of his actions, including the long-term effects his behavior might have on his victims, for instance. But another big problem is his motivational states; his urges and desires are a significant driver of his behavior, and seem to be a big part of the problem. Even if he knows what the consequences of his actions are, he may just not care enough about those consequences to overcome some of his urges. Or perhaps he cares enough most of the time, but sometimes has lapses. Maybe, then, we could offer him help in changing or better controlling his motivational states, such as his pedophilic urges and his concern for the consequences of his actions.

Suppose then that the educational programme, intended to improve his general thinking skills, is supplemented with therapy, intended to help him with his motivations, including his pedophilic urges. Some forms of therapy aim to improve patients' control over their thoughts and feelings—for instance, by helping patients to recognize and block a thought process before it causes problems. Perhaps using these tools, Jim could learn to recognize the urges and desires that may often lead him to unwanted behavior, and nip them in the bud. This would give Jim more control over his own mind by helping him to prevent situations where the urges continue to strengthen and dominate his thinking.

Consider, for example, one self-control strategy that we sometimes use when we recognize that our thoughts, feelings, or urges may be getting away from us, or when we feel overwhelmed: we close our eyes, take a few deep breaths, and perhaps count to ten. Doing so can help us to calm down, refocus on the bigger picture, or simply interrupt a vicious circle. There is presumably a complicated story as to how this works, and here we offer some speculations. Studies suggest that there is a limit to the amount of attention we can sustain at any given time; forcing ourselves to perform a task that requires a large amount of this attention means that there is much less attention to devote to other things. By taking deep breaths, we may be taking attention away from the strengthening desire, and the process that leads to its strengthening. Perhaps, instead, the change in oxygen levels is doing some significant work. Or, such a strategy might enable us to take a third-person perspective on some of our mental states, allowing us to have more control over them, in the moment. The complete story is not all that relevant for our purposes, and nor is it important whether Jim is aware of the full story. Many of our strategies for resisting desires are of this sort. They do not involve a careful reasoning process; rather, they involve our triggering some process, the inner workings of which we are unaware, that gets us the result we want.

So suppose we offer Jim a form of therapy that includes teaching and encouraging him to employ self-control strategies like the deep-breaths technique. This might give Jim better chances of reforming. But there's no guarantee it will work. There are many people like Jim out there, many of them receive therapy, and many of them still reoffend after being released from prison. We will just consider two reasons why such strategies might fail.

One reason is that people like Jim might not recognize the urge until it is too late for the strategy to have a significant effect, or may not recognize the urge at all. Now suppose that scientists' understanding of how the brain works has continued to progress to the point that they can monitor the brain and reliably detect the onset of such urges. Making use of this technology, they have created a device that Jim can wear, a device which warns him that the urges are about to arise. While Jim is wearing this device, it can detect precursors of his urges, and give him a warning; say, by making his watch vibrate. Using this device, Jim can avoid the risk of failing to recognize or react to the urge in time, since the device gives him a clear signal that he is probably about to get one.

Offering this device to Jim, we think, would be permissible. We can suppose that the device does not share information with anyone, and that the vibration on the watch is noticeable only by Jim. This sort of device would simply be an aid in improving the efficacy of the strategies he learns through the therapy; it would make Jim more effective at controlling his own urges.

The second reason why strategies like the deep breaths technique might fail is that, *even if* Jim recognizes the urge in time, and implements the strategy, the strategy may not be effective. Perhaps the urge this time around is too strong for the technique to significantly alleviate it. Or perhaps parts of the environment that triggered the onset of the urge persist, and maybe get more intense, thereby overwhelming the strategy. So suppose that there's more to the device; suppose that not only does it give Jim a signal when it detects a precursor of the urge, it also has a button that Jim can press. When Jim presses this button, the device releases a drug that is reliably effective at neutralizing these urges.[4] Thus, when his watch vibrates, Jim can choose to press the button and give himself a small injection of the drug. Alternatively, Jim can set the device to 'automatic' mode. In this mode, it releases the drug whenever it detects precursors to the urges, with no input required from Jim. We can further suppose that the drug is safe, and does not have significant side-effects.

Offering this amplified device to Jim, we think, would be permissible as well. Obviously, there is an important difference between these devices; the first device lets Jim know when the urge is likely to arise, allowing him to implement his preferred technique. The second device lets him use a drug in combination with, or in place of, this technique. But, we will argue, it's doubtful that this difference is in itself morally significant.

Let's begin by focusing on the similarities between the two devices. Both devices only 'kick in' when the problematic urge is about to arise. The goal of both devices is to prevent the urge from getting stronger, or leading to problematic behavior. You might think that there's an important difference in the way in which the devices achieve their goals. The drug, you might think, is problematic because it doesn't work by getting Jim to appreciate his reasons not to engage in inappropriate or illegal sexual behavior. However, it is not clear that self-control strategies like the deep-breaths technique do so either; we might just use such a strategy because of its results.

You might instead object to the drug-device in ways that some object to so-called 'motivation enhancers'. Motivational enhancers are intended to change a person's motivations for the better; for instance, by helping a person to achieve her goals, including the goal of being a better person. Many of the objections to them look quite a bit like the arguments against the use of smart drugs that we considered above. Consider motivational enhancements that increased students' motivation to study, or athletes' motivation to further develop their skills. One might worry that the use of such enhancements would devalue the achievements of these students or athletes, or that their use would be unfair to other students or athletes. But when we're considering rehabilitating Jim, he isn't in a competition with anyone, and we're not concerned with whether he deserves some accolade, or whether his achievements have merit. In the context of prisoner rehabilitation, it's reform that we want, so these arguments don't hold sway.

Alternatively, you might be concerned that Jim could come to rely on the device, and thus become worse at controlling his urges on his own. We have two points to make in response. First, in terms of avoiding recidivism, this would not be a problem if Jim has the option of using the device indefinitely. Relying on the device would only be problematic if the device might be taken away. Second, we wouldn't think this was a particularly powerful objection if Jim had an alternative strategy. Suppose, for instance, that instead of using a device, Jim develops a friendship, or a relationship with a counselor or priest, such that he can count on this person to help talk him down whenever his urges start to become strong. Few would think that this is a problematic way of preventing recidivism. And few would think that he should avoid forming the relationship because he might come to rely on the other person too much.

Another concern you might have is that the drug-device, when set on automatic, somehow leaves Jim's agency out of the process; and this is somehow a problem. When the device is on the automatic setting, Jim doesn't do anything; it is just the device detecting precursors of the urges and neutralizing them with the drug. We concede that, at the time at which the device neutralizes the urges, Jim is passive with regard to the process. However, we do not think that this means that Jim, as an agent, is no longer involved. In order for the device to be on the automatic setting, he needs to have changed the setting earlier. Compare this to some other strategies agents might use. Suppose that Jack, in order to prevent himself from driving drunk later, gives his keys to his friend, who agrees not to give Jack the keys if he is drunk. Or suppose that Jill is often late to lunch with her friends because she is sometimes distracted by the new devices at the electronic store on her way to the restaurant. She might decide, as she is leaving her house, to take a slightly different route which avoids the electronics store, thereby avoiding the temptation. Jack and Jill both do things to ensure that they don't have, or don't act on, certain urges or motivations later on, when they know that it will be harder to resist them. Jim's setting the device on automatic, we suggest, is similar. It is a case where he acts now to avoid certain actions later. Thus, we reject the view that the device, when set to automatic, somehow excludes Jim's agency in any important way.

Conclusion

Starting with a type of education programme that we think few would find problematic, we have progressed step-by-step through a range of interventions that might be offered to Jim. In each case, we have tried to show that it is hard to see why the intervention should not be offered, at least, if we accept the previously mentioned interventions. This pushes us toward a view according to which, if we accept the education programme, then we ought to accept all of the other interventions that we have discussed as well (as and when they become safe and technologically feasible). This would mean accepting a greatly expanded role for technology in our criminal justice systems, compared to what we see at present.[5]

Some might wish to resist this conclusion. How might they do so? One strategy would be to appeal solely to intuition. For example, someone could hold that, intuitively, the drug-based intervention with which we ended our discussion is so much more problematic than the educational intervention with which we began that we simply *must* accept that there is an ethical difference between them, even if we cannot say what the rational basis for this difference is. We find this strategy unappealing. After all, many people previously had the intuitions that slavery was unproblematic and some people now have the intuitions that mixed-race couples are objectionable or that women ought not to be allowed to work outside the home. Few of us would be willing to take these intuitions, without a rational basis, as indicative of what is actually morally acceptable or unacceptable—most of us would hold that, since they cannot be given any rational basis, these intuitions are mere prejudices. Perhaps our intuitions against the greater use of technology in criminal justice are mere prejudices too.

A second strategy would be to identify some morally significant difference between some of the interventions that we have proposed and others—some difference that we have overlooked. This strategy is more promising. Still, we find it hard to see what the neglected difference might be. So let us end by posing the reader with a challenge: either offer a good argument for drawing a line somewhere along the spectrum of interventions that we have discussed, or accept that there is, potentially at least, an expansive role for technology in crime prevention.

Further Reading

Ryberg, J., *Neurointerventions, Crime, and Punishment: Ethical Considerations* (Oxford University Press, 2019).

Notes

1. See L. Vieiratis, T. Kovandzic, and T. Marvell, The criminogenic effects of imprisonment: evidence from state panel data, 1974–2002, *Criminology and Public Policy*, 6/3 (2007), 589–622.
2. Other possible measures would include, for instance, limiting Jim's movement once he is released such that he cannot come within a certain range of a school, or requiring that he report to his neighbours as a sexual offender.
3. For an overview of this debate, see A. Giubilini and S. Sanyal, The ethics of human enhancement, *Philosophy Compass*, 10/4 (2015), 233–43.
4. If it helps, one can think of this device as using a similar mechanism as an insulin pump, intended for use by diabetics.
5. We have not, in this chapter, considered the possibility that technological interventions might be used to help criminals' rehabilitation *without their consent*. For a discussion of this possibility, see J. Pugh and T. Douglas, Neurointerventions as criminal rehabilitation: An ethical review. In J. D. Jacobs and J. Jackson (eds.), *The Routledge Handbook of Criminal Justice Ethics* (Routledge, 2017), pp. 95–110.

18

Artificial Wombs

Dominic Wilkinson and Lydia Di Stefano

It is the year 2030.

In her second trimester of pregnancy (21 weeks), Marci begins to suffer from abdominal pain and goes to hospital. She is found to be in extremely premature labour, and there are signs that delivery of the baby may be imminent. Marci and her partner are told that if she undergoes a normal vaginal delivery, even with the best medical care, her baby will die. This would be technically classified as a miscarriage.

However, a new technology has recently become available. It would involve having a Caesarean section to remove the baby before placing it in a liquid environment. The baby would stay in this artificial womb for at least four weeks, allowing its lungs and brain to mature sufficiently before a second 'birth'. Using this technique, her baby would potentially have an outcome similar to those of infants born prematurely at 25 weeks of gestation. About 80% of 25-week premature babies survive, and the majority of survivors have no or only relatively minor long-term disability. On the downside, having a Caesarean section this early in pregnancy is not risk free. It would increase the chance of complications for Marci in future pregnancies: she is likely to need repeat Caesarean sections for any future babies, and she would have higher risks of bleeding or other serious complications.

Ectogestation and Ethics

What are the ethical implications of the technology described in the case above? Is Marci ethically obliged to undergo this major surgery in order to give her baby a chance of surviving? What if she decided that she didn't want to do this? What are the wider ethical implications of this procedure? If extremely premature babies were able to survive in this form of artificial womb, would it have any implications for abortion?

The possibility of artificial wombs has been contemplated by novelists, filmmakers and philosophers for a century, perhaps most notably in Aldous Huxley's *Brave New World*.

> [T]here, in the crimson darkness, stewingly warm on their cushion of peritoneum and gorged with blood-surrogate and hormones, the foetuses grew and grew, or, poisoned, languished into a stunted Epsilonhood. With a faint hum and rattle the moving racks crawled imperceptibly through the weeks and the recapitulated aeons to where, in the Decanting Room, the newly-unbottled babes uttered their first yell of horror and amazement.[1]

The technology of developing a fetus from embryo to birth in an artificial environment is sometimes called "ectogenesis" ('ecto' from Greek—meaning external or outside, 'genesis'—meaning creation or generation). It is obvious that ectogenesis would have radical implications for the structure of our society as well as for male and female roles. Women would no longer be required to take time away from their career progression or bear the physical burden and complications of pregnancy. It would also allow women who do not have a functioning uterus, due to medical reasons or because they are transgender, and same sex male couples, to have children without the need for a surrogate. This could free women from various forms of gender oppression and liberate people from the constraints of anatomy. On the other hand, some feminists worry that this potential technology could undermine the importance of motherhood, render natural childbearing a luxury, and diminish the value of women's lives.[2]

Ectogenesis is likely to remain in the realms of science fiction for the foreseeable future. But the more limited development described above, in which Marci's baby was transferred to an artificial womb part-way through a pregnancy, might not be that far off. We could call this "ectogestation" ('ecto'—external, 'gestation'—to carry).[3]

For several decades, scientists have been trying to develop ways of caring for infants who are born prematurely in a womb-like environment. The potential benefit of such a technology is that it might improve the outcome for such babies. With current technology, premature babies can survive at as early as 22 weeks. Before that point, a baby's lungs are simply too immature to allow gas exchange, so survival appears impossible. Furthermore, extremely premature babies (those born below 28 weeks, who are more than three months early) are prone to many medical and developmental complications.

How close are we to ectogestation? Well, in 2017, researchers from Philadelphia successfully tested a type of artificial womb, called a "Biobag", on extremely premature lambs.[4] The lambs were delivered by Caesarean section at a level of lung maturity equivalent to humans at 23 weeks gestation, and were immediately transferred to individual Biobags where they received oxygen and nutrition via an artificial placenta. They were allowed to mature for up to one month in the bags before being delivered and then supported with conventional forms of medical care. The experimental lambs were found to have outcomes similar to newborn lambs who had stayed in their mothers' wombs for the same period. The researchers in Philadelphia, along with several other groups around the world, are continuing to develop artificial womb technologies, which they plan to test on extremely premature human infants in the next five to ten years.

Ectogestation would not radically change women's roles in society. If it were available, it would likely be used only in rare cases—for example Marci's situation—and women would still need to carry babies for the first half of pregnancy. However, it might have ethical implications in two different areas.

Ectogestation and Neonatal Ethics

Ectogestation could lead to some changes in decisions for premature babies.

When babies are born prematurely, parents usually have strong desires for doctors and nurses to do everything possible to save the baby, which will usually be unquestionably in the best interests of the newborn infant.

However, there's a significant chance that a baby born extremely early will die despite treatment. If they survive, there is a significant chance of them having some degree of life-long disability. In that situation, it is widely accepted that it is ethical, dependent on the wishes of the parents, to either actively resuscitate them, or to manage them with palliative comfort care (accepting that they will likely die). There are two ethical thresholds. The *lower threshold* is the point in pregnancy before which it would be unreasonable to even attempt medical care (because the baby's chances are so low). The *upper threshold* is the point past which it would be unreasonable to withhold resuscitation (because the baby's chances are so good). In between these thresholds, parents' wishes are important in determining the baby's care. With current technology, at the time of writing (2020), the *lower threshold* in many countries is about the 22nd week of gestation, while the *upper threshold* is around the 24th week.[5]

Ectogestation might reduce the *lower threshold* for newborn medical treatment. It might mean that it would be ethically permissible to try to save babies who would previously have been too premature to survive. That would mean that active management would potentially be an option for Marci's baby at 21 weeks gestation. However, ectogestation would not necessarily reduce the *upper threshold* (i.e. the point when it would be ethically mandatory to treat a premature baby). That is because of an important aspect of the way this treatment is expected to be offered. We mentioned above that the current approach to ectogestation necessarily involves delivery of the baby by Caesarean section. This is related to a major change in the physiology of the fetus between the uterine environment and the ex-utero environment. Normally, when the fetus is born, the circulation of the fetus transitions suddenly from obtaining oxygen and nutrition from the blood via the placenta, to obtaining oxygen through the lungs and nutrition through the gut. The change in the circulation is a little like a train being switched to another track; it is not easily reversed once it has occurred. In the ectogestation procedure, to prevent this switch from happening, the fetus is transferred directly (via Caesarean section) from uterus to artificial womb, where the fetus will receive oxygen through its blood rather than through the lungs. That probably cannot happen after a vaginal delivery.

We noted that Caesarean section (particularly very early Caesarean section) has significant implications for the mother. This means that Marci's consent would be crucial for ectogestation to occur. If Marci were to decide, for example, that she did not wish to undergo a

Caesarean section, it would not be possible to save her baby. The possibility of refusing this operation means that the *upper threshold* would not change. There can be no ethical requirement that the fetus be delivered by Caesarean and transferred to the Biobag, even if that would have a high chance of saving the life of the baby. It is widely accepted—throughout the world—that a mother, if she has capacity, has an absolute right to refuse obstetric interventions, including Caesarean section. That would apply even if the fetus was at full term, and so it would clearly apply in Marci's situation.

What if the technology developed further, so that Marci's baby could be delivered vaginally and then placed in a Biobag? That may well not be medically possible, but if it were, the argument relating to Caesarean section would no longer apply. If a baby was to be born by vaginal delivery at 20 or 21 weeks gestation with an 80% chance of survival, could the parents say that they did not wish for the baby to be treated? The answer might depend on several other factors.

First, what would be the burden of treatment for the parents? For example, if the treatment were extremely expensive (and the parents would be required to pay for it), it would be unreasonable to force them to accept that expense.

Second, would the healthcare system and wider community be able to care for the child if the parents do not wish to? If the community cannot pay for the child's treatment and adopt the child, it would be unwise to treat against the parents' wishes.

Third, and importantly, what do we consider is the moral status of a 20- or 21-week fetus? Do their 'interests' weigh as strongly as those of a more mature infant (for example a 25-week premature infant or a full term newborn)?

An 'interest' is a philosophical term referring to the degree to which someone or something is benefited or harmed. For example, if an entity is capable of perceiving pain, they would be harmed by painful stimuli. They have an *interest* in not being subjected to such stimuli. Some philosophers have argued that we only have an interest in continuing to live if we are self-conscious (i.e. aware of ourselves and our own existence over time). It is difficult to know when consciousness develops in the fetus. However, it is highly unlikely that a 21-week fetus is self-conscious. If the 20/21-week fetus morally lacks interests, or their interests have a lesser weight (than those of a more mature fetus), then we should potentially give greater ethical weight to parents' views about treatment.

Ectogestation and Abortion

Questions about the moral status of the fetus mid-way through pregnancy are also highly relevant to a different ethical issue—that of pregnancy termination (abortion).

One question is whether the possibility of ectogestation would change whether or when abortion is permitted. For example, imagine another woman, Maxine, arrives in hospital in 2030 at 21 weeks gestation and requests a termination of her pregnancy. Does it follow that if ectogestation is an option for Marci, then abortion should not be an option for Maxine?

The ethical issue of abortion remains highly controversial, and many societies are divided about it. Some regard the fetus as having full moral status from the point of conception. From that perspective, abortion is the moral equivalent of killing a newborn baby (or, indeed, an adult). On such a view, the development of technology such as ectogestation would have no implications, since those who hold a strict pro-life view would regard it as unethical to terminate even a very early pregnancy. Others take the opposite view. They hold that a woman has an absolute right to have a say over her health and body. Even if the fetus has full moral status, the woman's right to decide is the predominant ethical consideration. On such a view, again, technologies like ectogestation would have no implications for the ethics of abortion.

However, in practice, many countries have adopted a position somewhere between the strong pro-life and pro-choice positions. In these countries, abortion is permitted early in pregnancy, but restricted or outlawed after a certain point. Countries vary in where they draw this line. However, a number of jurisdictions link it to the point of fetal viability, either explicitly as a hard limit after which abortion is illegal (notably in the United States, where several states place an abortion limit at the gestational age of "viability"),[6] or implicitly. For example, in the UK, termination of pregnancy after 24 weeks gestation is possible only in restricted circumstances. In 1990 this was lowered from 28 weeks, reflecting changes in the survival of extremely preterm infants. The idea is that abortion is more ethically problematic for a "viable" fetus.

For those who hold this sort of view, ectogestation might be significant—since it potentially alters the point of fetal viability. However, much depends on what we mean by "viability" and why it is thought to be ethically relevant.

One intuitive way of understanding "viability" is that it reflects the ability of the fetus to survive outside the mother's womb. But do we mean the fetus will *possibly* survive, or will *probably* survive? And does it matter whether the survival of the fetus depends on advanced technology (such as the ectogestation technology or conventional newborn intensive care)? Some might think that the possibility of survival affects the fetus' moral status. Yet it is not clear why. Why would the development of a technological advance like ectogestation change our moral obligations to the fetus? More pointedly, it is not clear why the mere possibility of a fetus surviving *outside the womb* (if born prematurely) changes whether we should require the fetus to remain *inside the womb* (i.e. for the pregnancy to continue). Again, some might have the view that the fetus has moral status before viability. Others may have the view that the post-viable fetus lacks moral status (because of a lack of consciousness or because of the mother's autonomy). But it is not clear why viability itself changes the moral status of the fetus.

Here is another way of justifying the relevance of viability for abortion. One reason for thinking that viability makes a difference, and therefore that ectogestation might be relevant, is because of the ethical value of consistency. Some people might be troubled by the thought of Marci's baby receiving intensive life-saving treatment at 21 weeks gestation while in another part of the hospital Maxine's fetus is aborted at the same stage of pregnancy. They might believe that having an abortion cut-off at the point of viability is a way of making sure that neonatal care and obstetric care (particularly termination of pregnancy) are consistent.

Consistency is an important ethical principle. Yet, if the justification for limiting women's choice about abortion is based on ethical consistency, it should align with the point at which parental choice is limited in selecting non-resuscitation—in other words, the *upper threshold* for newborn resuscitation. Abortion might be limited or prohibited if a pregnancy has passed the point at which parents are no longer permitted to choose non-resuscitation for their premature baby. However, if that is right, this means that ectogestation should not alter policy around abortion in countries like the UK. That is because of the arguments that we have already discussed. We suggested that ectogestation might change the *lower threshold* for newborn resuscitation: it might make it ethically permissible to actively manage newborns more premature than previously. However, ectogestation would not change the *upper threshold* for resuscitation—it would not alter the point at which it would be ethically obligatory to resuscitate.

One final possibility is if the development of ectogestation makes it possible to respect the autonomy of pregnant women, while at the same time respecting the rights of the fetus, it could serve as an abortion compromise. Some might hold that if Maxine wished to terminate her pregnancy, her fetus could be transferred to an external womb, and then later adopted by another couple. However, it is not clear that this option provides an attractive compromise either for pro-choice or pro-life advocates.

First, as it is currently conceived, ectogestation would require Maxine to undergo major surgery—with significant risks for her future health and childbearing. She may wish to no longer be pregnant, but also to preserve her ability to deliver naturally in the future—in which case this compromise would hardly respect her autonomy.

Second, the child born and transferred to the artificial womb would potentially have a number of complications from being premature (ectogestation, as described, reduces but does not eliminate risks). They will potentially be harmed by the ectogestation procedure.[7]

Third, there are the costs of ectogestation. Conventional newborn intensive care is highly expensive; the lifetime medical costs of the extreme preterm can be as high as USD 450,000.[8] It is likely that ectogestation would be at least as costly (and potentially more so).

Who will bear the costs of this treatment? If Maxine is expected to bear these costs, that potentially creates an enormous financial burden for women contemplating terminating a pregnancy. If society is expected the bear the cost, then we, as a society, need to determine whether it is worth it to prevent the relatively small number of abortions that would otherwise occur at this stage of pregnancy. That takes us back to the question of the moral status of the

21-week fetus. Do we think that it is justified to use limited healthcare resources in order to save the life of a fetus halfway through pregnancy? If they have full moral status, perhaps it would be justified to not fund hip surgery or other medical treatments, in order to save them. However, if fetuses have no or reduced moral status, it would be a grave mistake to use scarce medical resources for this purpose.

Conclusion

Ectogestation, if it comes to fruition, might offer the extraordinary possibility of saving or improving the lives of babies born extremely early, barely halfway through a normal pregnancy. But like many advances in reproductive medicine and neonatal care, it is sure to be accompanied by challenging ethical questions. In practical ethics, it is useful to consider the ethical implications of technologies that may be developed in the years ahead. Sometimes that opens up new ethical concepts and questions. However, in many cases the questions may turn out to be familiar ones. The central ethical question raised by artificial wombs and ectogestation is the vexed one of the moral status of the fetus.

These uncomfortable questions do not mean that ectogestation should be avoided. But it should be the subject of ethical analysis, in which we identify the connections and overlaps with existing ethical debate.

Further Reading

Huxley, A., *Brave New World* (Chatto & Windus, 1932).

Notes

1. A. Huxley, *Brave New World* (Random House edition, 2016), p. 127.
2. Z. Buturovic, Formula feeding can help illuminate long-term consequences of full ectogenesis, *Bioethics*, 34/4 (2020), 331–7.
3. L. M. Di Stefano et al., Ectogestation ethics: The implications of artificially extending gestation for viability, newborn resuscitation and abortion, *Bioethics*, 34/4 (2020), 371–84.
4. E. A. Partridge et al., An extra-uterine system to physiologically support the extreme premature lamb, *Nature Communications*, 8 (2017), 15112.

5. Di Stefano et al. (2020).

6. L. Han, M. I. Rodriguez, I. Maria, and A. B. Caughey, Blurred lines: Disentangling the concept of fetal viability from abortion law, *Women's Health Issues*, 28/4 (2018), 287–8.

7. D. Wilkinson, L. Skene, L. De Crespigny, and J. Savulescu, Protecting future children from in-utero harm, *Bioethics*, 30 (2016), 425–32.

8. I. G. S. Cheah, Economic assessment of neonatal intensive care, *Translational Pediatrics*, 8/3 (2019), 246.

19

Genetic Immunisation

Tess Johnson and Alberto Giubilini

Suppose you could make sure that your child would be immune from some serious infectious disease, say COVID-19 or measles. Here are three questions:

1) Would you do it?
2) Do you have a moral obligation to do it?
3) Should you be held accountable for not doing it?

These questions are intentionally vague. Many people would probably answer that it all depends. Maybe immunity is not the only thing that matters. How difficult would it be to achieve immunity? Would it be achieved through 'natural' means? Would the intervention be pre- or post-natal? Would it entail risk? Would it require an act or an omission?

Take vaccination, for example. Although most vaccines are, in an important sense, natural substances (for instance, when they contain viruses that have been weakened or had their disease-causing capacity removed), in another sense they are not, because they are produced in laboratories. People committed to natural lifestyles might reject vaccination on grounds of its 'unnaturalness'. Secondly, the small risks from vaccines represent, to some people, sufficient reason to oppose them. Some parents would prefer their children were harmed as a result of an infectious disease (which is a consequence of non-vaccination, that is, an omission) than as a result of vaccination (an action). Finally, rather than vaccinate their children, some parents may prefer to rely on 'herd immunity'—that is, the protection from being in a population where enough other people are vaccinated that an infectious disease cannot spread. All these views will affect our answers to the three questions above, just in relation to vaccination.

But it gets still more complicated—what about immunity that isn't caused by vaccination after birth, but some pre-natal intervention? Suppose we discovered that some natural substance contained in apples, if consumed in large enough quantities, altered genes in the foetus in such a way that their future immune system became resistant to certain infectious diseases. Would women have a moral obligation to increase their intake of apples, if this avoided the need to vaccinate their children after birth? If we think that pregnant women have a responsibility to take folic acid (which protects babies against birth defects) during pregnancy, it seems plausible to conclude that they would have the responsibility to eat, say, two apples a day if that conferred immunity for their future children. The fact that the intervention would take place at the pre-natal stage, and that it requires an action instead of an omission, hardly seems an important objection in this specific case.

Consider now a third type of intervention: gene editing at the embryonic stage—that is, modifying the DNA of an embryo that codes for aspects of the future child's immune system. These changes are inherited by following generations, because they are made before the embryo's sex cells have developed separately from the rest of the cells in the body. Suppose we could genetically engineer the same kind of alteration to the immune system as apples did in our previous example. Gene editing has already been used for immunity: it has produced cattle that are resistant to mastitis-causing bacteria, by adding genes that code for a protein that kills the bacteria. These advances may lead to gene editing that could in principle prevent some infectious diseases in humans, too. With immunity to certain diseases from birth, the need for vaccines and antibiotics would be reduced in both animals and humans—this would have the additional and positive side-effect of helping to combat 'antimicrobial resistance', the resistance that evolves in certain infectious disease strains to drugs designed to kill them.

These interventions may sound like science fiction, but they are probably just around the corner. In fact, in 2018, gene editing was first used on babies brought to term, by Chinese scientist He Jiankui. He declared that he had managed to edit the embryos' genes to make them resistant to the HIV virus. The experiment was deemed both unsafe and unethical by the academic community—in part because of uncertainty about the risks involved in this modification—but it shed light on a new possibility: if we use gene editing to confer immunity, maybe we could eliminate infectious diseases that threaten our populations today. If gene editing technology was refined, properly ethically assessed, and made accessible to the public as a way of ensuring one's children's immunity, it might become as important as, or even preferable to, vaccination. We will refer to such a technique as 'genetic immunisation'.

In this chapter we want to examine the ethics of genetic immunisation with reference to the three questions with which we began. We will compare vaccination and genetic immunisation to see whether these different interventions provide different answers to these three questions. If they do not, then parents who would undertake vaccination for their child, who see a moral obligation to vaccinate their children, and who think that policy should hold parents accountable for not vaccinating their children, would be able to argue that the same should apply to genetic immunisation.

If We Should Vaccinate, Should We Genetically Immunise Our Children?

The disagreement about whether, and how, to vaccinate children is often based on members of the public holding different and sometimes incorrect factual beliefs. The vast majority of people, from 'anti-vaxxers' to those more informed about science and the benefits of vaccines, think that parents have a moral responsibility to protect their children's health. The disagreement is about how to achieve this. Some think that vaccines are ineffective or harmful, or that some infectious diseases are not particularly dangerous. Yet, most people agree that parents have a responsibility to preserve their children's health. If so, then given negligible risks and significant benefits of vaccines, failing to protect one's child against certain infectious diseases through easily available vaccination is like failing to provide children with adequate nutrition to prevent them from developing certain health conditions. One might go further and say that non-vaccinating parents are morally blameworthy even if the child does not get the infectious disease, because they have put their child at preventable risk of serious illness. Parents fulfil responsibility for their child's health once they make sure the child enjoys either direct (through vaccination) or indirect (through herd immunity) protection.

Parents are often encouraged to fulfil their responsibilities through social pressures or forms of non-coercive government action. For instance, even where vaccination is not mandatory, most governments promote vaccination uptake, if only by providing accurate information or subsidising certain vaccines. The existence of parental responsibilities and the encouragement of their fulfilment via government policy can be explained by appeal to 'paternalism', that is, the principle according to which certain individuals (in this case, children) ought to be protected regardless of whether they consent to it (direct paternalism) or whether those responsible for them consent to it (indirect paternalism). But there is another reason: we want parents to provide for their children's health not only because that is in their children's best interests, but also because we want to protect and promote public health. Arguably, vaccinating one's children constitutes a fair contribution to maintaining herd immunity.[1] This shared duty to contribute implies a *prima facie* duty to vaccinate our child for the sake of the community, even beyond our individual duty to our child as a parent.

Does the same moral requirement hold for genetic immunisation?

Vaccination and Genetic Immunisation: Similarities and Differences

1. Aims

The aim of vaccination policies is to protect individuals and reduce the spread of certain infectious diseases in society. These contribute to individual and public health but also to productivity and the economy. A pandemic of simple seasonal flu could cost a country like the USA around $45.3 billion in lost gross domestic product (GDP) with low vaccination rates; this number could come down by at least $10 billion with higher vaccination rates.[2]

Genetic immunisation could achieve the same result as vaccination and would be aimed at the same target—reducing the spread of disease by improving the ability of our immune cells to respond effectively to infection.

2. The Nature of Intervention: Genetic Modification and Enhancement

Genetic immunisation involves direct genetic modification (which we assume will be safe). Is parental responsibility and responsibility to society any different for direct modification as opposed to a vaccine, or eating apples to cause immunity? Whether the apples work by changing gene expression or the foetus' immune cells doesn't appear to be morally relevant. And if that's right, the directness of genetic modification doesn't seem a *morally relevant difference* when we compare genetic immunisation with vaccination.

What about whether each of the two interventions constitutes an 'enhancement' or a 'preventive measure'? Some people believe that an enhancement is either not permissible at all, or else less permissible than a treatment. Depending on how one understands the concept of 'human enhancement', vaccination could be taken to be either a preventive treatment or an enhancement. Vaccinations are preventive measures in that they do not treat a disease but create a new capacity for preventing certain diseases. In that sense, both vaccination and genetic immunisation count as preventive measures. But vaccination might also be termed an enhancement if we focus on the fact that the capacity does not exist in the natural, pre-vaccination population, unless they have acquired immunity by getting infected. In this sense, genetic immunisation is an enhancement, too. If the categorisation of vaccination as a form of enhancement does not make it morally unacceptable, the same holds true for genetic immunisation.

Worries that genetic immunisation is a form of enhancement might be a proxy for a different kind of concern, namely that genetic immunisation is 'eugenics'. This concern was voiced when He Jiankui announced the birth of the two first gene-edited babies.[3] More generally, the eugenics rhetoric is one of the most common strategies used to oppose human enhancement.[4] The rhetoric suggests analogies between the enhancement practices proposed today and the kind of practices carried out in Nazi Germany and elsewhere in the first part of the 20th century. Because of this dark history, the term 'eugenics' now carries a negative connotation, although the term itself is not inherently negative, if we look at its literal meaning ('good birth'). Making humans 'better' in certain respects, by exploiting our knowledge of genetics and heritability, is by definition a good thing. The disagreement is about what 'good' and 'better' mean (e.g. whether people with certain disabilities can have a good life) and about which means may permissibly be used to make humans 'better'. Where eugenics involves expressing disvalue toward those without a certain desired characteristic, for instance, ethical problems arise. They arise too if a process is enforced using state power to impose a certain way of life or to deprive citizens of individual liberties regarding reproduction or even life (as was the case in Nazi Germany).

But consider vaccination and genetic immunisation. Expressing disvalue toward certain groups is neither the goal nor a side-effect of inducing disease immunity, whether that be through vaccination or genetic modification. Nobody would say that when a state introduces a measles vaccination policy, it sends a negative message against those with measles. And immunising children against infectious diseases through gene editing would not express any negative attitude against people who are not immune any more than vaccinating children does.

The point about state use of power is more problematic. Certainly, we can see how compulsory genetic immunisation may be justified on the same grounds as vaccination, at least when it's relatively cheap and easily available to prospective parents already intending to use IVF. And it might be argued that this would constitute a coercive, imposing, or liberty-threatening practice.

To this concern we have two replies.

Firstly, if our major worry is about state imposition and limitation of individual liberties, then the simple response would be to accept that genetic immunisation, although a good thing in itself and perhaps even a moral obligation (the second question with which we started), should not be made compulsory (the third question)—nor for that matter should vaccination, on the same grounds. Of course, many people would still be willing to genetically immunise their children (first question) without there being a legal obligation, out of a sense of parental responsibility.

Secondly, not every form of state imposition is wrong, even if it does infringe individual liberties. Quarantine, vaccination, rationing allocation of scarce health resources, and taxation are a few examples of what are normally regarded as acceptable forms of liberty infringement. The real problem arises when the state uses its power to impose certain types of substantive values or norms on others—for example, values about what counts as a good life or a good human being. This is not consistent with the values of liberal, democratic societies. In such societies, the state should create conditions that enable individuals to develop and pursue their own values and life goals, so long as these are consistent with equal rights and liberties of others.

Would either compulsory vaccination or genetic immunisation impose a state's values on its citizens? Even if we think herd immunity and a decent level of public health are intrinsically good, they are also—and we would say, mainly—preconditions for citizens' abilities to pursue their own goals and values. Freedom from infectious disease is a health-related good that serves the pursuit of other goals. If that is right, then the eugenics objection loses its force.

3. Stage of Intervention

Perhaps an ethically relevant difference is between pre- and post-natal intervention. We might ask, for instance, whether parental responsibilities are affected by genetic immunisation's status as a pre-natal intervention.

However, assuming genetic immunisation is easily available and not too costly in the future, parents would seem to have as pressing a responsibility to pursue genetic immunisation as women would to eat disease-preventing apples during pregnancy. Equally, so long as the pre-natal intervention is safe and does not impose significant costs to the woman undertaking it, there doesn't seem to be a relevant moral distinction between the apples (pre-natal) and vaccination (post-natal) interventions.

The important costs caveat may, however, limit the scope for implementing genetic immunisation. Genetic immunisation would require prospective parents to use IVF to conceive a child. This involves invasive operations and over-stimulation of the ovaries to produce eggs, costs that for many prospective mothers may be morally significant. If so, then we should limit our investigation of genetic immunisation to cases where prospective parents already choose to undertake IVF.

4. Continuity of Intervention

We should also consider the continuity of the intervention. Genetic immunisation would be a form of *heritable* modification, with changes passed on to future generations. We are assuming that the kind of genetic immunisation we are concerned with would be safe and that the only change would be to an individual's and their descendants' immunity to a certain disease. Suppose there was high uptake of genetic immunisation, so that a few generations down the line significant parts of the global population would be immune from, say, measles—is this future problematic, somehow, compared to the same effect of a vaccination programme that eradicates measles a little later? The ultimate ambition of a vaccination policy is permanent immunity against certain infectious diseases. A safe heritable genetic immunisation producing the same outcome, but for multiple generations, seems at least morally equivalent to vaccination, if not better.

5. Bodily Integrity

Bodily integrity is a principle typically advanced against vaccination, especially compulsory vaccination. The claim is that forcing somebody to have a vaccine violates their bodily integrity—crudely, that is the right not to have one's body interfered with in ways that are considered too invasive.

Even if this charge has some merit, it is not necessarily a decisive principle. One could plausibly argue that the benefits of vaccination outweigh the slight invasion of a jab. In any case, for the purposes of this discussion, the real question is whether vaccination and genetic immunisation pose differing levels of threat to bodily integrity.

In the case of genetic immunisation, the 'body' that is interfered with is an embryo; it's not clear that embryos even have a 'body', or one whose integrity can be meaningfully violated. It may be argued that changes from genetic immunisation are carried through in the child's DNA, violating the child's body in the process. But even if this claim is granted, the genetic changes in the child seem equivalent to the changes incurred through vaccination. The only difference is that the former involves changes to DNA and the latter involves changes to cells. Genetic immunisation is no more a violation of bodily integrity than vaccination.

6. Alternative Measures and Cost

Genetic immunisation and vaccination may differ in cost and availability. At first glance, vaccination seems a more efficient means to cause immunity, given the portability of vaccines and the lack of equipment and expertise required. Genetic immunisation requires IVF and many associated costs, equipment, and qualified personnel. However, vaccines are not always an alternative option to achieve immunity, even in high income countries where they are easily available. Some people have adverse reactions (e.g. allergies) to certain vaccines, some are too young to be vaccinated and so cannot enjoy direct protection for a few months or years, and no vaccine is 100% effective. In that case, being born with immunity may be preferable to having to acquire immunity through vaccines.

What about the costs of each intervention? On a per-intervention basis, genetic immunisation is predictably more costly than vaccination. However, the cost of genetic immunisation will probably come down in future, and since immunity will be passed down to subsequent generations, the cost will be spread among the immune descendants of an edited individual, potentially making it comparable, or lower than, vaccination when considered per immune individual. What's more, such intervention may in the long run reduce the need for antibiotics, thus also reducing the impact and costs of antibiotic resistance.

7. Effectiveness

Although immunity from genetic immunisation would be heritable (unlike vaccination), this may not increase the effectiveness of the intervention, compared to vaccination. Disease strains evolve over time, so if diseases change significantly between one generation and the next, genetic immunisation may become obsolete. But this is the same with vaccines. New vaccines frequently need to be developed for fast-evolving disease strains such as flu viruses. Meanwhile, for slow-evolving diseases, we would still see the benefits of multiple generations inheriting immunity. For example, let's consider multi-drug-resistant tuberculosis (MDR TB). One of very few viable vaccines still effective against (non-pulmonary) MDR TB is neonatally administered bacilli Calmette-Guérin. This was first used in 1921 and has remained effective for 100 years. Although, like vaccination, genetic immunisation may not remain effective against fast-adapting diseases, we can assume it would show the same effectiveness at producing immunity per generation as vaccination.

What Do These Similarities and Differences Mean?

If vaccination is a moral obligation and should be compulsory, then our discussion suggests that parents would and should genetically immunise their children. However, any compulsory policy would have to be limited to those already undertaking IVF—otherwise too great a burden would be imposed on prospective mothers. As for the increased costs of genetic immunisation, this would seem to be balanced by its continuity into future generations. One might think that individuals have a moral responsibility to look after their own health, but that the state has no business in forcing them to live up to such moral responsibilities towards themselves or their children, especially when this is costly. But the cost issue is eliminated entirely if we consider the idea of publicly subsidised genetic immunisation, similar to the way we currently implement vaccination programmes. This may mean that parents undertaking IVF can be held accountable for not genetically immunising their future children.

When it comes to availability, we need to be realistic: it's unlikely that genetic immunisation will be an option for people in some areas of the world. This doesn't make it less morally required for those for whom it is available, but it does mean we need to make sure that vaccine development and distribution is not neglected *in favour of* a complete switch to genetic immunisation. Vaccine development will continue to be important for many years to come, and is a necessary alternative to genetic immunisation for those prospective parents not already intending to undertake IVF.

Is Genetic Immunisation the New Vaccination?

So is genetic immunisation the new vaccination? If parents would and should vaccinate their children, and if they should be held accountable for not doing so, does the same hold for genetic immunisation?

Overall, we think that genetic immunisation is *not* 'the new' vaccination. It must not replace current vaccination. However, with some caveats, it *is* a promising and morally justifiable new alternative to traditional vaccination. Vaccination must continue to be supported, but for parents who are already undertaking IVF, genetic immunisation may become the new vaccination. If so, it should be accompanied by the same aspects of parental responsibility and accountability—to the benefit both of individual future children, and of society at large.

Further Reading

Giubilini, A., *The Ethics of Vaccination* (Palgrave Macmillan, 2019).

Notes

1. See, e.g., A. Giubilini, *The Ethics of Vaccination* (Palgrave Macmillan, 2019); A. Giubilini, An argument for compulsory vaccination: The taxation analogy, *Journal of Applied Philosophy*, 37/1 (2020), 446–66.
2. F. Prager, D. Wei, and A. Rose, Total economic consequences of an influenza outbreak in the United States, *Risk Analysis*, 37/1 (2017), 4–19.
3. F. Huang, Letter: How China's penchant for eugenics led to CRISPR babies, *Caixin Global*, 17 December 2018, https://www.caixinglobal.com/2018-12-17/letter-how-chinas-penchant-for-eugenics-led-to-crispr-babies-101360013.html.
4. E.g. L. Kass, Defending human dignity. In The President's Council on Bioethics (ed.), *Human Dignity and Bioethics* (Washington, DC, 2008), p. 301.

20

Genome Editing in Livestock

Katrien Devolder

Recently developed genome editing technologies allow scientists to make very precise changes in the genome of livestock. These could be to the advantage of both humans and animals. If genome editing enables such a win–win situation, should we pursue it?

Hornless Cows

Most breeds of dairy cow have horns. These can cause serious injuries to other cows, as well as to the farmers handling them. To prevent such injuries, farmers routinely remove young calves' ability to grow horns by placing a hot iron on their horn buds, a very painful procedure that can also have detrimental long-term effects on the calves' welfare.

Some cattle breeds are genetically predisposed not to grow horns. This trait is called 'polledness'. Recently developed genome editing technologies that allow for very precise changes to an organism's genome have been used to insert this polledness trait into either the egg cells or the fertilized eggs (i.e. the early embryos) of horned dairy cows. The resulting calves do not grow horns, and, because polledness is a dominant trait, neither will their offspring. A painful procedure with long-term harmful effects can be avoided.

Disease Resistant/Resilient Pigs

Worldwide, more than a billion pigs are raised and slaughtered for meat each year. This enormous pig population is under constant threat of infectious disease. African Swine Fever, for example, is a deadly viral disease for which there is neither a cure, nor a vaccine. In 2019 alone, over one million pigs were culled to prevent its spread. Another dangerous viral disease is Porcine Reproductive and Respiratory Syndrome (PRRS), which causes reproductive failure, pneumonia, and increased mortality. The annual financial impact of the disease in Europe alone is estimated to be around €1.5 billion.[1]

Genome editing, and in particular the popular CRISPR-Cas9[2] technology, has been used to produce pigs that seem resistant to PRRS, and could potentially be used to produce pigs that are resilient to African Swine Fever, which means that though the pigs could get the disease, it wouldn't significantly affect them.

A Win–Win Situation

Should we pursue genome editing to produce hornless cows and disease-resistant or resilient pigs? At first sight, this would enable a win–win situation: it would be good for the farmers, as it would prevent enormous financial losses, and good for the animals, because it would prevent them from becoming seriously ill. Many people nevertheless object to, or are extremely suspicious of, the use of genome editing in livestock. In this chapter, I discuss some of the most serious concerns arising from the use of genome editing in livestock in cases where this could benefit both humans and animals. (I will not have anything to say about applications of genome editing that are clearly only to the advantage of humans, such as, for example, genome editing to increase meat per animal.)

Overstepping Divine or Natural Boundaries

One recurring worry about genome editing (and all technologies involving genetic modification) is that it oversteps the boundaries of humans' role in scientific research and development. These boundaries are thought to be set by either God (genome editing is then wrong because it amounts to 'playing God') or nature (genome editing is wrong because it is 'unnatural').

One problem is that we don't know, and cannot know, what God's plan is, if any such plan exists. Thus, we cannot know when we overstep some boundary set by God. Another problem is that referring to God won't appeal to those who do not believe in the existence of God.

How about overstepping some *natural* boundary? This objection, too, has little force, once we realize that we are constantly overstepping natural boundaries: when we wear clothes, use phones and computers, and use chemotherapy to treat cancer. For the objection to have some force, it would need to specify what is meant by 'unnatural' (artificial? unusual? unfamiliar?), explain why this kind of unnaturalness is morally problematic, and show that this understanding of 'unnatural' applies to genome editing but not to other practices that we accept, like mainstream medicine or travel into space. This is a challenge, especially in the context of agriculture, as current cows and pigs are the result of thousands of years of selective breeding and of the use of various technologies, including *in vitro* fertilization and cloning, that seem, on the face of it, to be unnatural. It is not obvious that genome editing would add significant unnaturalness to what is already far from a natural situation. Moreover, in the case of hornless cattle and African Swine Flu-resilient pigs, the genetic trait that is introduced occurs 'naturally' in some cattle breeds and warthogs. In the case of PRRS-resistant pigs, CRISPR-Cas9 is used to remove a small section of one protein; nothing is added. Thus, in the applications under consideration, either a small section of a protein is removed, or a protein (or a part of it) that 'naturally' exists in the species is added. This poses an extra challenge for those trying to formulate a convincing argument against genome editing on the grounds that it is unnatural.

Too Risky

Some may object to the use of genome editing because it is too risky. Genome editing may create a chance of a win–win situation, but there's no guarantee that it will work out. There could, for example, be 'off-target' effects—that is, unintended effects elsewhere in the genome. We might try to prevent horns from developing, but end up causing a disease. If cloning is part of the genome editing procedure, there are further risks, including a higher chance that the altered fetus will miscarry. Another worry is risk to humans. In two gene-edited calves, researchers found antibiotic resistance genes. Because these genes are present in most of the calves' cells, the risk is high that they will be transferred to bacteria, which in turn could be transferred to humans via direct contact, food preparation or consumption, or excretion in the environment This could pose a serious danger to human health as the infections they cause may be much harder, or impossible, to treat.

However, whilst safety concerns are clearly important, these problems may be resolved as research continues. One could significantly reduce the risks to both livestock and humans by conducting research cautiously, investigating the technology step by step. If the technology is eventually deemed sufficiently safe, we're left with the question as to whether we should apply it to produce, say, hornless cows and disease-resistant pigs.

Disrespectful

Some may think that genome editing in livestock would be disrespectful towards the animals. But what exactly does this mean? Respect is an opaque concept that requires explanation. What complicates matters is the fact that genome editing could happen before the animal comes into existence. For example, scientists might edit a skin cell, then insert this cell into an egg using cloning technology to create an embryo. Can genome editing be disrespectful to an animal when it is performed before it comes into existence?

When referring to respect, concepts like the 'intrinsic value' or 'inherent worth' of animals come to mind. Philosophers inspired by the 18th-century German philosopher Immanuel Kant might hold that it is wrong to use an animal merely as a means; that is, as an instrument to further one's goals. However, the applications of genome editing under consideration wouldn't involve using the animal merely as a means, since the aim would (also) be to improve the animal's welfare. Thus, the animal would also be treated 'as an end in itself'. This seems more respectful to the animal than current practices in factory farms that usually only take the animal's welfare into account insofar as it affects the quantity or quality of meat, dairy, and eggs that can be produced.

Another concept that comes up in debates about respect for animals is that of 'telos', which refers to the innate purpose or goal of an individual or being. The American philosopher, Bernard Rollin, famously applied this concept to animals. Rollin understands telos as "the unique, evolutionary-determined, genetically-encoded, environmentally-shaped set of needs and interests which characterize the animal in question—the 'pigness' of the pig, the 'dogness' of the dog, and so on".[3] According to Rollin, we disrespect an animal when we prevent it from realizing its telos. But producing hornless cows and disease-resistant pigs could be done in ways that do not make the cows any less cowish, and the pigs any less piggish, compared to their non-gene-edited variants. In the case of hornless cows, the cow would be hornless anyway, but as a result of a painful disbudding procedure.

Perhaps the contrast between the genetically altered cow and the farm cow today, misses the point. Perhaps we should instead simply be imagining and arguing for a world without factory farms? This brings us to the last, but, in my view, most important concern about genome editing in livestock.

A Technological Fix

Some may object to creating disease-resistant or resilient pigs and hornless cows, not because genome editing in itself is wrong, or because this would be disrespectful to the animals, but because it is *the wrong kind* of solution. Some may worry that it would be merely 'a technological fix' that superficially tackles the symptoms of the problem, while failing to address the 'real' or 'underlying' problem (e.g. our maltreatment of animals, or the social and economic structures that pull us towards factory farming).

Is this a convincing objection?

It's certainly true that creating, for example, disease-resistant pigs doesn't solve the more general problem of our exploitative attitude towards pigs, and livestock in general. But we accept many technological fixes that don't address the underlying problem. Cholesterol-lowering drugs don't solve the problem of unhealthy eating habits; a filter in a smokestack of a polluting factory doesn't address the existence of polluting factories. As long as one is clear about the target of a particular technological fix, it doesn't seem all that problematic that it only solves a narrow problem, or part of a problem, without addressing the 'real' or 'underlying' problem.

Perhaps the concern is not only that genome editing does not address the real or underlying problem, but that it might actually entrench the problem that it was meant to fix. A quote by an organic farmer expresses this worry:

> If gene editing is being used for disease resistance and it is not encouraging companies to change the way they keep their pigs so they don't get the disease in the first place, then it becomes a problem rather than a solution.[4]

The idea seems to be that genome editing to produce disease-resistant pigs will remove incentives to move towards a morally preferable solution to the spread of infectious disease, namely keeping pigs further apart.

An additional concern may be that not only will genome editing remove incentives to keep pigs further apart, it will also diminish incentives to abandon factory farms altogether. It could then be said that genome editing in livestock makes us complicit in ethically problematic agricultural systems that contribute to global problems, such as massive animal suffering, pollution, spread of infectious disease in animals and humans, and climate change. It takes us further from the ideal solution, which would be to get rid of factory farms altogether.

Nevertheless, at least two questions arise. First, can genome editing be expected to slow down the transition to better solutions, and second, if so, is this sufficient reason to justify not pursuing it?

Whether genome editing would slow down the transition to better solutions is an empirical question that is difficult to answer. Pigs are kept in close confinement for several reasons. At present, the threat of disease doesn't seem to be an effective incentive for keeping animals in factory farms further apart, so it seems unlikely that making them disease resistant would affect how they are housed.

How about incentives to move away from factory farming altogether? This is even more difficult to assess. It is a matter of time before factory farms cause a new pandemic, perhaps one that is even worse than Covid-19. If there is one thing that may stop factory farming, it is the fear of such a pandemic. But if genome editing prevents infectious disease in livestock, we would no longer have such a fear. And so, the argument runs, we would lose the main rationale for reducing our dependence on factory farming.

There is certainly something to this point. And the point is also somewhat specific to genome editing. Though there is some chance that *any* measure to improve animal wellbeing—even, say, providing larger cages for chickens—might delay the abolition of factory farms, the risk seems greater with genome editing. Providing larger cages goes much more against the spirit of factory farming. It comes much closer to what it would be like if animals were not contained in factory farms. Genome editing could be 'accused' of going along with the practice of factory farming—of facilitating it. This may entail more risk that it will indeed slow down a transition to alternative agricultural practices.

However, the effects of genome editing on incentives to move away from or towards factory farming are uncertain, and it seems reasonable to choose to pursue genome editing to almost certainly prevent disease, and thus a pandemic, rather than relying on the hope that the risk of a pandemic *may* motivate a move away from factory farms. Moreover, even if genome editing would *certainly* delay the abolition of factory farms, this is not necessarily a conclusive argument against pursuing it. For the same reasoning would suggest it was wrong to improve the welfare of slaves in the United States in the 18th and 19th centuries, which may have delayed the abolition of slavery. Even if it did delay abolition, we surely think that it was morally justifiable, even obligatory, to improve the slaves' lives whenever that was feasible.

Ideally, we should try to improve animal welfare when we can, and simultaneously support a move away from factory farms (at least factory farms as we know them now) through other means. For example, we could combine genome editing with higher taxes for meat, dairy, and eggs, or with financial and institutional support for the production of lab-grown meat.

Conclusion

Genome editing in livestock is around the corner. At least some applications seem to offer a win–win for the farmers and the animals. We considered the use of genome editing to produce hornless dairy cows or disease-resistant/resilient pigs. Concerns about overstepping some divine or natural boundary are unconvincing as it is difficult to find an interpretation of 'unnatural' such that unnaturalness is morally problematic *and* applies to the applications of genome editing under consideration but not to other practices that we accept. Safety concerns can be met by proceeding carefully with the research and the translation of this research to the practice. Concerns about disrespect for animals are also not strong enough to ground an objection to genome editing as the applications under consideration would (also) use the animals as an end in themselves, and would respect the animals' telos, at least to the same extent as current factory farming. Finally, the 'technological fix' objection raises the important point that we need to keep the bigger picture in mind. However, it is not clear that genome editing to produce hornless cows and disease-resistant or resilient pigs would move us away from morally preferable solutions. Even if they did, the best thing to do is to improve animal welfare *and* support measures that move us closer to a morally preferable solution, such as the abolition of factory farms.

I conclude that we should support research into applications of genome editing that would be to the benefit of both humans and animals, but that it is important to proceed cautiously. Simultaneously, we should do what we can to transform farming practices in other ways that improve animals' lives and reduce environmental damage.

Further Reading

Rollin, B., *The Frankenstein Syndrome: Ethical and Social Issues in the Genetic Engineering of Animals* (Cambridge University Press, 1995).

Notes

1. X. de Paz, PRRS cost for the European swine industry. Pig.333.com, 17 August 2015. https://www.pig333.com/articles/prrs-cost-for-the-european-swine-industry_10069/ (accessed 27 June 2020).
2. CRISPR is short for clustered regularly interspaced short palindromic repeats; Cas9 is a protein. CRISPR-Cas9 is typically used in an early embryo *in vitro* or in a fibroblast that is subsequently inserted into an enucleated cow egg by means of a cloning technique. The technology is popular because it is very precise, relatively simple, and cheap.

3. B. E. Rollin, Animal welfare, science and value, *Journal of Agricultural and Environmental Ethics*, Suppl. 2 (1993), 44–50.

4. P. Ghosh, Gene-edited farm animals are on their way, *BBC News*, 22 June 2018. https://www.bbc.co.uk/news/science-environment-44388038 (accessed 28 June 2020).

21

Brain Stimulation and Identity

Jonathan Pugh

Sam is a 63-year-old man living with Parkinson's Disease, a neuro-logical disease which causes severe motor impairments. He is a good candidate for a neurosurgical treatment called Deep Brain Stimula-tion (DBS). This treatment would involve Sam undergoing a neuro-surgical operation, in which electrodes would be implanted into an area of his brain that is malfunctioning. These electrodes would be connected to another implanted device that could be programmed to deliver low levels of electrical stimulation to Sam's brain. His doctor tells Sam that although there are some physical and psychological risks associated with this procedure, it has a good safety record, and has helped thousands of patients in his situation.

Sam agrees to undergo the procedure, and is delighted to discover that his motor impairments are significantly reduced when his doctors turn on the stimulation. He leaves the clinic very happy with the procedure.

However, at his one year follow-up, he tells his doctor that although the stimulation is still reducing his motor impairments, he has also noted some psychological changes, and that he feels like 'a different person' following treatment. He has become emotionally volatile and developed a new gambling habit, sustaining significant debts. His wife confirms these changes, and notes that it has placed a significant strain on their relationship. The doctor suggests that Sam is one of the extremely rare cases in which DBS may be associated with adverse psychological effects, and she recommends that they try ceasing Sam's stimulation. Sam agrees, and within a week he notices that his urge to gamble has subsided, but his motor impairments have returned.

*

Following substantial advances in our understanding of the brain, surgeons and neuroscientists have been able to develop powerful new medical interventions that aim to treat disease by modifying electrical activity in the brain. At present, Deep Brain Stimulation (DBS) is the most precise tool that we have at our disposal in this regard; it can target a cubic millimeter of brain tissue. In terms of precision, it stands in stark contrast to drugs that influence brain activity by affecting neurotransmitters across the brain. However, despite its precision, in some rare cases, DBS can have unintended side-effects. The example above is based on a real case[1]—elsewhere, there have been reports of patients exhibiting other behavioral and emotional changes following DBS, such as hypersexuality. Moreover, DBS is increasingly being investigated as an experimental treatment for psychiatric disorders, in which the express purpose of the treatment may be to modify the patient's emotional and motivational states. For instance, DBS might potentially be used to alleviate clinical depression, to reduce the compulsive behaviours of a patient with Obsessive Compulsive Disorder, or to lead an anorexic patient to engage in healthy eating behaviours.

As technology and understanding advances further, we might be able to exert even finer grained control over these states. To suppose that you could influence a person's behavior or emotional states simply by electronically stimulating the brain may appear somewhat far-fetched. Yet, there has been some progress in this general area, and the possibility of controlling motivational and emotional states has intrigued scientists since the earliest days of invasive neurostimulation.

However, this prospect raises profound ethical questions, regardless of whether such changes are intentional or an unintended side-effect of treatment. To what extent does it make sense to say that a medical intervention like DBS can change the recipient into 'a different person'? Why might that matter?

Concepts in moral philosophy can help us to answer these questions. Let's begin by thinking about the nature of identity and the self, and what someone might mean when they say that they have become a different person.

What Is a Person?

Perhaps, a natural place to start a philosophical enquiry about these questions is with so-called 'psychological theories' of personal identity. Think back to what you were like as a 14-year-old—whilst some readers' memories of that time may be hazier than others, hopefully you can recall a few things about what you were like then. Now consider the question, what is it that makes you the same person *now* as that 14-year-old?

The temptation is to say that you are the same person as the 14-year-old by virtue of the fact that you occupy the same physical body as the 14-year-old, even if it has undergone some significant changes. However, philosophers in the tradition of the British philosopher John Locke[2] have argued that occupying the same body is not really important for personal identity over time. Followers of John Locke stress the mental features of identity—that is to say, your identity-over-time with the 14-year-old requires that you maintain an overlapping chain of psychological connections; you are connected via a chain of shared memories, intentions, and desires, for example. Even if you are a little too old to remember much about what it was like to be a 14-year-old, perhaps you remember what it was like to be a 30-year-old. If, when you were a 30-year-old, you also remembered enough of what it was like to be the 14-year-old, then we might be able to draw a line of psychological continuity between those different points in time, in a manner that allows us to make sense of the idea that those points are different stages of the same person's life.

These psychological theories allow us to make sense of our intuitive reactions to familiar examples from science-fiction films involving 'body-switches', in which the consciousness of one character is transferred into another character's body. We tend to think that the identity of the character in these examples follows their consciousness, rather than staying with their body. However, on these psychological theories, if an individual's mental states change so much that we can notice a rupture in the chain of psychological connections over time, then it can make sense to say that the individual has ceased to exist, and become a completely different person. We might say that someone with a neurodegenerative disease (such as Alzheimer's Disease, which causes significant and wide-ranging changes to a large number of the individual's mental states) has become a new person in this way.

Regardless of the merits of these psychological theories of identity, it is not clear that they get to the crux of the concerns of a patient like Sam. Changes to identity on these psychological theories require wide-ranging changes to what we might call the individual's overall psychological economy, that is, the overall combination of the many mental states that together constitute personal identity on psychological theories. The limited scope of the changes to particular behavioral and emotional traits in Sam's case are not significant enough to threaten identity in the manner that the psychological theorist conceives of it. Since treatment has not significantly affected Sam's memories, he will retain significant psychological continuity with the pre-treatment Sam, even though he now displays some new character traits. The psychological theory thus cannot give us a theoretical explanation of Sam's sense that he has 'become a different person'.

Part of the reason for this is that philosophers like Locke use the psychological theory of identity to answer questions that are quite different to the concerns of someone like Sam. They are interested in the *metaphysical* question of what fundamentally constitutes a particular person as they persist over time. However, our concerns about identity are often quite different from this metaphysical question. This point is familiar from characters who undergo significant changes in film and literature. Consider the film *The Godfather*; we don't doubt that Michael Corleone is metaphysically the same person at the beginning of the film as the person at the end of the story. However, there is still a sense in which we nonetheless think that Michael has become a different person over the course of the film, changing from a quiet, heroic young man who renounces his family's criminal connections, to a ruthless mobster who is willing to kill anyone who stands in his way.[3]

One way of putting this is to say that we might be interested in 'who' Michael Corleone is at the end of the film, rather than 'what' he is in the strictly metaphysical sense.[4]

The Self—Who Is This Person?

Some philosophers have denied the existence of a unified self that persists over time. David Hume famously claimed that the self is nothing more than a bundle of our on-going perceptions.[5] However, it is a concept that is deeply rooted in our folk psychology. We use the terminology of the 'self' quite commonly in our day-to-day lives—you might, for instance, say that someone is 'back to their normal self' when they have recovered from a cold, or that you are 'not quite yourself today' when apologizing to a friend for being irritable. But, despite the common usage of the term, even those philosophers who agree that we can coherently speak of a unified self have understood the concept to mean quite different things. These different interpretations can have important implications for our understanding of cases like Sam and Michael Corleone.

We might begin by thinking about the self in very broad terms to encompass *all* of our emotional, behavioral, and cognitive traits. Indeed, we might extend the concept of self even further to incorporate non-psychological features, such as our physical characteristics; perhaps our self is partly constituted by our body. Such a broad model of the self can be useful for allowing us to illuminate all of the different kinds of impact that a medical treatment might have. Although the dramatic behavioral changes we see in Sam's case are striking, medical treatment can involve other smaller changes. For instance, like any invasive surgical procedure, DBS will leave the patient with a scar, and it may lead to minor side-effects like headaches and nausea. However, it is somewhat trivial to claim that DBS may change the self on this broad conception; this broader conception does not seem to do justice to the idea that there is something special about the changes that Sam reports. Although a scar changes the body, we may be reluctant to claim that it involves a change to who the person is, in the sense that Sam means.

Accordingly, we would do better to adopt a narrower conception of the self, one that distinguishes peripheral elements (that can be changed with little cause for moral concern) from elements that constitute the person's 'true self'. On such an approach, we should only be concerned if DBS threatens the person's true self. Why might changes to the true self be particularly significant? Well, it might be claimed that failing to live in accordance with this 'true self' is bad for a person's well-being. Second, it might be claimed that we should only respect a person's choices if they reflect the person's true self.

But how do we determine what constitutes a person's true self? One approach suggests that we each have a number of core characteristics that together constitute the essence of who we are, an essence that we cannot change, and that we must live in accordance with in order to live authentically, to be 'who we really are'. On this essentialist view, if one of Sam's core characteristics prior to treatment was that he was a careful, prudent individual who always put his family first, then the changes resulting from DBS treatment would be cause for concern.

However, the essentialist position is controversial. Even philosophers who reject David Hume's skeptical view may still be loath to claim that we each have some deep essence that is there waiting for us to discover. Were such a thing to exist, it is not clear how we are to identify which elements of a person's character constitute this true essence—for instance, how can we tell whether the true essence of Michael Corleone is that which is evidenced in the quiet war hero we see at the beginning of *The Godfather*, or in the ruthless criminal we see at the end?

Finally, it is also not clear why there is any moral value in acting in accordance with this essentialist conception of the self, or why we should only respect a person's choices if they flow from these core characteristics—indeed, it seems quite possible that one might not like one's core features, and might welcome the fact that they had changed. Some individuals living with certain psychiatric diseases sometimes identify very strongly with their disease—for instance, an anorexic patient might say that her anorexia is a crucial part of 'who she is', and that she would be a different person if she were not anorexic, even whilst recognizing that it would be good to receive treatment for her condition.[6] So, on this approach, the fact that Sam says that he feels like a different person may mean that something significant has happened to him, but it does not entail that he must take this to be a bad thing.

An alternative approach to understanding the self, which draws on themes from existentialist philosophy, claims that the self is a far more dynamic concept, something that we continually create and mold in accordance with our values. On this approach, the question of whether a change to our psychology is compatible with our true self depends on whether we endorse that change. For instance, in Sam's case, a great deal may turn on what Sam himself thinks of his new behaviours, and whether they are intelligible to him. If Sam is horrified by his gambling and distraught that his marriage is falling apart it would seem plausible to suggest that these behaviours are in some sense alien to him. In contrast, if Sam embraces his gambling, perhaps as part of a new zeal for life he has gained after finally being free from his motor impairment, then it is far less clear that the changes amount to him becoming a different person in a morally significant sense.

Such existentialist-inspired theories can offer a straightforward explanation of why inauthentic changes might matter; if they are not endorsed by the agent, then they are likely to be experienced negatively, and on some accounts of autonomy, the agent may not be autonomous with respect to the behaviours that they do not endorse. However, the precise implications of these theories for people like Sam turns a great deal on the sort of endorsement that they require. In the above example, we considered a scenario in which Sam either did or did not embrace his behavioral changes after treatment. But why suppose that his endorsement at this point speaks for Sam's true self? Perhaps there is a case for claiming that it does if the endorsement is grounded in a set of values that Sam has held for a great deal of time already, and which he can now use to articulate the endorsement of his new behaviours. However, what if Sam's endorsement appeals to a set of values that themselves appear to be very different to those that we would have expected from Sam prior to surgery? Suppose that prior to surgery, Sam clearly valued his life as a committed family man and that he extolled the virtues of financial prudence. If after surgery, he claimed to now value a life of spontaneity, in which the thrill of gambling takes precedence over his relationships, then it might seem tempting to claim that DBS has directly changed both Sam's values and his behavior, and that no matter how much he now endorses the changes, this is just 'not Sam'.

However, there are two problems with this line of argument. First, it is not easy to establish whether the DBS caused the change of values or behavior. The reason for this is that there is a host of other causal factors that could be contributing to the changes in question; rather than directly inducing these changes, DBS might be causing these changes only indirectly, by virtue of the fact that it has relieved Sam from a chronic health problem.[7] Successful treatment for a chronic health problem can lead to significant behavioral and emotional changes in some patients, as they rebuild their lives and cope with the so-called 'burden of normality'.[8]

Second, even if we could establish that DBS was directly causing the changes in question, it is not clear why this should preclude the possibility that the changes could be authentic. In Sam's case, the changes in question were an unintended side-effect of treatment; as such, part of the problem is that he did not fully authorize the changes to his behavior and values, even if he was aware of the risks that this might occur following surgery. However, some individuals who have undergone substantial changes to their behavior, emotional states, and values may be in a very different position. For instance, in psychiatric applications of DBS, the therapeutic aim of treatment may well be to change dysfunctional emotional or motivational states. Looking further forward, there may be a time where it is possible for people to choose to use forms of neurostimulation to intentionally fine-tune their own behavioral and emotional states.

If living authentically is a matter of self-creation (as the existentialist claims), then why should the means that people use in order to mold their characters have any bearing on whether or not the changes they bring about are authentic? Indeed, if a person makes an informed choice to bring about significant changes to their emotional and motivational traits using neurostimulation, such a change could be far more intelligible to the person than the subconscious forces that conventionally mold a person's character traits in their social environment. Perhaps then, a person might choose to use extreme methods to change themselves quite significantly, without becoming a different person in any morally significant sense.

So what of Sam? What matters most for the question of whether Sam has changed as a person is not what he now *does*, but what he now values. In cases where patients clearly retain the same values after treatment but exhibit new (and perhaps even unwelcome) behavioral traits, it is plausible to say that we are talking about the same person, even if such patients might describe themselves as 'having become a different person'. So, if Sam knows that continued stimulation will mean that the new behaviours will also continue, then we can sensibly hold him accountable for those behaviours, if he chooses to continue stimulation on the basis of values he held prior to surgery; perhaps being able to move freely has always been one of the most important things in his life. However, it is also true that a person can change some of their values over time and still retain their identity, if the nature of the change is endorsed by the person, and the process of change is intelligible to them by virtue of other values and beliefs that the person has retained across the change. So, if Sam chose to continue stimulation after his follow-up, and to continue gambling on the basis of an apparently new 'lust for life', we can make sense of him being the same person if he now endorses his new outlook on life and how he came to have it.

Further Reading

Levy, N., *Neuroethics* (Cambridge University Press, 2007).

Notes

1. H. M. M. Smeding et al., Pathological gambling after bilateral subthalamic nucleus stimulation in Parkinson disease, *Journal of Neurology, Neurosurgery & Psychiatry*, 78/5 (1 May 2007), 517–19, https://doi.org/10.1136/jnnp.2006.102061.
2. J. Locke, *An Essay Concerning Human Understanding* (Clarendon Press, 1975).
3. F. Ford Coppola, *The Godfather* (Paramount Pictures, Alfran Productions, 1972).
4. M. Schechtman, *The Constitution of Selves* (Cornell University Press, 1996).
5. D. Hume, *A Treatise of Human Nature*, 2nd ed., with text revised and variant readings by P. H. Nidditch (Clarendon Press, 1978).
6. J. Tan et al., Competence to make treatment decisions in anorexia nervosa: Thinking processes and values, *Philosophy, Psychiatry, & Psychology*, 13/4 (2006), 267–82.
7. J. Pugh et al., Evidence-based neuroethics, deep brain stimulation and personality—deflating, but not bursting, the bubble, *Neuroethics*, December 2018.
8. F. Gilbert, The burden of normality: From "chronically ill" to "symptom free". *New Ethical Challenges for Deep Brain Stimulation Postoperative Treatment*, 1 July 2012, 408–12.

Future Death

22

What Is Death?

Mackenzie Graham

In early 2019, a group of scientists from Yale University partially restored function to the brains of 32 pigs which had been dead for four hours.[1] Using a system called BrainEx to provide the pig brain cells with a hemoglobin-based solution, they found that the cells began to consume oxygen and glucose, and produce CO_2—signs of brain-wide metabolism restarting. Further, they found that some cells could still fire, suggesting that, at least in principle, these cells remained capable of neural activity.

The pig brains did not show any signs of the sort of organised activity necessary for consciousness, and researchers were prepared to administer anesthesia and lower the brains' temperature in case any evidence of awareness began to emerge. Nevertheless, their results challenge fundamental assumptions about how the brain responds to the loss of oxygen. What was assumed to be the irreversible loss of brain cell function may one day turn out to be not so irreversible.

Most of us would be confident in saying that these pigs were no longer alive, despite the restoration of some activity in their brain cells. But we might be less confident about *why* we feel this way. The bright line between life and death has been blurred by advances in science and technology. What does it mean for an organism to die, including organisms like us?

History of Death

For much of human history, determining death was a straightforward process. When illness or injury caused the irreversible loss of heart, lung, or brain function, their mutual interdependence meant that the other vital functions would inevitably cease within a matter of minutes. A physician could declare a patient dead simply by showing the absence of a heartbeat, breathing, or reaction of the eye to light (a proxy for brain function).

The introduction of new medical procedures in the 1950s, including mechanical ventilation and cardiopulmonary resuscitation (CPR), meant that a person whose heart had stopped beating, or lungs had stopped breathing, could be kept alive. Patients who had sustained brain damage that would have been fatal in the past could have circulation and breathing maintained artificially. These patients presented a problem for the traditional understanding of death because they had irreversibly lost some vital functions, but not others. To classify these patients as alive or dead, a new definition of death was required.

Death Defined

To understand the nature of human death, we must begin by defining the concept: what is it for any living thing to die? Having answered this metaphysical question, we can move to an epistemological one: what is the appropriate standard for judging that something has met the definition of death? Finally, we require criteria and tests to affirm that the epistemological standard has been met: when can we confidently say that someone is dead?

The most widely accepted definition of death is that it is 'the irreversible loss of functioning of the organism as a whole'. Two features of this definition are worth emphasizing. The first is that death is a unitary phenomenon. Organisms are living things which are made up of constituent parts of varying degrees of complexity (e.g. cells, tissues, organs). Organisms function as an integrated unit of these constituent parts, exhibiting properties which are not reducible to the properties of the individual parts. The life status of the organism as a whole is different from that of its constituent parts. An organism can survive the death of some of its parts or die while some of its parts remain alive.

The second feature of the organismic definition is that death is a biological phenomenon common to all organisms. Whether an organism is a tree, an insect, a whale, or a human, the word 'dead' has the same meaning: the irreversible loss of functioning of the organism as a whole. As we will see, both features—the biological and the unitary—pose difficulties for the various standards of death.

The Whole-Brain Standard and the Circulatory-Respiratory Standard

By the 1960s, a growing proportion of the medical and scholarly community considered patients that had lost all brain function but were being sustained using artificial means to be truly dead. In 1968, an ad hoc committee of the Harvard Medical School proposed a set of neurological criteria for death. According to these criteria, a patient who had sustained irreversible cessation of all functions of the entire brain was dead, even as heart and lung function persisted.

This 'whole-brain standard' for death received rapid uptake by the medical and legal communities, partly because it provided a way to lawfully withdraw physiological support in hopeless cases, and also because it had the potential to increase the number of suitable candidates for organ donation. Despite continued debate in the academic community about whether brain death is equivalent to human death, it remains the *de facto* standard in most developed countries.

It was only years after the neurological criteria for death were proposed that the organismic definition was offered by philosophers as a justification for this standard. After whole-brain death (or after the death of the brain stem) the body can no longer be sustained as an integrated organism, even with the aid of technology. Thus, the irreversible loss of functioning of the whole brain (or the brain stem) is sufficient for the irreversible loss of functioning of the organism as a whole. In some jurisdictions, the traditional circulatory-respiratory standard (i.e. the irreversible loss of heart and lung function) also remains a valid standard for determining death in addition to the neurological standard.

However, evidence accumulated over the last several decades has cast doubt on the claim that a functioning brain is necessary for the integrated functioning of a human organism. Most of the brain's functions are not directed towards the integration of the organism, and most of the body's integrative functions are not mediated by the brain—and have been found to be possessed by at least some patients satisfying the whole-brain standard for death. These integrative functions include: homeostasis (the balancing of chemical conditions in the body), elimination of cellular wastes, energy balance, maintenance of body temperature, wound healing, fighting of infections, and response to painful stimulation.[2]

Two widely publicized cases exemplify this weakness in the whole-brain standard. Jahi McMath was a 13-year-old girl who suffered severe neurological damage following complications from a tonsillectomy in 2013, and was declared brain-dead. While she initially fulfilled all standard criteria for a diagnosis of brain death, McMath eventually began showing signs that her hypothalamus—the portion of the brain responsible for regulating organ function through hormones—continued to function. Court records indicate that beginning eight months after her injury, she began to undergo puberty. After a legal decision granting her release from hospital, McMath continued to survive at an undisclosed location until 2018.

Marlise Munoz was a 33-year-old woman who was 14 weeks pregnant when she sustained devastating neurological damage from a pulmonary embolism. Munoz also fulfilled the standard neurological criteria for death but was sustained on life-support in accordance with state law. She continued to carry her fetus for an additional eight weeks before being removed from life support. While rare, there have been dozens of recorded cases in which a viable child has been delivered via caesarean section from a mother satisfying the neurological criteria for death.[3]

It will strike many of us as odd, at the very least, that a child could go through puberty, or a woman gestate a fetus, if they were *really* dead. Does this mean we need to abandon the whole-brain standard? It is possible that a proportion of patients that satisfy the clinical criteria for brain death have not sustained irreversible cessation of function of the whole brain. By expanding the clinical criteria for brain death to include testing for functions not currently assessed— such as a functioning hypothalamus—we can avoid cases like Jahi McMath, who seemed to maintain integrative function despite satisfying the criteria for brain death.

But there is a more serious objection to the whole-brain standard, namely that the human organism does not begin its existence with a brain. The basic structures of the brain, along with the spinal cord, appear roughly four weeks after fertilization. Surely this is a living human organism prior to four weeks, which suggests that although the brain is an important part of the human organism, it is not essential for integrated functioning.

In an effort to address these worries, proponents of the whole-brain standard have offered alternative formulations, according to which death is defined as the 'permanent cessation of the *critical* functions of the organism as a whole', and the corresponding standard as 'the permanent cessation of the *critical* functions of the whole brain'.[4] Given the kind of complex organism human beings are, the critical functions of our organism are brain-controlled respiration and brain-regulated circulation, the capacity for wakefulness, and the capacity for self-awareness. A human being dies upon losing all these critical functions.

Critical Functions

This revised standard seems promising, insofar as it picks out just those functions which seem essential to human life. Even if the brain does not mediate every integrating function of the human organism, the fact that it is central to the most important functions of the human body suggests that a functioning whole brain is essential to human life.

Nevertheless, the revised standard has weaknesses. By defining human death in terms of the critical functions of the human organism, the revised standard shifts from a biological claim about what functions are essential to organismic functioning, to a value judgement about which functions are important or critical for human life. Why should we think that functions not mediated by the brain, such as hormone regulation or fighting infection, are any less critical to organismic functioning than respiration or awareness? Who has the authority to determine these critical functions? And supposing we could reach a societal consensus on those functions that are critical for a human life, these functions may not overlap perfectly with the whole-brain standard.

One might go a step further and argue that determining the critical functions of the human organism is a matter of individual choice; people should be free to choose for themselves when they are dead.

But to do so would be to treat the moment of death as a matter of convention, rather than a biological fact. It could also lead to strange circumstances in which a person is left in limbo, neither alive nor dead, as relatives attempt to determine an appropriate standard of death, or where a person declared dead could be 'brought back to life' simply by crossing a jurisdictional boundary with a different standard of death.

The Higher-Brain Standard

One might think that there is an important difference between the death of the *body*, and the death of the *person*. When one loses the capacity for consciousness, and all the important human capacities which consciousness underlies (e.g. reason, imagination, emotion, autonomy, communication), this constitutes the end of our psychological lives, and thus, the death of the person. Accordingly, the appropriate standard for death is the irreversible loss of the capacity for consciousness. This typically occurs after the destruction of the cortex, the part of the brain responsible for 'higher' brain functions.

On some interpretations, the capacity for consciousness is essential to our continued existence because we are essentially persons (i.e. 'person essentialism'). Personhood requires the capacity for relatively complex forms of consciousness, including self-awareness and reasoning. When we lose the capacity for consciousness, we lose these essential capacities and cease to exist as persons. On other interpretations, we are essentially 'minds'—beings with the capacity for consciousness—and we die when we lose this basic psychological capacity (i.e. 'mind essentialism').

The higher-brain standard has radical implications. For example, patients in a permanent vegetative state—who retain sufficient brain-stem function to allow spontaneous breathing and heartbeat, and who go through sleeping and waking cycles—as well as patients in irreversible coma, would be considered dead because they lack the capacity for consciousness. Moreover, on a person-essentialist view, someone who suffers from severe dementia and eventually loses the capacity for the complex forms of consciousness necessary for personhood, will cease to exist at some time before their progression into coma. Similarly, because infants lack the capacity for complex consciousness, person-essentialism suggests that you came into existence at a time *after* your physical birth.

Conversely, if human beings are essentially minds, what is the precise relationship between 'us' and our associated human organism? We cannot be identical to our organism because it can survive without us, as in the case of patients in a coma or permanent vegetative state. (This also implies that the very definition of death is different for organisms, and for persons/minds.) Perhaps we are 'constituted' by our organism, in the way that a statue is constituted by pieces of bronze without being identical to them.[5] On this view, I am essentially a thing that can attribute first-person thoughts to myself, such as "I wonder what *I* will have for dinner", or "I wish *I* could buy a new car." But our organisms can presumably think such first-person thoughts too, given that they have functioning brains. If they can, this implies that there are two first-person thinkers in one organism, and we can't be sure which one *we* are.

Irreversible or Permanent?

Determining the precise time of death is most often discussed as an ethical issue in the context of organ donation. It is a widely accepted ethical norm that organs must only be procured from donors after they have been declared dead (the so-called 'dead donor rule'). The majority of organ donation occurs after the donor has been declared dead according to neurological criteria, but as many as 40% of donations in some countries occur after a declaration of death using the circulatory-respiratory standard. When the patient's heart has stopped, indicating that circulation has ceased, the physician must wait to ensure that the heart will not spontaneously restart (i.e. 'autoresuscitation') before pronouncing death. This is argued to be sufficient to ensure cessation of both circulation and, by proxy, cessation of brain function. The time required to rule out autoresuscitation is controversial, and recommended wait times range from as little as 2 to 5 minutes in the United States to as much as 20 minutes in Italy.[6] This wait time is critical, as every second risks damage to the organs.

However, there is a worry that these donors may not be truly dead. First, 2 to 5 minutes may not be sufficient to ensure that autoresuscitation will not occur. Moreover, the growing adoption of procedures like normothermic regional perfusion—mechanically supplying oxygenated blood to preserve organs for transplant—poses serious complications for existing standards of death. These procedures use what is called 'extracorporeal membrane oxygenation' (ECMO) to recover donor blood, oxygenate it, remove carbon dioxide, and return it to the donor's body, to maintain circulation after the donor has been declared dead. A clamp or inflatable device is used to direct blood flow from the heart and prevent circulation to the brain. Yet the fact that circulation is restored clearly shows that the cessation of circulation was not irreversible. There is also a risk of inadvertent blood flow to the brain, which could revive the donor.[7]

A popular line of argument in response to this worry is to interpret 'irreversible cessation' as 'permanent cessation'.[8] Permanent cessation means that the function will not be restored because it will neither return spontaneously, nor will resuscitation efforts be attempted. In the case of normothermic regional perfusion using ECMO, provided there continues to be a permanent loss of brain function, the donor is considered dead.

However, permanence is not an acceptable replacement for irreversibility in the case of organ donation. In day-to-day practice, physicians regularly declare death before they can know that the loss of circulation is irreversible because the difference between 'dying' and 'dead' is immaterial; nothing of consequence will happen to the patient prior to the cessation of circulation becoming irreversible. However, when the minutes immediately following the loss of circulation involve surgical incision and removal of vital organs, the difference between 'dying' and 'dead' is critical.

Moreover, the distinction between alive and dead is an ontological one, describing two different states of the world. Which state a person is in cannot be dependent on the intentions of others, as the permanence condition suggests. Suppose a person suffers a heart attack and collapses, and no one nearby can perform CPR. Assuming they will not autoresuscitate, this person is dead on the permanence condition. But if a doctor should happen by, and agrees to perform CPR, the person is no longer dead, but merely dying, although nothing about their physical condition has changed. This is nonsensical.

Death and Death Behaviours

Understanding human death is not as straightforward as it appears. Despite widespread acceptance in the legal and medical community, the whole-brain standard of death does not cohere with biological reality. Yet if we abandon this standard, and take up the view that human death refers to the death of a person or mind instantiated by the 'higher-brain', we are led to highly counter-intuitive conclusions about who is dead and who is not.

I think the organismic definition of death is ultimately sound: a human being has died when the integrated functioning of the organism as a whole has irreversibly ceased. The death of the whole brain does not appear sufficient to meet this requirement; patients meeting the criteria for whole-brain death are severely damaged human organisms, but they are not truly dead. The circulatory standard seems to be the most plausible standard for determining human death. Unlike any functions of the brain, the irreversible cessation of circulation will inevitably lead to the cessation of the organism as a whole. Thus, at the moment circulation irreversibly ceases, the human organism is dead.

Unfortunately, this means that we cannot be *exactly* sure when a person has died, because we have no means of precisely determining when the cessation of circulation has become irreversible. It might even be theoretically possible that circulation irreversibly ceases prior to the death of the brain, meaning that a person could be biologically dead, but still conscious. This is essentially the worry presented by the pig brains in the introductory case. I argue that in such a case, the organism is dead, but a part of it (albeit a highly complex one) continues to function; transplanting an organ from a deceased donor does not mean that the donor remains alive, although the organ continues to function.

It also means that most cases of organ donation—both after brain-death and circulatory-death—involve procuring organs from a donor who is not known to be dead. However, the biological reality of death does not entail that we must accept traditional assumptions about the moral significance of death. What is much more important than the moment of death itself is when it is appropriate to engage in certain 'death behaviours': when it is appropriate to begin mourning the loss of the person, when care can be withdrawn, when a married person becomes widowed, when inheritance or life insurance is conveyed, and when organs may be procured for donation, to name a few. Under normal circumstances, a family rightfully begins to grieve the death of a loved one as soon as they stop breathing and having a pulse. What is important to the family is probably not whether the person has irreversibly ceased to function as an organism, but rather that they will never again interact with that person. Thus, any discrepancy between death in the biological sense, and death in the conventional sense, is insignificant. Conversely, an emergency room physician rightfully engages in the 'death behavior' of halting efforts at resuscitation when it becomes clear that spontaneous circulation will not return, even though circulation has not yet *irreversibly* ceased.

In the case of organ donation, the relevant moral concern is not whether donation is the cause of the donor's biological death, but whether procurement harms the donor or violates their autonomy. Given that both donation after brain death and donation after circulatory death occur after the withdrawal of life-sustaining treatment, the donor's death is imminent regardless of whether donation occurs. Thus, it is difficult to see how the donor is harmed through procurement of their organs, provided the appropriate consent is given. In fact, there may be far fewer cases than we would expect where certainty about when a patient is *truly* dead is required, such as for legal (e.g. murder) or religious reasons. And unlike the case of organ donation, in these cases there is unlikely to be any time pressure preventing a cautious approach to confirming death.

Looking Forward

We began with the case of a pig brain having partial function restored four hours after the animal had died. From a technical standpoint, this technique could one day be adapted to humans. What would the capacity to 'restart' a human brain mean for our understanding of death? In one respect, I don't think it would mean much. Given that a functioning human brain is not essential to the functioning of the human organism, the ability to revive a human brain would not change who was biologically dead. However, it could significantly change our death behaviours. Would a family be willing to accept that a loved one satisfying the whole-brain standard for death be removed from a ventilator, if it were possible that their brain function could be restored? Could a patient's brain be removed after a declaration of death, and then revived so it could be studied for medical research? Careful thought will need to be given to these kinds of questions.

Scientific and technological advances may not only change what biological processes are irreversible, but also change what it means to be a human organism. Bionic devices, which replace or enhance human organs or parts with mechanical versions, already include cochlear implants to restore hearing, artificial hearts, bionic eyes,[9] and bionic arms[10] and legs.[11] If one day it becomes possible to replace much of our bodies with mechanical devices, integrating them into our organism, this may change what it means for the human organism to function as a whole, and what it means for this functioning to cease.

Finally, the possible development of new forms of being could also require a re-examination of what it means to be alive, and thus, what it means to die. For example, many experts accept that computers will eventually achieve human-like intelligence. If a computer became conscious, and had feelings and desires, would we say it was alive? How would this cohere with the organismic definition of death? And perhaps more importantly, what kinds of death behaviours would be appropriate for an entity like this?

Developments in medical technology have saved countless lives but have also made it much more difficult to determine when human life has ended. Given the complexity of human life, perhaps we should not be surprised at the complexity of human death.

May we all go peacefully in our sleep.

Further Reading

Bernat, J. L., Brain death and the definition of death. In J. Illes (ed.), *Neuroethics: Anticipating the Future* (Oxford University Press, 2017).

DeGrazia, D., The definition of death. In *The Stanford Encyclopedia of Philosophy*, https://plato.stanford.edu/entries/death-definition/.

Veatch, R. M. and Ross, L. F., *Defining Death: The Case for Choice* (Georgetown University Press, 2016).

Notes

1. Z. Vrselja, S. G. Daniele, J. Silbereis, F. Talpo, Y. M. Morozov, A. M. M. Sousa, et al., Restoration of brain circulation and cellular functions hours post-mortem, *Nature*, 568 (2019), 336–43.
2. D. A. Shewmon, The brain and somatic integration: Insights into the standard biological rationale for equating "brain death" with death, *The Journal of Medicine and Philosophy*, 26/5 (2001), 457–78.
3. M. Esmaeilzadeh, C. Dictus, E. Kayvanpour, F. Sedaghat-Hamedani, M. Eichbaum, S. Hofer, et al., One life ends, another begins: Management of a brain-dead pregnant mother—A systematic review, *BMC Medicine*, 8/74 (2010).
4. A. P. Huang and J. L. Bernat, The organism as a whole in an analysis of death, *The Journal of Medicine and Philosophy*, 44/6 (2019), 712–31.
5. L. R. Baker, *Persons and Bodies: A Constitution View* (Cambridge University Press, 2000).
6. M. Lomero, D. Gardiner, E. Coll, B. Haase-Kromwijk, F. Procaccio, F. Immer, et al., Donation after circulatory death today: An updated overview of the European landscape, *Transplant International*, 33/1 (2019), 76–88.
7. A. Manara, S. D. Shemie, S. Large, A. Healey, A. Baker, M. Badiwala, et al., Maintaining the permanence principle for death during in situ normothermic regional perfusion for donation after circulatory death organ recovery: A United Kingdom and Canada proposal, *American Journal of Transplantation*, 20/8 (2020), 2017–25.
8. J. L. Bernat, Point: Are donors after circulatory death really dead, and does it matter? Yes and yes, *Chest*, 138/1 (2010), 13–16.
9. E. Mullin, Blind patients to test bionic eye implant. *MIT Technology Review*, 2017. Available https://www.technologyreview.com/2017/09/18/149107/blind-patients-to-test-bionic-eye-brain-implants/.
10. M. Ortiz-Catalan, E. Mastinu, P. Sassu, O. Aszmann, and R. Branemark, Self-contained neuromusculoskeletal arm protheses, *New England Journal of Medicine*, 382 (2020), 1732–8.
11. F. M. Petrini, G. Valle, M. Bumbasirevic, F. Barberi, D. Bortolotti, P. Cvancara, et al., Enhancing functional abilities and cognitive integration of the lower limb prothesis, *Science Translational Medicine*, 11/512 (2019).

23

Should We Freeze Our Bodies for Future Resuscitation?

Francesca Minerva

In 2016, the story of an English girl (referred to in court as JS) who had died of cancer at the age of 14 was widely reported by the media. What attracted interest to her tragic death was the legal quarrel surrounding it. A few months before dying, JS had carried out an internet search looking for something that could offer her a glimmer of hope while she contemplated her mortality. She discovered that a few hundred people in the world had been "cryopreserved"—that is, fully immersed in liquid nitrogen at −196°C—in the hope that science will eventually discover a therapy for the disease that has killed them, and that future technology will succeed in bringing them back to life. Cryopreservation is usually performed soon after the heart has stopped beating, and after the individual has been pronounced legally dead. 'Cryonics' can only work if the lack of oxygen has not caused any brain damage, a process that starts only a few minutes after the heart stops pumping blood.

It works as follows. Soon after legal death has been pronounced, the blood circulation and respiration are restored, so as to keep the tissues intact. The body temperature is slowly lowered using ice-baths, and the blood is replaced with a special substance that prevents the formation of ice and the subsequent destruction of the cellular structure. Being immersed in liquid nitrogen is essential in order to prevent the body from continuing those metabolic processes that eventually cause decomposition. Ultimately, what cryonicists want to achieve is the preservation of the information stored in the individual's brain, because that information is, to a large extent, what makes each of us a unique individual with a distinctive set of ideas, memories, preferences, and mental states. According to the criterion for death shared by cryonicists (the so called "information-theoretic account of death"), death only occurs when the information stored in the brain is lost forever. Insofar as the information remains stored in the brain, even if the body is not functioning normally, a person is not dead, but rather "paused".

After searching the internet, JS, the young British girl, concluded that cryonics was her only chance to gain back a few more years of life, even though she knew that these extra years might only be returned in the remote future, if ever. Her mother immediately supported her request to be cryopreserved, but her father refused to grant her permission to choose cryonics as an alternative to the more traditional burial. Being underage, she needed her father's permission to be cryopreserved, so she eventually resorted to legal measures. The judge involved in her case, Mr Justice Peter Jackson, asked her to write a letter explaining why she wanted to undergo cryonics, and so she wrote: "I am only 14 years old and I don't want to die, but I know I am going to die. I think being cryopreserved gives me a chance to be cured and woken up—even in hundreds of years' time. I don't want to be buried underground. I want to live and live longer and I think that in the future they may find a cure for my cancer and wake me up. I want to have this chance. This is my wish."

Cryonics Is "Weird"

The desire of the girl to take a chance on cryonics is understandable, since the death of a person that young is undoubtedly a tragedy. We can all empathize with her desire to die with the hope of living again in the future, rather than with the knowledge that she will be gone forever.

Her father's scepticism towards cryonics is also understandable, at least insofar as it seems to be the most common reaction to cryonics, which is often labelled as "fictional", "crazy", or "weird", as a quick Google search can confirm.

Indeed, the root of many objections to cryonics seem to be its perceived weirdness. If we look at the history of other biotechnologies developed over the last fifty years, hostility towards what is new and "weird" is not surprising. For instance, the first heart transplant was performed in South Africa in 1967, and even though nobody is hostile to it now, it was initially considered a quite controversial intervention. The same goes for in vitro fertilization of human foetuses: in 1978 Louise Brown was born as the first "test-tube baby" in the world. Back then, many people opposed the idea that a baby could be "created in a laboratory", rather than conceived by her parents and, ultimately, by God. And yet it has been estimated that, since 1978, more than eight million babies have been born through IVF, suggesting that objections to the weirdness of the technology were quickly overcome once its usefulness became apparent.

So, we know from past experience that technologies perceived at first to be weird are not necessarily bad; and that the perception of what constitutes a weird technology can shift quickly over time. This might conceivably happen with cryonics if, for instance, more and more people decide to be cryopreserved, or if there is a major breakthrough in research providing more evidence of its feasibility.

Is Cryonics a Scam?

Another major objection to cryonics is that it's a waste of money, or a scam, i.e. a way to make money by promising dying people something that cannot possibly be achieved.

Like most new technologies, cryonics is not free, and is available only in the private sector without any state subsidization. The cost of cryopreservation is between $20,000 and $200,000, depending on whether the fee includes the transportation expenses, and other services, such as a contribution to a trust fund to be accessed once revived. The fact that cryonics is relatively expensive, though, does not per se prove that it is a scam, nor that it is a complete waste of money. What people mean when they say it's a scam, or a waste of money, is that it could not possibly succeed in bringing people back to life, so that paying for cryonics is paying for a service that will never yield any benefit.

At the moment, we don't know whether a cryopreserved body will ever be revived. The technologies currently available are not advanced enough to revive the people who are currently cryopreserved, and we can't predict if the necessary advancements will ever be achieved. More importantly, we can't know if scientists will ever be able to revive not only the body, but also a sufficient number of mental faculties for a revived person to be able to recognize themselves as the same individual who chose to be cryopreserved decades or centuries before. Without this continuity of mental faculties before and after cryopreservation, cryonics would be a rather useless technology that could do little more than ship a body from $Time_1$ to $Time_2$.

Uncertainty surrounding the possibility that cryonics will succeed may explain why many people are very suspicious about it, especially given the costs. However, the fact that we don't have such technologies right now doesn't mean that we won't have them in the future.

Cryonics as a Step towards Immortality

Most of the people who want to be cryopreserved and have signed a contract with a cryonics facility are not as young as the English girl whose case ended up in court. Her young age made a particularly compelling case for cryonics. But what about those who want to undergo cryonics after dying at a much older age? Why do they want to be cryopreserved? Would they not soon die of old age after they restarted living?

To understand what cryonics is, we need to see it as a component of a more ambitious project aimed at indefinitely extending human life-span. Many people choose to be cryopreserved because they want to extend their life via rejuvenating technologies that are not available yet but that might be developed at some point in the future. It is not clear yet how such technologies would work in practice, but some scientists believe it is possible—in principle—to turn back our biological clock. Given that many deadly diseases are caused by cellular ageing, indefinite life extension could be achieved by reversing or stopping this process. If indefinite life extension were achieved through cellular rejuvenation or other technologies, someone undergoing cryonics today could wake up in a future where their life expectancy would be much greater than today.

So, a person choosing cryonics is gambling a relatively large sum of money on a small chance of living indefinitely in the distant future, which is a bit like buying a rather expensive lottery ticket knowing that the chances of winning are extremely small, but that the prize would be exceptionally valuable.

Cryonics Is Selfish

Perhaps the decision to spend large sums of money on cryonics in the hope of extending one's own life indefinitely is reprehensible regardless of how likely cryonics is to succeed, and regardless of the number of life-years that could be gained. Perhaps such money should instead be donated to charities and used to help people who live in poverty.

Although this is quite a powerful objection, it is an objection that can be made against anyone spending money on non-necessary items. Most of the people who have spare money keep it for themselves and use it to make their lives more comfortable. So, if buying an expensive car is not immoral, then cryonics isn't either.

More importantly, if cryonics could help people to increase their life-span indefinitely, it would be inappropriate to compare it to a luxury good. It should, instead, be considered an investment in one's health, and we don't usually blame people for their selfishness when they spend money on healthcare, or when they choose to undergo expensive experimental treatments to gain a few more years of life.

Of course, cryonics might never work and so any money invested in it would not have a return for the person who paid, but this is also true for many other kinds of medical treatments. We usually accept that uncertainty is the hallmark of human existence. We can never know for sure if the time and the effort we put into building a career, or developing a relationship, will produce the results we hope for. In this sense, cryonics is not so dissimilar from other investments we make, though the degree of uncertainty about the outcome, as well as the magnitude of the outcome, is much higher than with other choices we make.

Life After Life Could Be Horrible

One could argue that cryonics is different from other investments that don't pay off because, even if everything proceeds as hoped, the outcome might still be negative overall.

We can imagine a scenario where the revived person has been successfully brought back to life and finds herself alive again after hundreds of years. Her new life could pose some unexpected difficulties that might make her regret the decision to undergo cryonics. For instance, she might struggle to feel happy in a world where she doesn't know anybody, and where everybody she used to know had died a long time before she was revived. If not many people opt for cryonics, then the few who do might feel isolated and lonely. There could be some people genetically related to her, some great-great-grand-children, but the connection would be very weak and perhaps not sufficient for these relatives to feel any genuine affection or interest towards her.

Moreover, the world and the people inhabiting it could be very different from how she remembered them. Let's imagine that some-one who had died just thirty years ago were brought back to life today: she would probably struggle to adapt to a digitalized world where the internet serves as the main medium through which we work, socialize, and entertain ourselves. To someone coming from the past, our dependency on our laptops and smartphones would look bizarre.

The differences between life today and life in a few hundred years could be even more profound, since biotechnologies might be used to radically engineer human DNA. Future humans might merge with machines, or perhaps they will be genetically modified to be much smarter than we are. Their emotions could be different as well, and so could the way they understand human relationships and perhaps even morality. If this were the case, it would be difficult for revived humans to interact with future humans, and it would be particularly difficult for meaningful relationships to be established between them; even basic interactions could then become difficult, even dangerous. If future humans weren't able to appreciate that the revived humans are intelligent and capable of experiencing pain and pleasure, or if they perceived them as a threat or as competitors for scarce resources, the revived ones could end up being abused, mistreated, or killed.

One could imagine numerous eventualities in which the life of a revived human turned out to be much worse than they expected, and perhaps not worth living. But they are not any more plausible than alternative outcomes where someone is revived and finds herself in a world that is much better than the one in which she got cryopreserved: future people might be nicer and more compassionate than current ones, and they might have discovered the secret to eternal happiness. Cryonics is also a gamble in this respect: at present nobody can tell which kind of scenario is more likely to come true. There is no particular reason to believe that the dystopian scenarios are more likely to materialize than the utopian ones.

Who Wants to Live Forever?

Philosophers have often argued that an immortal life would be necessarily bad—and it would be bad no matter how blissful the future world might be.

Bernard Williams,[1] for instance, believed that an indefinitely long life would be unbearable, because we would exhaust those desires that propel us into the future, such as the desire to get a degree, or to start a family, or to write a book. Once we satisfied all of those desires, Williams claimed, we would lose any interest in remaining alive.

Samuel Scheffler[2] argued that we attribute value to our existence and to the good things in it (such as health, success, and achievements) because we know that we have limited time. So the scarcity of such things, as well as the scarcity of the time available to achieve them, is what makes us appreciate what we have and attribute meaning to what we do.

Another philosopher, Shelly Kagan,[3] has based his objection to immortality on concerns about the boredom that would necessarily arise after living for too many years. Meanwhile, Todd May[4] has expressed a similar view: no matter how intense our passion for interests, hobbies, and relationships, it would eventually be eroded by the passage of time.

It is hard to tell if existential boredom, tiredness, or exhaustion of all desires would eventually surface during a very long life and make death preferable to more life. Leaving death open as an option certainly seems like a reasonable idea. Perhaps, though, we would all enjoy life more if we knew that the decision about when to go was up to us. Maybe having more control over our death would be better than living in fear that tomorrow death might claim us. After all, living without the constant reminder of human mortality is what we do as children, and there is no reason to believe that we wouldn't enjoy such a carefree existence as adults too.

JS

Eventually, the judge decided that JS's last wish should be granted, and she is now cryopreserved in one of the few cryonics facilities around the world. Nobody knows if she will ever be revived, or when, and what kind of society would welcome her back if she returned from the world of the dead. But in all this uncertainty, at least we know that she died hoping to be able to enjoy a few (or very many) years of life at some point in the future, and this thought may have provided some comfort during her last days. Perhaps in the future there will be ways to avoid ageing and dying, and future generations will look at a past where people died, no matter their age, as tragic. Some people want a chance to live in that future and cryonics might be the closest thing we have today to ship us there. There is no good reason not to let people try it.

Further Reading

Ettinger, R. C. and Rostand, J., *The Prospect of Immortality* (Sidgwick & Jackson, 1965).
Minerva, F., *The Ethics of Cryonics: Is it Immoral to be Immortal?* (Springer, 2018).

Notes

1. B. Williams, *Problems of the Self: Philosophical Papers 1956–1972* (Cambridge University Press, 1976).
2. S. Scheffler, *Death and the Afterlife* (Oxford University Press, 2013).
3. S. Kagan, *Death* (Yale University Press, 2012).
4. T. May, *Death* (Routledge, 2014).

24

Posthumans

Anders Sandberg

"Here is my offer: the TransLife Medichine 3000™ is a brand-new life support system. It supplements your immune system, removing any viruses, bacteria and parasites. The database is constantly updated and shared—if anybody with the medichine encounters a new pathogen anywhere in the world, you will become immune overnight. It filters out toxins and can supply you with any legal drug or medication. Since it also removes cancer, senescent cells, plaque and repairs intercellular matrix, it stops ageing. If you upgrade to the Proteus™ version it can also repair wounds and regenerate lost tissue, do cosmetic surgery or change your sex while you sleep. Then we have the Athena™ boosting your working memory to 70 items, +50 IQ, allowing downloading memories and skills from our MindStore™ or other users, removing the need for sleep, plus giving you conscious control over your weight setpoint, pain perception, and empathy. And did I mention the backup feature?"

"So where is the catch?"

The salesperson is persistent. Should you buy their medichine? And does there have to be a catch?[1]

Fixing the Human Condition

All things considered, the human condition has many things going for it. Unfortunately, there are some problems. The need to sleep. Hangovers. Pain. Forgetfulness. Bad judgement. Cruelty. Depression. Ageing. Mortality. To name a few.

One approach is to try to accept these limitations and pains. Learning to live with adversity can sometimes be good for a person—it might teach them perseverance or humility . . . Unfortunately, adversity can also numb, harden, or crush us—and surely we should not just accept cruelty or ignorance as a fact of life.

Another approach is to try to fix our limitations and problems. This is the goal of human enhancement: if we are forgetful, maybe we can improve our brains to forget less, for example by taking drugs that increase neural plasticity. To counteract ageing we might use gene therapy to increase production of enzymes that decline with age, remove aged and ill cells, or add fresh stem cells.

Human enhancement is all around us. The morning coffee or tea contains stimulating caffeine that counteracts sleepiness. Vaccines are a form of collective, global immunity against illnesses we may have never encountered. Less invasively, most of us live our lives with smartphones connecting us to a sizeable fraction of humanity and its knowledge. We are never alone, never lost, never bored, able to record anything. Our medieval ancestors would find our (long, healthy, rich) lives superhuman.

What Is Enhancement?

Defining enhancement is not straightforward. Some contrast enhancement with what is 'natural'. There are "natural" ways to become better at sport, like training and diet, yet many of the activities that elite athletes and serious meditators engage in don't seem very natural—simulated high altitude training, regimented diets, watching a wall intently for days. The tools used are not relevant (although we tend to get more exercised when they are new and fancy technologies rather than, say, learning intricate memory-arts from the Renaissance).

Another approach is to compare enhancement to what is "normal". Are my glasses an enhancement, since my natural eyesight is myopic? Most would say the use of glasses is therapy, restoring my sight to normal. But some people have better eyesight than normal people. A pill that made me as smart as Einstein would still keep me within the human intelligence range, yet the improvement (trust me!) would be vast.

Many try to distinguish between therapy restoring us to health, and enhancement as moving beyond it. But defining enhancement as "better than well" requires us to figure out what being healthy is. This is contentious, with many contradictory answers. Intriguingly, the definition from the World Health Organisation (WHO):

> Health is a state of complete physical, mental and social well-being and not merely the absence of disease or infirmity

implies that *nobody* has so far ever been healthy. Were we to become as healthy as WHO dreams, we would be living in a fantastic world.

There are also extensions that are not boosting traits we already have, but giving us *new* traits. Some people have implanted magnets that allow them to sense magnetic fields, or devices that signal remote earthquakes. Those in the body modification subculture want to alter their bodies to fit their identities, even when that includes forked tongues, horns, whiskers, and scales. Our smartphones give us "radio-telepathic" abilities to communicate afar.

It might be useful to call enhancements things that improve the functions we already have—memory, staying healthy, emotions— while extensions add new functions—sensing magnetic fields, radio. But whether we're discussing enhancements or extensions, some improvements are trade-offs: sometimes it is vital to feel pain, but not always. Sometimes it is nice to be less sharp, which is why many drink alcohol. We gain something at the expense of something else, but usually prefer it to be temporary. The key thing is that we become better at something we think will improve our well-being or be useful.

Human, Transhuman, Posthuman

In the future we are likely to become much better at enhancement than we are currently. We are figuring out our bodies and minds, learning how to use surgery, genetic engineering, nanomachines, and software to assist and boost our abilities. Doubtless some people will avail themselves of these opportunities (and equally predictably, others will say they're a very bad idea). Over time, we will as a species figure out what changes are helpful and which ones are merely expensive dead-ends.

We may call somebody who is very enhanced compared to us current humans a 'transhuman' (someone with the TransLife Medichine 3000™ may count as transhuman). They are clearly better at a lot of things, even if they are not better people in a moral sense.

Transhumans may find that with greater power comes greater responsibility. They might not have to dress up in capes and fight crime, but if you can foresee something bad happening and you can prevent it, you have reason to do so. A transhuman smarter than normal humans may hence have an obligation to do things from which humans are excused. Some of these responsibilities may be naturally motivating: if you expect to live for centuries you have a good selfish reason (in addition to all the unselfish ones) to maintain the environment and civilization. Conversely, we may hold transhumans to a higher moral standard: by virtue of their intelligence or self-control they ought to behave better. To some this may sound like a reason to avoid enhancement, but usually if something is good to do, we should wish to be better able to do it. Being a moral or good person (whatever that actually means!) seems to be a thing we should always try to achieve—even if it means installing an ethical co-processor in the brain.

But could we turn ourselves into a new species, a posthuman species?

Actually, making a new biological human species is easy. To do it we need just a group of people who refuse to have children with outside people, and wait long enough. If they keep up their reproductive isolation they will speciate just like any other animal or plant: random genetic changes will eventually make them genetically incompatible with the rest of humanity and they will become their own biological species. It is just that this process would take a long time, require dedication that fortunately seems unlikely, and most importantly, just produces a new human species that functions just like the rest of us. They might look slightly different but it's unlikely there will be any truly fundamental difference.

But what if we enhance ourselves so life actually is fundamentally different? One definition of a posthuman, from Nick Bostrom,[2] is a being:

> that has at least one posthuman capacity. By *a posthuman capacity*, I mean a general central capacity greatly exceeding the maximum attainable by any current human being without recourse to new technological means.

"General central capacities" are things that are general in that they cover many aspects of life in an open-ended way and central in that they are necessary to have a life. He gives healthspan, cognition, and emotion as examples, but this list is not exhaustive. A non-ageing human would be a posthuman, since healthspan is a general central capacity, but someone who never needs to sleep would merely have enhanced something relatively specific. Being strong does not make you posthuman since it only affects parts of life, but if you had super-intelligence it would likely affect everything you did.

What about entirely new general capacities? Maybe there could be ways of thinking or being conscious that are general enough to make their bearers count as posthuman, even if they are not on any current list of human capacities. They are not central to human life: they would only be central to posthumans.

Is It Good to Be a Post-Ape?

Could we really become posthuman? We can consider that we are post-apes, and got here through blind natural evolution. It could happen again, although, as I discussed above, it is we ourselves who are most likely to cause it.

As post-apes we are not that extreme. Most of our lives involve the same general central capacities—we get angry or excited just like them, we have most of the same needs as them, though we get our food and health in fancier ways. But some aspects of human life are utterly alien to even our close relatives the chimpanzees. We experience the world through language, which allows us to transmit feelings and knowledge not just to neighbours but to future generations. We have a cumulative culture where stories, advice, and technology are gradually built up. No other species has that. We are also much smarter (most of us) than chimpanzees and can solve problems they cannot solve and think about things they are entirely unable to recognize. We know we are a species, we write poetry about our emotions, we dream about what we may become in the future.

We can playfully imagine some apes once discussing whether it would be good to become post-apes. They might note that being smarter tends to lead to foraging success, so post-apes would have a lot more bananas—obviously a good thing! These apes would have been right: humans plant and produce more bananas than the apes could ever have imagined possible. Most of us also enjoy eating bananas. Yet the apes might have been dismayed at noting that besides our amazing banana-powers we are wasting our time on other things. We sit around with books and computers, we have long meetings that do not seem to be fun (despite the fruit bowl on the table), and much of the human world would seem pointless to an ape.

So maybe we have failed at becoming successful post-apes?

Most humans would respond that while we do like many ape-pleasures, from bananas to sex to being with friends, we also have human pleasures: sports, art, science, religion, philosophy . . . they are valuable in ways apes cannot understand, but being humans we can appreciate them. The apes just have to take our word for it. These mysterious things come from our slightly expanded capacities for thinking, and we are still just beginning to explore where art and science can lead us.

When we think about whether becoming posthuman is a good idea, the same reasoning should apply. Yes, posthumans will have vast abilities for art, science, and other valuable activities—including perhaps enjoying bananas—but most of the value may come from things that we cannot understand. We are simply not smart enough to see what is beyond science and philosophy, our emotions may be too crude to go beyond ethics, our lifespans so short that we do not notice some important patterns in the world that are obvious to anybody paying attention for a few millennia. So the posthumans may mostly value things we are unable to care about. But this is fine! In fact, it is probably better than just having a lot more of what we currently have. Bananas are nice, but we don't want to cover the Earth with them.

I Am That I Am . . . I Think?

There is still a problem: what if enhancement makes us not ourselves? If somebody offers to replace you with a super-person who is better than you in every respect, you may still reasonably refuse: it would not benefit *you*, even if everybody else were happy with it. Similarly, people might not want humanity replaced with a super-humanity which bore no relationship to us humans.

Generally, we seem to be fine with enhancements of functions that are not fundamental to our self-image. Better memory, learning new languages, becoming more alert? Bring it on! But in one survey, only

9% wanted to take an enhancer for kindness.[3] You could argue that the nay-sayers are just wrong: we ought to try to become more kind. But if there is a value in remaining oneself, and changing one's emotions and personality too much makes one a different person, it might be reasonable to abstain from the kindness pill.

How much change would make us a different person? Most adults claim they are the same person they were as kids, despite having different bodies and seeing the world utterly differently. Their kid-self would likely hardly recognize them, and might not even endorse their views and actions (just ask any kid about their views of normal adults). The reason adults think they are the same person as they always have been is that they remember being kids. They can tell a story about how they grew up and became who they are. This is also why the kid may not recognize the adult: the adult self is just one among many possible futures.

This gives us some sense of how radical personal change can be without being too radical. It also shows that it is asymmetric: the before-the-change version of us and the after-the-change version look at it differently. In many ways, this is similar to the previous discussion of posthumans, who may value things we do not value. If becoming posthuman is like growing up, it would be unproblematic.

We usually have no problem with changing gradually. If we dislike the change, we often think we can return to our old selves. Deliberate changes are made based on what we currently value, and after the change we will still value nearly the same things: our past and future selves agree. The worry with radical change is that it may affect our values and identity so much that even if the change was bad (by our standards before) the new version would not recognize it, and we will have lost our entire future.

The same may be true for humanity. Few people are worried about the fact that if humans survive they will eventually genetically drift and become very different from us. We may be worried that drift or selection could produce some degenerate humanity that lacks what we value—the brutish cannibal Morlocks and ineffectual Eloi in H. G. Wells's *The Time Machine* come to mind—and take steps to ensure we do not mis-evolve in that direction. But change itself is not bad. A future in which humans gradually become better (more moral, more capable, with new abilities) sounds great.

A sudden jump to that state may lose a continuity we value (when visiting a museum it is a wonderful experience to recognize a shared emotion across millennia, or to feel a sense of pride in having built on the achievements of past civilizations). Worse, the jump may change how we evaluate things, making future humanity unable to recognize that it had lost something important. This is the great fear of some critics of enhancement, like Francis Fukuyama.[4]

Not everybody agrees on what changes would change how we evaluate ourselves. In fact, people differ enormously in what they regard as defining their own existence, so a change that is fine for one person may be too radical for someone else. The best we can do is to respect different choices, making sure they are well considered and informed. Similarly, we may want to have some daring souls explore posthuman paths, reporting back what they find so the rest of us can decide if it sounds like a good idea or not. There is no need for all humans (or transhumans or posthumans) to be alike. In fact, it might benefit us to have even more diversity, if we can handle it socially. Enhancing tolerance may be one of our current top priorities!

Returning to the pushy salesperson with the TransLife Medichine 3000™, most of the offered enhancements look like they are just improvements. We want health no matter what our life projects; whether the ideal lifespan is 80 or 800 years might depend on who we are, but it is good to have the option of a longer life rather than one cut short after a mere century. Whether the ability to produce drugs, change appearance, or go without sleep improves your life may depend much more on who you are. The real challenges may come from being able to download memories and make backups of yourself—these are the features that can actually change who you are in nontrivial ways. You should probably try them out cautiously if you want to go that far.

In the end, the medichine may not be that radical compared to the shift from ape to post-ape.

Have a banana.

Further Reading

Moravec, H., *Mind Children: The Future of Robot and Human Intelligence* (Harvard University Press, 1988).

More, M. and Vita-More, N. (eds.), *The Transhumanist Reader: Classical and Contemporary Essays on the Science, Technology, and Philosophy of the Human Future* (John Wiley & Sons, 2013).

Naam, R., *More than Human: Embracing the Promise of Biological Enhancement* (Broadway Books, 2010).

Savulescu, J. and Bostrom N. (eds.), *Human Enhancement* (Oxford University Press, 2009).

Notes

1. In practice there are always problems with any technology—price, privacy, bugs, and so on—but in philosophical thought experiments we can wave those problems away to look for fundamental issues. Actual enhancement and approaches to posthumanity will of course have to deal with the real problems too.
2. N. Bostrom, Why I want to be a posthuman when I grow up. In *Medical Enhancement and Posthumanity* (Springer, 2008), pp. 107–36.
3. J. Riis, J. P. Simmons, and G. P. Goodwin, Preferences for enhancement pharmaceuticals: The reluctance to enhance fundamental traits, *Journal of Consumer Research*, 35/3 (2008), 495–508.
4. F. Fukuyama, *Our Posthuman Future: Consequences of the Biotechnology Revolution* (Farrar, Straus and Giroux, 2003).

About the Editor and Contributors

David Edmonds is Distinguished Research Fellow at Oxford University's Uehiro Centre for Practical Ethics. He is the author, co-author, or editor of over a dozen books including *Wittgenstein's Poker* (with John Eidinow), *The Murder of Professor Schlick*, and the children's book *Undercover Robot* (with Bertie Fraser). He is the host of *Philosophy247* and *Social Science Bites* and he co-hosts *Philosophy Bites* (with Nigel Warburton), a podcast which has had 42 million downloads.

*

Anne Barnhill is Core Faculty at the Johns Hopkins Berman Institute of Bioethics, where she is part of the Global Food Ethics and Policy Programme. Dr. Barnhill is a philosopher and bioethicist who works on the ethics of food and agricultural policy, public health ethics, and the ethics of influence.

Steve Clarke is Associate Professor of Philosophy in the School of Humanities and Social Sciences at Charles Sturt University in Australia as well as a Senior Research Associate in Ethics and Humanities in the Wellcome Centre for Ethics and Humanities, the Uehiro Centre for Practical Ethics, and the Faculty of Philosophy at the University of Oxford.

John Danaher is a Senior Lecturer in Law at the National University of Ireland (NUI) Galway. He is the author of *Automation and Utopia* (Harvard University Press, 2019), co-author of *A Citizen's Guide to Artificial Intelligence* (MIT Press, 2021) and co-editor of *Robot Sex: Social and Ethical Implications* (MIT Press, 2017). He has published dozens of papers on topics including the risks of advanced AI, the meaning of life and the future of work, the ethics of human enhancement, the intersection of law and neuroscience, the utility of brain-based lie detection, and the philosophy of religion.

Gabriel De Marco is a Research Fellow at the Oxford Uehiro Centre for Practical Ethics at the University of Oxford.

Katrien Devolder is a Senior Research Fellow at the Oxford Uehiro Centre for Practical Ethics and a Fellow at Reuben College. Her research lies in applied ethics. She currently holds a Wellcome Trust Research Fellowship to work on her project 'The Ethics of Genome Editing in Livestock'. She regularly makes video-interviews with renowned philosophers, which can be viewed on The Practical Ethics Channel on YouTube.

Lydia Di Stefano is currently undertaking the final year of her Doctor of Medicine (MD) at Monash University. In the past she has worked as a research assistant with the maternal health group at the London School of Hygiene and Tropical Medicine, where she also completed an MSc in Reproductive and Sexual Health Research. In 2018, she undertook a BMedSc (Hons) as a visiting student at the Uehiro Centre for Practical Ethics at the University of Oxford, which is where she began her research into the ethics of artificial wombs.

Thomas Douglas is Senior Research Fellow and Director of Research and Development at the Oxford Uehiro Centre for Practical Ethics, University of Oxford, and Hugh Price Fellow at Jesus College, Oxford. He trained in medicine and philosophy and works primarily in philosophical bioethics.

Brian D. Earp is a philosopher and cognitive scientist who studies, among other things, sex, sexuality, gender, and the self/identity. Brian is Associate Director of the Yale-Hastings Programme in Ethics and Health Policy at Yale University and The Hastings Center, a Research Fellow at the Uehiro Centre for Practical Ethics at the University of Oxford, and an Associate Editor of the *Journal of Medical Ethics*. With Julian Savulescu, Brian is co-author of *Love Drugs: The Chemical Future of Relationships* (Stanford University Press, 2020; published in the UK by Manchester University Press as *Love Is the Drug: The Chemical Future of Our Relationships*).

Ruth R. Faden is the founder of the Johns Hopkins Berman Institute of Bioethics. Dr Faden's research focuses on structural justice theory and on national and global justice challenges in multiple sectors, including food and agriculture. Currently, she is working on these challenges in COVID-19 response. Her latest book, with Madison Powers, is *Structural Injustice: Power, Advantage, and Human Rights*.

Alberto Giubilini is a Senior Research Fellow at the Oxford Uehiro Centre for Practical Ethics and at the Wellcome Centre for Ethics and the Humanities, University of Oxford. He has published on different topics in bioethics and philosophy, with a particular focus in recent years on public health ethics (including the ethics of vaccination, of antibiotic resistance, of challenge studies, and of coerciveness of public health measures more generally). He recently published the book *The Ethics of Vaccination* (Palgrave Macmillan, 2019).

Mackenzie Graham is a Senior Research Fellow at the Wellcome Centre for Ethics and Humanities, University of Oxford, and the Junior Research Fellow in Humanities at St Catherine's College, University of Oxford. He received a PhD in Philosophy from the University of Western Ontario in 2016. His research interests are in bioethics, and the ethics of artificial intelligence and 'big data'.

Tess Johnson is a DPhil candidate at the Oxford Uehiro Centre for Practical Ethics; Tess gained her Master of Bioethics from Monash University, Australia, and a Bachelor of Arts / Bachelor of Science in biology and linguistics at the Australian National University. Her current research focuses on gene editing for human enhancement, but more broad research interests include the ethical assessment of new reproductive and medical technologies, and issues of autonomy in public health interventions.

Angeliki Kerasidou is a bioethicist with a background in theology and philosophy. She studied in Greece, Germany, and the UK, and gained her DPhil at Oxford University in 2009. Her research interests are in the ethics of data-driven technologies (e.g. genomics, artificial intelligence, 'big data') in health research and in healthcare. Her current research focuses on the issues of trust, empathy, and efficiency in AI-augmented healthcare. She is an NDPH Senior Fellow at the Ethox Centre, and a Fellow at Reuben College, Oxford University.

Xaroula (Charalampia) Kerasidou is a researcher in the fields of feminist science and technology studies and media and cultural studies with a special interest in exploring how new technologies challenge us to reconceptualize the ontologies and power relations between the human and the machine, and to understand what this means for ethics, politics, and policy. She currently leads the project 'Configuring Ethical AI in Healthcare' funded by the Wellcome Trust at Lancaster University.

Professor Seumas Miller holds research positions at Charles Sturt University, TU Delft, and the University of Oxford. His recent authored books include: Shooting to Kill: The Ethics of Police and Military Use of Lethal Force (Oxford University Press, 2016), Institutional Corruption: A Study in Applied Philosophy (Cambridge University Press, 2017), Dual Use Science and Technology, Ethics and Weapons of Mass Destruction (Springer, 2018) and (with T. Bossomaier) Ethics and Cybersecurity (Oxford University Press, 2021).

Francesca Minerva is a researcher at the University of Milan. She was a Postdoc at the Universities of Melbourne, Ghent, and Warwick. She is the author of The Ethics of Cryonics: Is it Immoral to be Immortal? (Palgrave, 2018).

Erica L. Neely is a philosopher specializing in issues pertaining to technology. Her work primarily focuses on the ethics of video games, virtual worlds, and emerging technologies.

Jonathan Pugh is a Parfit-Radcliffe Richards Senior Research Fellow and Manager of Visitors Programmes for the Oxford Uehiro Centre for Practical Ethics, University of Oxford. He recently led a Wellcome Trust-funded project entitled 'The Ethics of Novel Therapeutic Applications of Deep Brain Stimulation'. His research interests lie primarily in issues concerning personal autonomy in practical ethics, particularly topics pertaining to informed consent. He has also written on the ethics of human embryonic stem cell research, criminal justice, human enhancement, and gene-editing.

Stephen Rainey is a Research Fellow in Neuroethics at the Oxford Uehiro Centre for Practical Ethics. His recent work has focused on ethical issues concerning brain–computer interfaces, and how these impact upon control over, and responsibility for, actions. Dr Rainey also carries out research in areas where technology and governance interface, including how to regulate new and emerging technologies such as artificial intelligence, 'big data', and financial technology.

Rebecca Roache is Senior Lecturer in Philosophy at the University of London. Her research is in applied ethics, philosophy of language, philosophy of psychiatry, and occasionally metaphysics. She hopes one day to finish the monograph on swearing that she's been working on for too long.

Anders Sandberg is Senior Research Fellow at the Future of Humanity Institute at the University of Oxford, where he researches the ethics of human enhancement, reasoning under uncertainty, global risks, and very long-term futures. He is also Research Associate at the Oxford Uehiro Centre for Practical Ethics and the Institute for Future Studies in Stockholm.

Julian Savulescu is trained in medicine, neuroscience, and philosophy. He holds the Uehiro Chair in Practical Ethics at the University of Oxford. He directs the Oxford Uehiro Centre for Practical Ethics and co-directs the Wellcome Centre for Ethics and Humanities. In Australia, he is Visiting Professorial Fellow in Biomedical Ethics at the Murdoch Children's Research Institute and Distinguished Visiting Professor in Law at Melbourne University.

Carissa Véliz is an Associate Professor at the Faculty of Philosophy and the Institute for Ethics in AI, and a Tutorial Fellow at Hertford College, University of Oxford. She works on privacy, the ethics of technology, moral and political philosophy, and public policy. She is the author of *Privacy Is Power* (Bantam, 2020) and the editor of the forthcoming *Oxford Handbook of Digital Ethics*.

Jess Whittlestone is a Senior Research Fellow at the Leverhulme Centre for the Future of Intelligence at the University of Cambridge, where her research is motivated by ensuring the long-term development of AI is safe and beneficial for society. She has a PhD in Behavioural Science from the University of Warwick, a first class degree in Mathematics and Philosophy from Oxford University, and previously worked for the Behavioural Insights Team advising government departments on their use of data, evidence, and evaluation methods.

Dominic Wilkinson is Director of Medical Ethics and Professor of Medical Ethics at the Oxford Uehiro Centre for Practical Ethics, University of Oxford. He is a consultant in newborn intensive care at the John Radcliffe Hospital, Oxford. His co-authored books include *Medical Ethics and Law, Third Edition* (Elsevier, 2019) and *Ethics, Conflict and Medical Treatment for Children, From Disagreement to Dissensus* (Elsevier, 2018). He is also the author of *Death or Disability?: The 'Carmentis Machine' and Decision-making for Critically Ill Children* (Oxford University Press, 2013).

Bridget Williams is a medical doctor specializing in public health medicine, and has worked in public health roles in research, government, and the World Health Organisation. She is an adjunct research fellow with the School of Public Health and Preventive Medicine at Monash University and an MSt in Practical Ethics candidate at the Oxford Uehiro Centre for Practical Ethics.

James Williams is a Research Fellow at the University of Oxford in the Uehiro Centre for Practical Ethics, University of Oxford. He works on the philosophy and ethics of technology, especially questions of attention, persuasion, and wellbeing. His first book, *Stand Out of Our Light: Freedom and Resistance in the Attention Economy*, was published by Cambridge University Press after winning the inaugural Nine Dots Prize in 2017. Previously, James worked for over ten years at Google, where he received the Founders' Award, the company's highest honour. He received his DPhil from Oxford in 2018.

Hazem Zohny is Research Fellow in Bioethics at the Uehiro Centre for Practical Ethics at Oxford University. He has a PhD in Bioethics from the University of Otago and has published a number of academic papers related to enhancement, disability, and well-being. Previously, he worked as an Editor at Nature Publishing Group, and has extensive journalistic experience with publications in *Scientific American*, *Slate*, *Aeon*, *Quillette*, and many others.

Index